Teaching English to Young Arabic Speakers

Also available from Bloomsbury

Identity, Motivation, and Multilingual Education in Asian Contexts,
Mark Feng Teng and Wang Lixun
Language Learning Strategies and Individual Learner Characteristics,
edited by Rebecca L. Oxford and Carmen M. Amerstorfer
Teaching English to Young Learners, Janice Bland
The Value of English in Global Mobility and Higher Education,
Manuela Vida-Mannl
Video Enhanced Observation for Language Teaching, edited by Paul Seedhouse
Performative Language Teaching in Early Education, Joe Winston
Rethinking TESOL in Diverse Global Settings, Tim Marr and Fiona English
Teaching and Learning the English Language, Richard Badger

Teaching English to Young Arabic Speakers

Assessing the Influence of Instructional Materials, Narratives and Cultural Norms

Irma-Kaarina Ghosn

BLOOMSBURY ACADEMIC
LONDON • NEW YORK • OXFORD • NEW DELHI • SYDNEY

BLOOMSBURY ACADEMIC
Bloomsbury Publishing Plc
50 Bedford Square, London, WC1B 3DP, UK
1385 Broadway, New York, NY 10018, USA
29 Earlsfort Terrace, Dublin 2, Ireland

BLOOMSBURY, BLOOMSBURY ACADEMIC and the Diana logo are
trademarks of Bloomsbury Publishing Plc

First published in Great Britain 2023
Paperback edition published 2024

Copyright © Irma-Kaarina Ghosn, 2023

Irma-Kaarina Ghosn has asserted her right under the Copyright, Designs and
Patents Act, 1988, to be identified as Author of this work.

For legal purposes the Acknowledgements on p. xiii constitute an
extension of this copyright page.

Cover design: Charlotte James
Cover image © FatCamera / Getty Images

All rights reserved. No part of this publication may be reproduced or transmitted in
any form or by any means, electronic or mechanical, including photocopying,
recording, or any information storage or retrieval system, without prior
permission in writing from the publishers.

Bloomsbury Publishing Plc does not have any control over, or responsibility for, any
third-party websites referred to or in this book. All internet addresses given in this
book were correct at the time of going to press. The author and publisher regret any
inconvenience caused if addresses have changed or sites have ceased to exist, but
can accept no responsibility for any such changes.

A catalogue record for this book is available from the British Library.

Library of Congress Cataloging-in-Publication Data

Names: Ghosn, Irma-Kaarina, author.
Title: Teaching English to young Arabic speakers : assessing the influence
of instructional materials, narratives and cultural norms / Irma-Kaarina Ghosn.
Description: London; New York : Bloomsbury Academic, 2023. |
Includes bibliographical references and index.
Identifiers: LCCN 2022039653 (print) | LCCN 2022039654 (ebook) |
ISBN 9781350260474 (hardback) | ISBN 9781350260535 (paperback) |
ISBN 9781350260504 (adobe pdf) | ISBN 9781350260511 (epub)
Subjects: LCSH: English language–Study and teaching (Elementary)–Arab
countries. | English language–Study and teaching (Elementary)–Arabic speakers.
Classification: LCC PE1068.A65 G46 2023 (print) | LCC PE1068.A65 (ebook) |
DDC 372.652/109174927–dc23/eng/20220913
LC record available at https://lccn.loc.gov/2022039653
LC ebook record available at https://lccn.loc.gov/2022039654

ISBN: HB: 978-1-3502-6047-4
PB: 978-1-3502-6053-5
ePDF: 978-1-3502-6050-4
eBook: 978-1-3502-6051-1

Typeset by Newgen KnowledgeWorks Pvt. Ltd., Chennai, India

To find out more about our authors and books visit www.bloomsbury.com
and sign up for our newsletters.

*To my granddaughter, Kiira,
whose language development has been a joy to observe!*

Contents

List of Figures	ix
List of Tables	x
Preface	xi
Acknowledgements	xiii
List of Abbreviations	xiv
Transcription Conventions	xv
Introduction	1

Part 1 Some Theoretical Considerations

1	Cultural Norms and Expectations versus Teaching Materials	9
2	Narrative and Children's Language Learning	25
3	Meeting the Challenge of English-Medium Instruction with Stories	39

Part 2 Insights from Classroom Research

4	Teacher Questions versus Learner Engagement	55
5	Classroom Discourse and the Role of Teaching Materials	65
6	Influence of Instructional Materials on Reading Comprehension	83
7	Influence of Instructional Materials on Receptive and Productive Vocabulary	97
8	Instructional Texts as Models for Writing	107
9	Literate Language from Storybooks	121
10	Transfer from Arabic to Children's English Writing	129

Part 3 Teachers and Students in Action

11	Whole Language Experiences in Kindergarten	151
12	The Flexibility of Story-Based Instruction in the Classroom	165
13	Teacher Effectiveness and Learner Engagement	181

Conclusion	193
Notes	201
References	203
Index	221
Children's Book Index	225

Figures

4.1	Continua of teacher questions	58
10.1	K's spelling at age five	136
10.2	K's spelling at age six	137
10.3	K's spelling at age seven	138
10.4	Letter positions in Arabic words	139
10.5	Children's handwriting	144
11.1	(a, b) Children's scribbles	158

Tables

1.1	Preferences of Egalitarian versus Hierarchical Cultures	14
1.2	Tolerance for Uncertainty and Ambiguity	15
3.1	Activating Academic Language Functions with Stories	41
4.1	Examples of Questions	58
5.1	Basic Exchanges with Teacher Negotiation of Form	67
5.2	Three Types of Exchanges	67
5.3	About Prefixes and Suffixes	68
5.4	Figuring Out Vocabulary and Negotiation of Meaning	69
6.1	Sample Text Excerpts	92
6.2	Sample of Six Children's Progress	93
9.1	Literate Language Features	123
9.2	Literate Language Features in the Two Groups	124
9.3	Literate Language in Children's Narratives Before and After Intervention	125
10.1	Grammar Errors	132
10.2	Gentry's and Bear and Templeton's Stages	135
10.3	Children's Spelling Error Categories	140
10.4	Errors According to Bear and Templeton	140
13.1	Scaffolding Vocabulary Learning	186
13.2	Scaffolding a Concept	187

Preface

As the practice of teaching English to ever younger children is spreading, the concern of suitable instructional materials arises. How motivating children will find the language learning materials determines how well they engage in the lessons and how much language they will learn.

This book is an amalgam of research studies, classroom experiments and years of classroom observations and discussions with teachers. Its early origins are in my doctoral dissertation in which I argued that story-based, reading-focused coursebooks produce better outcomes than the communicatively oriented coursebooks with dialogue practice. I have not changed my mind about that – after all, worldwide research strongly supports this view – but have since considered other factors as well, including culture. After developing a course on cross-cultural communication and conflict for a university Liberal Arts core curriculum, I took another look at my dissertation and began to think that cultural conflict was a factor in the classroom discourse in many cases. After more observations and classroom research, a pattern emerged between the expectations regarding instructional approaches and cultural norms. During hundreds of hours of teacher development workshops I have delivered in Lebanon, Syria, Jordan and the UAE, many teachers have expressed concerns about the materials they were using. In this book, I am attempting to view the classroom as a unique ecosystem within which multiple bi- and multidirectional relationships are at play and which is situated within a web of nested systems that influence what goes on in the classroom. In each chapter, there is some evidence to support story-based instruction. Each chapter also provides some suggestions for both teachers and materials developers. It is my hope that the book will be thought-provoking and generate discussion and more research on the different factors explored.

Regrettably, as this manuscript is heading to the publisher, the financial crisis in Lebanon is changing what materials teachers will have available. Because parents are responsible for purchasing children's textbooks and other materials, to alleviate the burden, schools are abandoning imported coursebooks. Already, at least five of the schools where data were collected for this book have made the switch from story-based reading books to either imported young learner ELT books or locally published books. Based on the findings in this book, one has to wonder what influence these changes will have on students' language learning and their ability to follow English-medium instruction in the upper grades.

Monsif, Lebanon, January 2022

Acknowledgements

I wish to thank all the teachers who have welcomed me into their classrooms over the past twenty years and allowed me to observe and tape their lessons, as well as all the children who completed assigned activities and tests without complaints. Appreciation is also due to the several principals who have given me access to their schools and allowed me not only to observe classes and carry out research but also invited me to present workshops for teachers. Names of children, teachers, schools and students have been changed to prevent any identification of individuals or schools concerned.

Abbreviations

EFL	English as a foreign language subject
ELL	English-language learner
ELT	English-language teaching
EMI	English-medium instruction
ESL/EAL	English as a second/additional language in countries where English is the language of daily communication or an official language
FLAPPS	Foreign language for academic purposes in primary school
IRF	Initiation-response-feedback
LOI	Language of instruction
TEVYL	Teaching English to very young learners age six and below
TEYL	Teaching English to young learners ages seven to twelve
VYL	Children age six and below
YL	Children between seven and twelve

Transcription Conventions

T	teacher
S	student
Ss	two or more students
Italics	in classroom episodes students reading from the book
Brackets (xxx)	unintelligible words or phrases
Double brackets (())	non-English words or phrases
Square brackets []	actions or behaviours during the episode
Words in CAPITALS	incorrect spelling in written work

Introduction

How nice it would be if we could only get through into Looking-glass House!
Lewis Carroll – *Through the Looking Glass*

The practice of teaching English to young learners and even very young learners (TEYL and TEVYL, respectively) is rapidly spreading around the world, and Arab World is no exception. Several Arab countries now introduce English instruction in lower primary school, many as early as year one (age six to seven), and in Lebanon already in kindergarten (age four to five). This book was prompted not only by the changing landscape of TEYL but also by the prevailing perception that pupils' English-language achievement in the MENA region is less than satisfactory. For example, a call for a 2020 conference in Oman, *Emerging Trends and Contemporary Issues in Language Learning: The EFL Context*, opened with the following quote:

> As most countries in the Middle East and North Africa (MENA) region have adopted English as the lingua franca, competence in the language is an essential requirement for a successful academic and professional life. There is a vast influx of students entering the western university system through satellite campuses located in the MENA region. However, the language proficiency of Arab EFL learners entering tertiary education is often inadequate to meet the requirements of a higher education system in which English is the language of instruction and assessment. (*Emerging Trends* 2020)

There are, indeed, numerous English-medium universities in the MENA region, many of them satellite campuses of American, British, Canadian and Australian universities and colleges. Clearly, considerable competence in English language is required for students to succeed in these institutions, and it is not clear if this goal is reflected in English-language curricula and instructional materials in the region. For example, Lebanon's language policy requires schools to use a foreign language in key school subjects, such as mathematics and sciences, the two most common languages of choice being French and English. Yet, there is no specific training for subject matter teachers on how to teach their subject to young learners in English (or French). Similarly, TESOL (teaching English to speakers of other languages) methods courses do not typically include guidelines on how English teachers can support development of academic language. Use of foreign language as the medium of instruction has been tried also in some other Arab countries, but with less-than-satisfactory results. For example, O'Sullivan (2015) notes that in the UAE, students' English-language level, despite bilingual education, is too low for many of them to follow the imported curricula in English.

O'Sullivan identifies a mismatch between the imported instructional approaches and locally prevailing norms as one possible reason for low student achievement. There is a strong possibility that this is, indeed, one of the reasons for low student performance. Both the North American and British cultures, where internationally marketed TEYL and TEVYL courses are primarily developed, differ greatly from the Middle Eastern ones in terms of cultural norms and expectations. One of the aims of this book is to examine young learner classrooms through cultural lenses to explore this possible mismatch and how that may influence classroom discourse, learner engagement and language learning.

Several theories have been posited over the years about how second language learning happens in and out of classroom settings. Trying to make sense of the many theories reminds one of the ancient Jain parable about the blind men and the elephant in which six blind men were introduced to an elephant. After examining the elephant by touch, each man offered a different description of the elephant, which lead to an intense argument. A wise man then explained to them: 'All of you are right. The reason every one of you is telling it differently is because each one of you touched the different part of the elephant. So, actually the elephant has all the features you mentioned.' Over decades, researchers have similarly examined many variables to determine how language learning best happens. Reinforcement, motivation, role of L1, learner aptitude, different methods and materials, and classroom interaction are some of the variables examined. It is likely that all these variables, and most likely many others, play a role in how well learners acquire the new language. Therefore, we need to look at as many aspects of the 'elephant' as possible to try to really understand what influences instructed second language learning and learner output and achievement in a TEYL classroom.

Systems theories are applied in many different fields from engineering to biology, psychology and social work. Systems are defined as a complex set of interacting and interrelated components together with the relationships among them (Sexton and Stanton 2016: 213). Bronfenbrenner's (1979) bioecological systems theory of child development assumes that within a given system there are numerous mutually interactive forces that all influence the eventual outcomes. The strength of a given influence is often not predictable because of the complexity of the system, and although global patterns can be identified, the local details of the pattern cannot be accurately predicted. An example of this is Horowitz's (1990) theory of resilient versus vulnerable infants and their respective ability to withstand the stresses placed on them by the environment. To apply this theory to a classroom, it is not possible to estimate, for example, the extent of the influence of negative classroom experiences on learners, since children differ widely in their emotional resilience.

In an adaptation of Bronfenbrenner's theory to a classroom, we can view the classroom as an ecosystem comprising multiple interactive microsystems of individual learners and their teachers. Both learners and teachers are influenced not only by their personal characteristics and each other but also by the instructional materials and other classroom resources. This classroom ecosystem is influenced by elements outside the classroom with which the individuals are in direct contact. In this mesosystem, children are in direct contact with family, friends and the school and community language environment while teachers are in direct contact with their colleagues and the principal, as well as their family situation. This mesosystem, in turn, is nested within a wider exosystem with which individual microsystems are in indirect or infrequent contact. For example, for language learners, the exosystem may include occasional visits to an English-speaking family while the teacher's exosystem may include professional development courses. The macrosystem is the broader sociocultural and sociopolitical context within which all the other systems are situated influencing each other. For example, overarching economic and sociopolitical factors may influence educational policies, publishing policies, teacher preparation programs and teachers' working conditions. Culture may influence how teaching as an occupation is viewed, how teachers are expected to perform and how much autonomy they are allocated, as well as how well they are remunerated. From this perspective, the foreign-language classroom can be viewed as a small, unique ecosystem with many mutually interactive microsystems, which, in turn, are influenced by wider systems. When attempting to examine the causes of learner achievement, it is not possible to consider all the elements across the systems that may have a direct or indirect bearing on student learning.

Culture has also potentially significant influence on the classroom ecosystem as well as the individual learners. As already mentioned, TEYL and TEVYL courses marketed internationally are developed primarily in the UK and the United States. Most of these courses are structurally organized around communicative language practice and feature topics and concepts familiar to learners in the British and American culture. How these courses are used in the classroom is influenced by not only individual teachers but also students' background knowledge, and the cultural norms and expectations that guide teachers' approaches and interactions with learners. When content and expected approaches of the instructional materials are culturally unfamiliar to the end users, the outcomes may be different from those expected by materials developers.

The aim of this book is not to propose yet another theory but to explore a variety of interrelated factors within the classroom system through cultural lenses to understand what influences teacher approaches, classroom discourse and student learning outcomes. More specifically, the chapters explore reciprocal relationships between culture, instructional texts and activities, the role of narrative, teacher questioning strategies and feedback to learners and overall teacher effectiveness and how these influence learner engagement and achievement. The conclusion links the findings to different layers of the complex system. While the complexity of the system does not allow all possible variables to be considered, the incomplete web nevertheless illustrates the influence of some of the interrelated variables on classroom discourse and children's language learning.

Data presented comprise systematic recorded observations, classroom observation notes, standardized tests, experimental studies, student work samples, as well as informal teacher interviews. Data come from twenty-one different Lebanese classrooms of sixteen teachers in kindergarten to grade six. From the data, a picture of a complex, multifaceted web-like system emerges that links together cultural expectations, instructional texts, classroom discourse, individual teacher strategies, learner engagement and their ultimate achievement. While pointing out some problematic aspects of traditional language teaching practice activities, this book also showcases some excellent examples of effective and engaging teaching.

Although the data presented come from Lebanese classrooms, the findings are applicable not only in the MENA region but also in other non-Western cultural contexts where internationally marketed TEYL and TEVYL courses are used. Young learner materials developers may find the book interesting and thought-provoking and gain some insight into how their materials may or may not be used and how they might take it into consideration when developing coursebooks and accompanying teachers' guides.

Part 1
Some Theoretical Considerations

1

Cultural Norms and Expectations versus Teaching Materials

'Explain yourself!' 'I can't explain myself, I'm afraid, sir', said Alice, 'because I'm not myself, you see'.

Lewis Carroll – Alice in Wonderland

Lily and Rima are both English-language teachers in Lebanon and teach in small-town schools with seven hundred to eight hundred students. Their students have begun learning English in kindergarten at age four to five and are now learning English six 50-minute sessions a week. They are also receiving English-medium instruction (EMI) in math and science. In the first lengthy episode, Rima's fifth-graders are working through a dialogue practice to talk about their favourite seasons. The book provides some suggestions for seasonal activities, some of which are not familiar to the children in the class. (Italics denote student reading from the book.)

Episode 1.1

S1:	*What do you do in the fall?*
S2:	Fall I go bike
T:	Bike riding
S2:	*I play in the leaves.*
T:	Okay. Rami and Boutros. Please do the conversation number four.
S3:	*What is your favourite season?*
S4:	*My favourite season* [pronounced as 'favrit']
T:	My, Rami, my favərite
S4:	*My favourite season is spring.*
S3:	*Why?*

S4: *I like warm, rainy days.*
S5: *What is your favourite season?*
S6: (xxx)
S5: *Why?*
S6: I want
T: Hady, when he asks you why, you will answer by 'because', 'because'
S6: Because to swimming
T: Because I go
S6: I go to swim
T: I go swimming
S7: *What is your favourite season?*
T: Ok. Now Rania, you answer him.
S8: *My favourite season is winter.*
S9: Why do you like winter?
S8: Because it's cold.
T: Because it's cold or because you like to play in the snow?
S8: *I like to play in the snow.*
T: Now, Hani and Zeina, you do the conversation.
S9: *What is your favourite season?*
T: [to S10] and don't say winter!
S10: [no response]
T: What is your favourite season? (Ghosn 2017: 218–19)

Clearly, there is a mismatch not only between coursebook authors' expectations and the prevailing cultural norms but also between concepts and children's experiences. Lebanese culture is hierarchical than egalitarian, and Rima expects to be in control and wants students to follow the book, and students are not really working in pairs to practice the dialogues as intended. Rima's expectation seems to be that children should memorize the dialogues and stick to the script of the book. Note how her correction gets S2 to revert to the safety of the book, and how Rima is not satisfied with S6 response 'I go to swim', despite it being correct but insists on 'go swimming' offered in the book. Similarly, she does not accept S8's response of liking winter 'because it's cold' and insists the student chooses the book alternative for winter, 'playing in the snow'. One should note that although it snows abundantly in the mountains in Lebanon, in the locale of this particular school, it snows very rarely, if ever, so many of the students may have never experienced 'playing in the snow'. One of the other suggested activities, 'playing in dry autumn leaves' is similarly unfamiliar in an area where there are not enough deciduous trees to result in piles of dry leaves and where many mothers would strongly frown upon such behaviour.

Contrast the above with Lily's fourth-grade class in another EMI school, where students have read Judith Viorst's classic, *Alexander and the Terrible, Horrible, No Good, Very Bad Day*, where Alexander ponders the following:

> There were two cupcakes in Philip Parker's lunch bag and Albert got a Hershey bar with almonds and Paul's mother gave him a piece of jelly roll that had little coconut sprinkles on the top. Guess whose mother forgot to put in dessert? It was a terrible, horrible, no good, very bad day. (Viorst 1972: n.p.)

This is how the discussion went:

Episode 1.2

T: Why did Alexander think it was such a bad day?
S1: Miss, because, Miss, his mother not put ((sweets)) for him!
S2: Miss, what it mean 'cupcake'?
T: Uh, cupcake, cupcakes are little cakes ((cake)) baked in a paper cup.
S3: Miss! Miss! What 'jelly roll'? Is the same Jello?
T: Jelly roll, no, it's a little bit like … it's also a little cake but with a kind of jam inside, it's not Jello.
S3: Miss, like a donut?
T: Yeah, something like a donut, yes. OK, now. If you were in Alexander's place, how would you feel?
S1: If me, if I am Alexander, I will be very sad when I see all my friends eat cookies.
T: Uhuh, so you would be sad if you had no cookies for dessert.
S2: Miss, me, me! Me, I angry because my mother she did not put any cookies.
T: Oh, so if you were left without dessert, you would be angry. Uhuh.
(Ghosn 2004: 118–19)

Alexander's disappointment, although situated in the American culture, is clearly something to which children in this class could relate. At the same time, the text offers an excellent opportunity for explicit learning about the target language culture, as well as a natural context to practice past tense verb forms and pronouns, for example. Even though some of the content is unfamiliar to these children, they are clearly curious and quite able to ask questions about it.

However, their role is that of an observer rather than an imaginary participant in the situation. Yet, despite the children's eager contributions and questions, the teacher is clearly maintaining her instructor role while also entertaining children's vocabulary questions.

How Cultures Differ

One might be tempted to argue that the different discourse observed in the two episodes is simply a result of the lessons' content, one of dialogue practice and a story, as the author has argued elsewhere (Ghosn 2001). However, to better understand the young language learner classrooms and their dynamics, it will be helpful to examine them from a cultural perspective and consider all the interactive influences involved. Classroom interactions, like all human interactions, are social events (Allwright 1984), and therefore complex and culture-bound. In *Appropriate Methodology and Social Context*, Holliday calls for acknowledgement of the diverse classroom cultures and the social dynamics within them in language teaching. He notes that 'any methodology in English language education should be appropriate in the social context within which it is to be used' (Holliday 1994: 1).

In terms of methodology or content, in many internationally marketed coursebooks there is little evidence of the cultural diversity that characterizes the global English-language teaching (ELT) world. When reviewing several popular courses, Arnold and Rixon (2008: 51) found the cultural content to be 'Western-specific'. When reviewing Western-produced ELT coursebook used in Japan, Dickinson (2010: 12) also found some of the content 'irrelevant' to his Japanese students. Understandably, this is because the constraints of international publishing and marketing policies make it difficult, if not impossible, to consider all 'the learners' real worlds with all their cultural behaviors' (Holliday 1994: 173). However, when materials developers use only their own cultural reality as a reference point, inappropriate assumptions about the similarity of experience may result in texts and activities that inhabit a world different from the one of the teachers and learners using them. What teachers and learners bring to the situation may 'alter classroom practices in ways that are unintended and unexpected by curriculum designers or textbook producers' (Kumaravadivelu 2002: 16), as we saw in the case of Rima's class, for example.

Since classrooms are microcosms of the prevailing culture, they can, therefore, be expected to reflect the communication patterns typical in the culture. Understanding of cultural differences in interpersonal communication is not only crucial in intercultural communication but is also an important consideration when developing instructional materials that will be used in diverse cultural contexts. For example, concepts to which children across cultures can relate include happiness, disappointment, sibling rivalry, cooperation, competition, etc., albeit expressed differently in different cultures. This will give children the opportunity explore how children elsewhere might experience and react to such emotions or situations. While language-teaching textbooks provide necessary structure, they are culturally loaded, both in terms of content and approach to instruction (Damen 1987). Internationally marketed 'global' coursebooks feature settings and topics common in the Anglo world, which is quite appropriate from the culture learning perspective. However, when the proposed approach aims to involve learners in dialogues about culturally situated unfamiliar topics and situations, problems may arise. First, talking about unfamiliar topics will restrict students to the few options provided in the book that might not be very meaningful to them, if at all. Second, the approach proposed may not fit within the prevailing culture. As Holliday points out, 'knowledge of how culture works generally can reveal much about the workings of classroom interaction' (1994: 23).

Taxonomies of Cultural Patterns

Research since the 1980s has identified a number of taxonomies of cultural patterns, with Geert Hofstede's extensive research leading in the field. In his landmark study of over forty national cultures, he provides indexes for a number of different dimensions of culture (Hofstede 1980). Although some of his findings have been contested, several large-scale replication studies involving more than thirty countries by Hofstede (2002), Kolman et al. (2003) and others provide a robust empirical basis for his theory. The cultural dimensions should be viewed as existing along a continuum from one extreme to another, with several gradations in between. They should not be taken as stereotypes but rather as central tendencies within a given culture, because not all individuals in a given culture fit within the central tendency for one reason or another; there are always individuals who are 'outliers' and deviate from the central tendency to a lesser or greater degree.

Two dimensions of culture are particularly important when attempting to understand classroom events, which are jointly orchestrated by the teacher,

Table 1.1 Preferences of Egalitarian versus Hierarchical Cultures

Characteristics	Egalitarian – Low PDI	Hierarchical – High PDI
Power distance	Small power distance	Large power distance
Social class/inequalities	Minimizing social/class inequalities important	Hierarchy and inequality appropriate (even desirable)
Attitude towards authority	Questioning/challenging author acceptable	No questioning or challenging of authority
Use of power	Only for legitimate purposes	Those with status can use power for whatever purpose and in whatever way

Source: Summarized from Lustig and Koester (1993).

learners and the textbook. First is the level of hierarchy in interpersonal relations, or what Hofstede calls 'power-distance preference', which can range from highly egalitarian to highly hierarchical, with several gradations in between. 'Power-distance-index' (PDI) measures how far a given culture is from the neutral (see Table 1.1). Where hierarchy and formality guide social interactions, teachers and learners have rather clearly defined roles to which they are expected to conform. Lustig and Koester, authors of *Intercultural Competence*, describe the teaching-learning situation in hierarchical cultures which score high in power-distance-index, or PDI:

> Students in high-PDI cultures are expected to comply with the wishes and request of their teachers, and conformity is regarded very favorably. As a consequence, the curriculum in high-PDI cultures is likely to involve a great deal of rote learning, and students are discouraged from asking question because questions might pose a threat to the teacher's autonomy. (Lustig and Koester 1993: 139)

Hierarchical cultures also often place a high value on the authority of books, with students being evaluated based on how closely they can 'recall and repeat the words of the teacher and the words of the book' (Wurzel and Fischman 1995: 44).

The level of tolerance for uncertainty and ambiguity is another dimension relevant in the classroom context. Hofstede calls it uncertainty avoidance, and cultures where individuals prefer to avoid uncertainty tend to be characterized by many strict rules that govern social behaviours and by elaborate rituals with precise form or sequence. 'Uncertainty and ambiguity tolerance index' (UAI) measures how far a given culture is from the neutral (see Table 1.2).

Table 1.2 Tolerance for Uncertainty and Ambiguity

High Tolerance for Uncertainty and Ambiguity – Low UAI	Low Tolerance/Aversion to Uncertainty and Ambiguity – High UAI
Tolerates uncertainty, ambiguity and deviance well	Prefers to avoid uncertainty and ambiguity by establishing structures and rules governing social conduct and behaviour
Minimize rules and rituals governing social conduct and behaviour	Desire or demand consensus about social goals
Consensus for social goals not necessary	Low or no tolerance for dissent or deviation from established norms
Few established social rules, rituals and regulations	Characterized by rigid rules, rituals and regulations

Source: Summarized from Lustig and Koester (1993).

In cultures high in UAI, classroom routines are often fixed and rigid, and insistence on one correct answer for each question is typical. Richards and Lockhart's quote from a teacher in Egypt reflects preference to avoid uncertainty:

> When I present a reading text to the class, the students expect me to go through it word by word and explain every point of vocabulary or grammar. They would be uncomfortable if I left it for them to work it out on their own or ask them just to try to understand the main ideas. (Richards and Lockhart 1994: 108)

Hofstede's scores from the UK and the United States (as well as Canada, New Zealand and Australia) reveal that individuals in these countries are more at ease living with ambiguity and uncertainty than those in Mexico, Turkey, France, Argentina and Japan, for example, which are countries scoring high UAI (Hofstede 1980: 315). In classroom discourse, a hierarchically oriented teacher will not be comfortable with students proposing their own ideas but will insist on them to use the options offered in the coursebook even when unfamiliar to students, as we saw in Rima's case. As already mentioned, in each country or cultural group, individuals differ in these dimensions to varying degrees, as we will see later on in some other classes.

Culture in the Classroom

As mentioned earlier, internationally marketed TEYL/TEVYL courses are produced primarily in the United States and UK, both egalitarian cultures scoring low in Hofstede's PDI, whereas many of the user countries represent hierarchical cultures, scoring high in PDI. Malaysia, Brazil, Mexico, China and the Arab countries are some examples of hierarchical cultures. In other words, in many of the end-user countries, social status, rank, gender, age and other factors determine the expected, appropriate classroom role behaviours, which are often quite different from those appropriate in the producer countries. For example, in an egalitarian culture low in PDI, it is not unusual for the teacher to take on a facilitator or observer role as learners work in pairs or small groups, as we will see later in Joanna's class. However, in a hierarchical culture, the expected role of the teacher is to provide knowledge and information as learners listen to and learn from the teacher. The communicatively oriented TEYL materials, originally devised for older learners in Western countries with relatively small and well-resourced classes, do not, therefore, always work in the intended ways in hierarchical cultures. As Holliday warns, there are elements in this approach that are not 'culture-sensitive' because they 'are *not* adaptable to any social situation' (1994: 169) (emphasis in the original).

A good example of what may happen when the content is not relevant to learners and where teachers represent hierarchical approaches was observed in Tanya's fourth-grade class. Students (age nine) were working on an 'ask and answer' activity presented in their lesson, in which two, Rick and Lisa, are talking about pocket money:

'My dad gives me pocket money. He gives me three pounds every week. I buy books, comics, and sweets. Sometimes, I save my money and buy a computer game.' 'My mum gives me pocket money. She also gives me three pounds every week.' (Holt 2005: 34)

Tanya instructed students to take turns to practice the dialogue and corrected every error students made. When one student read the answer offered in the book *He gives me three pounds*, the teacher instructs him to say how much his father gives him, the student shyly says in Arabic that he does not get any pocket money, which is not uncommon in Lebanon. So, the teacher asks him to pretend he gets about three thousand Lebanese pounds (two US dollars at the time). The student again proceeds to read the answer from the book, which generates giggles from the class as the items mentioned would cost far more than the three pounds. The teacher does not recast the student's L1 response to English but guides the student to pretend he gets pocket money. This prompts the student to return to the book, and an opportunity to validate the student's frank (and possibly embarrassing) response is lost. For example, the teacher could have said something like 'OK. Not all children everywhere get pocket money. In some countries children can earn pocket money for doing chores, like taking out the trash or washing dishes.' An interesting discussion could have ensued within which language could have been practiced in a real conversation before reverting back to the book. The resulting outcome here was 'routine teaching characterized by a heavy reliance on the textbook with few opportunities for spontaneous communication or interaction' (Holliday 1994: 103).

Clearly there was a mismatch between the material writers' perceptions about reality in some of the classrooms where their books are used. To quote Holliday, many teachers face a difficult dilemma: 'How to be in a classroom which is her own while at the same time belonging to others' (Holliday 2002: 4). Instead of monitoring student–student interactions, as clearly intended by the materials' writers, teachers monitor the accuracy of their production, as Rima did in the first episode at the beginning of the chapter, as did the teacher in the above example.

While adhering to the book provides not only structure but also security in terms of what is perceived 'correct' or expected, it leaves students with little opportunity to personalize the new language.

Teachers and students also bring into the classroom their personal perceptions about their roles, which may differ from the mainstream cultural tendencies. For example, a teacher working in a hierarchical culture may have lived or studied in a country where more egalitarian interactions are observed and will thus have acquired a more egalitarian approach to teaching. In such a case, the teacher may find it easier to implement the Western-style communicative language teaching approach presented in typical TEYL coursebooks than a teacher who has lived and studied only in a hierarchical culture. Let us take Joanna as an example. She moved to Canada as a very young child and went through school and college there. She had moved to Lebanon only two years before the recorded lessons in her class. In Episode 1.3, her fifth-graders are working on a restaurant dialogue in their ESL book. Student desks are pushed together to create an open space in the front of the room and students are sitting on the floor in a circle. Their task is to write dialogues between a waiter and a customer, using vocabulary from the word bank in their book. Each one starts with a sentence, passes the paper to the next student and so on, until the dialogues are complete. Joanna sits on the floor with students. When the dialogues are completed, students take turns to perform the dialogues as Joanna observes them, making occasional comments:

Episode 1.3

S1: And for you a soup, soup with rice.
T: Uh uh! You already ordered, so the 'for you' means (xx) for you. So she wants the soup and rice [indicating a student]
S1: A soup with rice
S2: Do you want des-desert, dessert [giggles]
S1: No thank you
S1: Thank you for everything.
T: OK. Thank you. Now who is going to roleplay?
S3: *Are you ready to order?* [reads from his paper]
S4: Yes, I am ready (xxx) [giggles]. Yes, I am ready. What's … soup
T: What's Tony's mistake here?
Ss: [several simultaneous comments] Tony should say (xxx)
T: Tony should say 'What's the soup today?'
S4: What's the soup today?
S3: The soup is (xxx) tomato and rice
S4: OK. I'll take it.
S5: I take an salad eggs
T: Egg salad
S5: Egg salad
S3: Anything for dessert?
S4: I take ice cream.
S5: I don't want
T: I don't want what?
S5: Dessert
F3: Do you want anything else?
S4: No thank you
S5: Give us the bill, please.
S3: It's five thousand
S4: That's ten thousand.
S5: Here's your change [laughter as customer reads the waiter's line]
S3: Here's your change.
S5: Keep the change [student's spontaneous addition not in the written dialogue]

Students are all paying attention and participate eagerly. Although Joanna does intervene and much of the vocabulary and phrases are from the word bank in the book, her interventions are more guiding than rejections, enabling the flow of the dialogue to continue. Although some of the menu items may not have been very familiar to the children, such as 'egg salad', for example, they knew the words. The activity proceeded very much in the way it was apparently intended by the author/s of the book. The mood of the session was quite different from the one observed in Rima's and Tanya's classes. Presumably Joanna's Canadian background had shaped her perceptions about the roles of teachers and students, as Rima's and Tanya's Lebanese background had shaped their views.

'Culture-Friendly' Materials

Contrary to what was observed during Rima's season dialogue and Tanya's pocket money dialogue, when teachers work with stories, even many quite hierarchical teachers engage their students in more meaningful interactions than during the dialogue practice. It seems that stories are more 'culture-friendly' than the culturally situated dialogue practice. This is illustrated in the following episode from Rima's fourth-grade class. The class is discussing the *Wizard of Oz*, of which an abbreviated form was presented in their coursebook. Rima had also managed to show the class a full feature film of the story, and the discussion happened the day after children had watched the film.

Episode 1.4

- **T:** What did you like about the story?
- **S1:** I liked the good witch.
- **T:** You liked the good witch. Why did you like the good witch?
- **S1:** Because IT is very good.
- **T:** What did she do that was good? She did something special.
- **S1:** Yes.
- **T:** Uhhuh. Do you remember what it was? What was special about her?
- **S1:** She was ((generous))
- **Ss:** Generous!
- **T:** Did she give something to other people?
- **S2:** The good witch gave to Dorothy the slippers.
- **T:** Uhhuh. Slippers.
- **S2:** Yes.

T: What kind of slippers?
S2: Uh, red magic slippers.
T: Why did she give slippers to Dorothy?
S2: Because can help her when she is in trouble.
T: OK. So, they were very special slippers.
S3: Teacher!
T: Yes?
S3: Why she put slippers outside? (Ghosn 2003a: 12)

Although Rima is in control of the discourse and clearly has in mind the correct answers she expects from her students, the discourse is interactive and connected, students are engaged and some negotiation is also taking place. Rima's feedback is affirming rather than rejecting, and she does not correct the student's use of pronoun 'it' for the witch but validates the response and repeats the pronoun 'she' twice in her feedback.

Observations have consistently confirmed the distinct difference in discourse and teacher feedback related to the instructional materials used. Even when students offer 'incorrect' responses to factual questions about stories, teachers rarely reject them outright, as in 'No, it was not …'. Rather, they engage in some sort of negotiation of topic like, 'Hmm, are you sure?', 'Oh, did she …?' or 'Tina said that … do you all agree?' And when students respond to such prompts, they do not recite text from the book, but either try to rephrase their responses, turn to their neighbours for ideas or try to scan the text to find where they could check the information. In contrast, when students engage in so-called conversation practice, teacher focus zeroes in on form errors, and subsequently, students read their parts mechanically from the book rather than attempting to express their own ideas.

Discussion and Conclusions

Culture determines how people perceive interpersonal relations, authority and their roles as teachers and learners. How teachers approach the lessons will influence how students respond, how the classroom discourse will take shape and determine, to a large extent, how students engage with the lesson and how quickly they pick up new vocabulary and structures. Cultural differences in levels of hierarchy and subsequent communication patters have implications in a language classroom. First, during dialogue practice, a hierarchical teacher is more likely to overtly correct learner errors and provide negative feedback than an egalitarian teacher, which in turn will affect learner engagement. While an outgoing, self-confident student may not mind being overtly corrected in front of their peers, a more timid and less confident student may avoid participating in order not to be embarrassed or ridiculed. This may have a negative impact on participation and consequently on learning.

Second, since language learning is now widely believed to be facilitated by negotiated interactions, one needs to understand what factors the young learner classrooms encourage and invite negotiated interactions and which might hinder them. If there is a mismatch between materials writers' expectations about how their materials should be used and what the prevailing culture the end-users perceive as appropriate, awkward situations may arise that do not necessarily promote optimal learning. If the teacher's adopted approach goes contrary to the prevailing cultural values and expectation, the teacher may face resistance not only from students but also from parents and administrators, as many teachers have reported to be common. For example, a Lebanese teacher, whose class had been assigned a communicatively oriented coursebook, stated the following when questioned why she did not follow the teacher's guide:

> When I first started teaching at [the school], I tried to follow the teacher's book and I think students liked it ... but anyway, the coordinator told me to stop doing it because some parents were complaining. They said my class was out of control and that I wasn't teaching the children anything, and that they were just talking to each other and playing games. So, now I don't do that anymore. (Ghosn 2004: 114)

In contrast to the communicatively oriented language materials that expect learners to take on roles of American or British children and talk about sometimes culturally unfamiliar topics, story-based instruction can be more 'culture-friendly' in that talking about stories allows the interlocutors to remain in their own comfortable cultural roles, as we saw in Lily's fourth-grade class. Culturally situated stories can also provide learners with information about the target language culture and illustrate what is common among people everywhere, such as Alexander's disappointing day.

To sum up, cultures differ widely in the ways interpersonal relationships are perceived, and these perceptions influence communication patterns, including language classroom discourse. Culture determines how people perceive interpersonal relations, authority and their roles as teachers and learners. In egalitarian cultures, language teachers are comfortable taking on a facilitator role, monitoring student–student interactions, as Joanna did during the restaurant dialogue and what is clearly expected by the authors of the dialogue. In contrast, a hierarchically oriented teacher, like Rima, is the authority figure and provider of knowledge, with students expected to take in that knowledge without questioning. Although the discourse in her class during the episode about the *Wizard of Oz* was more natural and interactive than that observed during the dialogue about seasons, Rima clearly had in mind the answers students should provide. While Lily's cultural background is the same as Rima's, Alexander's story content intrigued the children, and they initiated questions, which Lily answered. The discourse was genuine while Lily still remained in her teacher role.

Recommendations for Practice

Teachers

- If the coursebook presents dialogue practice with culturally unfamiliar topics, teachers can prepare their students for it in advance. Before doing dialogues about free time activities, for instance, the teacher can encourage students to talk about their *own* free time activities that are common in their life, as in the following hypothetical example:

    T: Let's talk about our free time activities. What do you do when you are at home and have finished your homework, or on days when there is no school. What do you like to do?
    S1: I like go ((camel races))
    T: OK. So, you like to go and watch camel races. Nice. Who else likes to watch camel races?
    S2: Me and my friends we play basket.
    T: Ah, you play basketball with your friends. Basketball is a popular sport. Do you also watch basketball games on TV?
    S2: Yes, we ((support)) Tigers.
    T: I see, you support the Tigers. Who else supports the Tigers?
    S3: I play Barbies with Nancy.
    T: You and Nancy play with Barbie dolls. Nice, my daughter also likes to play with Barbies. Do you collect them? Do you have many of them?

Students can then use their own free time activities in their dialogues if the provided options are not relevant to them. This way, the dialogues could be personalized, at least in part. After all, the aim of such exercises is not to learn all the activity vocabulary, such as coin collecting or gardening, for example, but to practice asking questions and using the present tense to describe habitual actions.

Materials Developers

- Include in the teachers' guides suggestions on how teachers can adapt the dialogue content when it is too unfamiliar to the students.
- Include more culturally diverse topics and activities in the word bank options in the dialogues.

2

Narrative and Children's Language Learning

'And what is the use of a book', thought Alice, 'without pictures or conversation?'

Lewis Carroll – *Alice's Adventures in Wonderland*

Why We Need Stories

We humans are storytellers, or *Homo narrans*, a term coined by German folklorist Kurt Ranke in the 1960s. Lehman (2014) notes that for Ranke, storytelling was a basic human need, while philosopher MacIntyre actually suggests that we experience life as 'a series of narratives, conflicts, and characters, with beginnings, middles, and ends' (MacIntyre, quoted in Dégh 1994: 245). In fact, Bruner (1986) considers narrative as the primary mode of thought and a fundamental way in which we encode and make sense of our experiences. Beach, Bissell and Wise (2016) extend Bruner's notion arguing that narratives are not only a natural mode of thinking, but narrative thought equals 'mind', and that the need to think narratively reflects known neurological processes.

It is therefore not surprising that human interest in stories goes back thousands of years. The importance of stories for children was recognized already by Plato, who in his *Republic* calls stories as 'soul-shaping forces for children' and advised storytellers to 'select their stories whenever they are fine and beautiful' and to 'persuade nurses and mothers to tell their children the ones we have selected, since they will shape their children's souls with stories' (Plato *c*.377/1992: 60–1).

Stories are equally important to adults, because without narratives we would not have our memories and our histories. Aidan Chambers explains why stories are essential for us:

> In every language, in every part of the world, story is the fundamental grammar of all thought and communication. By telling ourselves what happened, to whom, and why we not only discover ourselves and the world, but we change and create ourselves and the world too. (Chambers 1985: 59)

Livo and Riertz see story somewhat differently but equally as important, arguing that

> a universal mirror that shows us the 'truth' about ourselves – who and why we are. When we look into this mirror, we see daily routine and mundane circumstances transformed into something profound. 'Story' takes the ordinary … revealing the significance of the trivial. (Livo and Riertz 1986: 4)

Vandergrift makes an important argument when she says that for children 'literature is an exploration of life and living, a chance to try life on for size as a confirmation, an illumination, or an extension of life experiences' (Vandergrift 1990: 160). Escott in turn points out that 'stories offer children the chance to consider representations of the world and its values … allow them to consider, with a safety of distancing that fiction allows, new circumstances and possibilities' (Escott 1995: 20). In the words of Bruner (1986), narratives develop children's 'landscape of consciousness', the ability to think about the mental states of other people. Story narratives will also develop language children need to refer to mental states, for example, noun clause complements (deVilliers and deVilliers 2000), such as 'he thinks monsters are real' or 'she could not believe what she saw'.

Reading the classic *Cinderella* story may offer the young reader insight into what Cinderella might have thought about the stepsisters, as well as how it might feel to be bullied. When reading Farley's *The Black Stallion*, young readers can be guided to discuss Alec's feelings and fears, and imagine how they might have reacted in a similar situation. Gackenback's delightful *Harry and the Terrbile Whatzit* is a story about courage and overcoming one's fear and encourages children to talk about Harry worrying about his mother, and what he felt when he saw the Whatzit. Garvie (1990), in fact, views stories as vehicles for language and culture learning, saying that story is 'going somewhere and the learner wants to reach the end of the journey' (Garvie 1990: 31).

Although the word 'story' is used in many ways ('The story of the day'; 'What's your life story?' 'Let's hear your side of the story'), the terms 'story' and 'literature' are here used interchangeably and are understood to be accounts 'of imaginary or real people and events told for entertainment' as defined by the *Oxford Dictionary* (online). A story narrative has a defined setting and characters, whether animal, human or objects. Children's stories often feature animals and toys or other objects as characters such as *Peter Rabbit*, *Winnie the Pooh* and *Corduroy*. A story also has a plot and a logical, satisfying conclusion, and it is told in the past tense, unlike sports commentaries, which are typically delivered in the present tense. Just as any good children's story, language learning stories (referred to some as language learner literature) should feature amusing, repetitious refrains that will provide language learners with useful chunks of language. Ideally, stories would also conform to Goforth's definition of good children's literature as works that 'authentically and imaginatively express the thoughts, emotions, experiences, and information about the human condition, offer insight and/ or intellectual stimulation, relate to the experiences, developmental levels, and literary preferences of the intended audience' (Goforth 1998: 3).

Rich Language of Children's Literature

'Life of literature is in its language,' says Vandergrift (1990: 160), and English children's book market features a vast array of titles that not only present rich, contextualized language and fit Goforth's above criteria, but that are also suitable in a primary school language class. Because story is the fundamental grammar of all thought and communication (Chambers 1985), stories can provide a link between languages, enabling learners to move beyond word and sentence-level awareness of language to a more 'overall awareness' – differences in discourse sequence, the ways words link and the understanding of inferences (Lazar 1994). In other words, stories can teach language learners something about '*how* language means' and not only '*what* it means' (Carter and McRae 2002: 10) (emphases in the original). Literature is full of examples of different life situations – whether realistic or fantastical – providing language in a variety of registers within clearly defined contexts of discourse. When children are exposed to different literary genres (poems, realistic fiction, fantasy, humour, etc.), they will gain knowledge about vocabulary, language patterns, idioms and metaphors. For example, idioms are notoriously difficult for second language learners, but if young ELLs read or listen to the hilariously funny *Amelia Bedelia* stories by Parish, they can accumulate a good collection of idioms. They will also begin to develop an understanding of how not to interpret idioms literally as Amelia did when she was asked to 'dress the chicken' and 'draw the curtains', for example.

Good children's authors know how to select their words and offer those that 'tumble and scramble and fall, engaged with meanings' (Butzow and Butzow

2000: 14). Therefore, literature can also promote awareness of language use, which Widdowson (cited in McKay 1986) has defined as knowing how to use language rules for communication. It may also help learners to internalize the language by providing them with access to a much more extensive experience of contextualized linguistic items than what is offered in the typical primary school language coursebooks. Nick Butterworth's delightful *One Snowy Night* offers a good example:

> It was a fox! He looked very cold and hungry. 'Can I come in, too?' he asked. Percy scratched his head and thought for a minute. 'Well, if you promise to behave,' he said. 'I promise,' said the fox, and he squeezed into the bed next to all the other animals Bump! Oops! The squirrel fell out. 'Who did that?' asked the squirrel crossly. (1989: n.p.)

Although not intended for language teaching, it is not difficult to imagine how advanced beginners will be caught in the storyline. Even if they don't understand every word, the illustrations provide enough context for the meaning to become clear. Children will readily act out especially the above exchange over and over again, with each repetition reinforcing the chunks of language, helping children pick up some of them for their own use. One can easily see the immediate usefulness of structures such as 'can I come too?' 'if you promise' and 'who did that?' for primary school children.

Another delightful story that features simple, but captivating, repetitious refrains is Slobodkina's old classic, *Caps for Sale*. In the story, a cap peddler encounters a troop of mischievous monkeys who confiscate his caps while he takes a nap under a tree.

> 'You monkeys, you', he said, shaking his finger at them. 'You give me back my caps'. But the monkeys only shook their fingers back at him and said, 'Tsz, tsz, tsz'. ([1940] 1987: n.p.)

As the peddler gets angrier and angrier, he shakes his fists and stomps his feet, only to find the monkeys up in the tree mimicking his every move. Finally, in desperation, he throws his own cap to the ground and – you guessed – gets all his caps back. The story's popularity is evident from the fact that it is still in print after more than seventy years of its original publication. Children love the story, and it is perfect for total physical response (TPR) activities, offering also opportunities for contextualized language practice.

Fortunately, as mentioned, the body of English-language children's literature is vast and many stories are available that contain rich, natural language and repetitious refrains, which children can pick up and use in their own communication efforts. Motivation to read – or to listen – is kept high as the reader is eager to confirm their predictions, and new structures and vocabulary are acquired, not as a result of drill and practice, but as an outcome of the reader–text interaction. Very appropriately, Bassnet and Grundy argue that

> literature is a high point of language usage; arguably it marks the greatest skills a language user can demonstrate. Anyone who wants to acquire a profound knowledge of language that goes beyond the utilitarian will read literary texts in that language. (Bassnet and Grundy 1993: 7)

Although Bassnet and Grundy have older learners in mind, their argument is equally valid for young learners; why would we want to leave young second language learners at 'the utilitarian' level of English, particularly in FLAPPS context (Ghosn, 2001, p. 19)? It is, therefore not surprising that an increasing number of young learner coursebooks feature storylines. There is, however, a problem with some of the lower level books, which delay the introduction of the past tense verbs for the first two or three levels, even in stories. This not only renders the 'story' unnatural but also denies young learners access to past tense verbs they would need to produce their own narratives. For example, if the teacher wants to encourage learners to share something about their weekend or holiday experiences, it would be difficult without simple past tense verbs.

An exception to the practice of simplification and adherence to present tense verbs is *Amazing English* by Addison-Wesley, a series which unfortunately went out of print in the wake of publishing house mergers in the 1990s. In this series, even the first-level kindergarten book featured past tense, as shown in the rebus story *The Gingerbread Man* (in the book the words in square brackets are presented as pictures):

> Once upon a time, a [woman] made a [gingerbread man]. When she opened the oven door, out jumped the [gingerbread man]! Away he ran. 'Stop!' cried the [woman]. But the [gingerbread man] just laughed. (1987: n.p.)

The verbs 'made', 'opened', 'jumped', 'ran', 'cried', 'laughed', 'saw', 'came' and 'said' appear several times each, and the illustrations help make sense of the meaning.

The Rabbit and the Turnip, from the same Addison-Wesley series, is another good example of language teaching story that fits also Goforth's earlier identified criteria of literature, albeit written for didactic purposes. The story features Little Rabbit, who in the middle of winter finds two turnips and decides to share one with another hungry friend, Little Donkey. Little

Donkey comes home with some potatoes and is surprised to find a turnip on his doorstep and decides to give it to Little Sheep, and the turnip eventually finds its way back to Little Rabbit. The language has repetitious refrains in a natural context, and the past tense verbs make it a true narrative. The underlined phrases in the following excerpt are repeated a number of times in the course of the story:

> It was winter. It was snowing very hard. It was very cold. … Little Rabbit found two turnips. He gobbled one right up. He wanted the other turnip. Then he thought of his friend Little Donkey. 'Little Donkey is probably hungry, too. I'll take this turnip to him.' Little Donkey was not at home. [Little Donley comes home.] He had some potatoes to eat. 'How kind of someone to give me this turnip', he thought. (Walker 1987: n.p.)

Children can easily relate to story's theme of sharing and thinking of others. Some basic food items are introduced (turnip, potatoes, lettuce, carrots), and the repetitious chunks of language can serve as useful shortcuts to children's own communication efforts. Depending on the context, vegetables familiar to the particular children could be substituted or added. The past tense verbs are particularly important for children, as they will enable children to develop their own narratives about their experiences in the new language.

When in a TESOL Conference in the late 1990s, I lamented the lack of past tense verbs in the early levels of young learner coursebooks, a well-known applied linguist (whom I shall not identify) argued that 'you cannot teach them the past tense before they know the present tense of a verb'. However, that notion is based on the observed emergence of grammatical forms in language learners' output. We should not confuse emergence with exposure. Exposure to structures need not mirror the observed emergence of grammatical forms. Imagine if caregivers would refrain from exposing young first language learners to natural language; how long would it take for children to acquire language. Second language learners in naturalistic settings have exposure to by far richer, grammatically not sequenced language than what they are able to produce. With frequent exposure and opportunities to use the language, correct forms will gradually emerge.

Motivating Power of Story

Good children's literature has long been an inherent part of successful first language literacy and reading programs in North American schools, and it is equally justifiable in an English-language program. First, children are naturally drawn to stories, which with their primarily narrative form respond to the universal human need for narrative (Hardy 1978). Hence stories provide a potentially highly motivating medium for language teaching. The rich, contextualized language of high-quality storybooks facilitates language learning, and story discussions can activate many of the language functions associated with academic subject matter learning, as we will see later on.

Eric Carle's classic picture storybook *The Very Hungry Caterpillar* is a good example of how good stories keep children motivated. In Lebanon, the story kept a kindergarten class of four-year-olds intensely occupied for four weeks, as we will see in Chapter 11, and Machura (1995) reports advanced twelve-year-olds enthusiastically working through the same story in Hungary. The appeal of this story to such a large age span demonstrates the power of skillfully constructed narrative represented through the language that is both rich and predictable in its repetitious features. Carle's superb illustrations undoubtedly add to the appeal as they not only clarify and extend the language but provide a visually aesthetic experience as well.

Bettelheim (1986) recognized the significance reading material has for the developing child and the way children learn to understand the world and themselves. He says if reading material is 'so shallow in substance that little of significance can be gained', reading 'becomes devalued when what one has learned to read adds nothing of importance to one's life' (Bettleheim 1986: 4). Although Bettelheim's remarks refer to first language context, one needs only to alter his argument a little to make it apply for second language learning: if language teaching materials are so shallow in substance that little of significance can be gained, language learning becomes devalued when what has been learned adds nothing of importance to one's life (Ghosn 2013). Exton and O'Rourke's concerns in second language context resonate with Bettelheim: reading and language activities generated by the typical basal reader texts fail to offer readers any satisfaction and may actually foster a notion that 'reading and perhaps language in general involves the expenditure of effort upon texts that give back neither pleasure nor information in return' (Exton and O'Rourke 1993: 27–8). In a second language class, there is the danger that the learners will see the new language in this light. However, when teachers engage learners with quality stories and picture storybooks, motivation is likely guaranteed and learning the new language will be enjoyable and meaningful.

Developmental Significance of Narrative

Stories are narratives, and Barbara Hardy of the University of London suggests convincingly that narrative is the way we order our world. She says,

> We dream in narrative, day-dream in narrative, remember, anticipate, hope, despair, believe, doubt, plan, revise, criticize, construct, gossip, learn, hate, love by narrative. In order to live, we make up stories about ourselves and others, about the personal, as well as the social past and future. (Hardy 1978: 13)

Narrative is also believed to form a significant if not a vital part of children's cognitive development (Beach, Bissell and Wise 2016; Bruner 1986; Meek 1988; Wells 1986). Understanding story narratives is a complex mental activity, requiring the integration of linguistic, cognitive and social abilities, and the more children have opportunities to listen to and read stories, the better they develop their understanding of the world. The Bristol Language Project (Wells 1986) found that children who had had the most stories read to them by age seven were much more competent at subjects requiring symbolic thought than their age peers with less story experiences. This resonates with Bruner's argument that story plays an important role in developing thought processes in children.

It is obvious that cognitive development is critical for academic success, and there is evidence from multiple sources that reading of narratives enhances cognitive development. For example, studies on college-level students reveal a link between narrative reading habits and their grade point average (GPA) (Chen 2007; Gallick 1999), and their ability to examine issues from multiple perspectives (Facione 2004; Miller 2003). It is safe to assume that students in these studies had not suddenly picked up the reading habit in high school or college but most likely had been readers in childhood. The earlier learners are exposed to narrative texts, the more likely the positive influence on their cognitive development.

One might reasonably argue that different modes of thinking are required in formal reasoning typical of academic discourse than what is involved in narrative texts such as children's stories. However, Bruner (1986), one of the foremost cognitive psychologists, argues that the cognitive processes involved in making sense of narratives, such as sequence, cause-and-effect relationships, connections between related ideas, perspective-taking and reflection, form a basis for the kind of thinking involved in academic discourse. According to Facione (2004), Oatley (2002) and others, because these cognitive processes are fundamental in academic writing, mastery of narrative is also a precursor to academic writing.

Perspective-taking, the ability to reflect on and understand the thoughts and behaviours of others, is essential in strategies of academic rhetoric, such as predicting and refuting counterarguments (Whalen 2010). Perspective-taking ability and fantasy narrative seem to be correlated and carry over to real-world situations (Mar 2004; Oatley 2002; Vine and Faust 1992). Mar et al. (2006) have also found a high correlation between students' reading of fictional narratives and their reading of non-fiction, and Whalen suggests that 'developing fantasy through narratives prepares students to engage with academic texts' (Whalen 2010: 13). The more practice readers have making sense of fantasy, the better they are able to recall previous knowledge and connect it to new information (Brookfield 2005; Tennant and Pogson 1995). While this is true about both fiction and non-fiction, according to Oatley (2002) fictional narratives result in better recall than non-fiction narratives.

Research has clearly shown that children's narrative ability is predictive of both later language proficiency and academic achievement (Bishop and Edmundson 1987; Dickinson and McCabe 1991; Fazio, Naremore and Connell 1996; Hemphill, Picardi and Tager-Flusberg 1991; Roth and Spekman 1986), and plays an important role in developing academic discourse and literacy and is positively related to school engagement (Diez-Itza et al. 2018). Based on their research, Pauls and Archibald (2022) suggest that due to the cognitive demand of narratives, language interventions based on narratives can have a positive influence also on academic skills of children with developmental language disorders. Given that, one could argue that because of their narrative structure of stories, story-based instruction can have a positive influence also on young second language learners.

These findings resonate with Wells, who argues that 'stories provide a major route to understanding' (Wells 1986: 206), positing that constructing stories 'in the mind is one of the most fundamental means of making meaning; as such it is an activity that pervades all aspects of learning' (ibid: 194), a view shared by many other researchers. In other words, narrative should not be thought of as a mere recount of experience.

Narrative constitutes also a foundational skill in children's writing development (Kaderavek and Sulzby 2000; Roth and Spekman 1986). Although writing in academic subjects arguably differs in structure from narrative, narratives provide young second language learners with an important basis for later writing. Bearne argues that children's narrative writings 'carry the seeds of other, non-narrative forms of writing' (Bearne 1995: 14), and she presents a compilation of research studies that support her argument. Rosen (1985, quoted in Bearne 1995: 12) also suggests that 'inside every narrative there stalk the ghosts of non-narrative discourse ... inside very non-narrative discourse, there stalk the ghosts of narrative'. Among emergent literacy variables, children's oral narrative competence has been found to be the only significant predictive of later competence to produce structured, coherent and cohesive written narratives (Pinto, Tarchi and Bigozzi 2016). In later chapters we will examine the influence of storybooks on young English learners' written expression and literate language.

Moreover, stories present a variety of discussion topics, with the possibilities ranging from the literal to those that transcend the story and allow children to link the story to their own lives, at times making sophisticated generalizations, as McConaghy illustrates: After listening to her first-grade teacher read Jewell and Himler's *Bus Ride*, young Ada said, 'That story reminded me of when I go to the doctor's office. Sometimes I meet a friend and we play and then she goes into the doctor and I go into mine and we never see each other again' (quoted in McConaghy 1990: 36). Yet, the story is not about going to the doctor's but about a young girl travelling by herself and during the bus ride meets an elderly lady. During the ride they develop a friendship that sadly comes to an end when the little girl reaches her destination and gets off the bus. Ada's comment reveals that she has not only recognized the theme of short-term relationships but also linked it to her own experience.

Children can also develop insight from stories. This is how a ten-year-old Lebanese English-language learner compared Steptoe's *Mufaro's Beautiful Daughters* and San Souci's *Talking Eggs* (text left uncorrected):

> 'Talking Eggs' and 'Mufaro's Beautiful Daughters'
>
> The two stories are similar by that Nyasha and Blanche escape from home, but they different that Nyasha went to the King. But Blanche went to an old woman's house and help her. Manyara should learn that not to be a show off because maybe she would have good luck without cheating. (Ghosn 2006: 24)

Clearly, the writer has given Manyara's behaviour some thought and her comment reveals insight into Manyara's character.

Let us also look at Gregory's 'knowledge centre' model. She proposes that storybooks can provide scaffolding for young English-language learners by developing what she refers to as 'knowledge centres', the development of which is facilitated by stories. For example, she suggests that the lexical knowledge centre reinforces collocation and word association, the orthographic/graphophonic knowledge centre helps develop awareness of letter and sound patterns, and the syntactic knowledge centre provides useful chunks of language. What is particularly relevant in Gregory's model for young learners in FLAPPS context is not only the development of linguistic knowledge centres but also the semantic knowledge centre, which widens the learners' range of awareness of cultural concepts, different ways of life and universal values. In addition to the culturally oriented knowledge that Gregory considers, literature can also broaden learners' knowledge base of history and social issues, depending on the titles selected.

Stories rich in rhyme and onomatopoeia will contribute to development of orthographic knowledge centre, while stories that present collocations and lexical sets will contribute to lexical knowledge centre. Syntactic knowledge centre is broadened by stories that feature chunks of language, such as '*I knew it will be a terrible, horrible, no good very bad day*' from Viorst's Alexander and *Terrible, Horrible, No Good, Very Bad Day*. The same often repeated sentence in the story will also reinforce the lexical knowledge centre with the multiple expressions meaning 'very bad'. The story can also add to learners' semantic knowledge centre, presenting the universal concept of disappointment and hurt caused by teasing, as we all as common daily life experiences of a young American boy.

Finally, when reading story narratives, readers learn to understand characters' emotions in different situations, and research shows that emotional perception ability correlates with Scholastic Aptitude Test (SAT) scores (Mayer and Geher, cited in Whalen 2010). Emotional perception ability is also important in peer relations, and the importance of peer adjustment in middle childhood cannot be underestimated, and this adjustment has been linked to narrative ability. Davidson et al. (2017: 891) argue that attention to sequence of events, cause effect connections between events, and motivation and moral significance of human behaviours may be precursors for establishing and maintaining positive peer relationships during primary school years. They found that writing personal narratives about peer interactions which had 'chronological and thematic coherence and reports of moral concerns' contributed to more positive perception of peers and lower levels of loneliness. In a second language class, story-based instruction can foster the skills required to understand characters' motivations and emotions and thus promote social adjustment.

Conclusion

Because stories are of fundamental importance to us humans, and no less so for children, carefully selected illustrated children's stories can provide a rich medium for language teaching. Stories have a strong motivational power to draw children to them and keep them engaged in lessons evolving around good stories. Story narratives contribute also to children's cognitive development, and should, therefore, have a central place in TEYL and TEVYL curricula. It is particularly important to introduce paste tense verbs, as they not only mirror language used in the real world but are also necessary to enable young learners to craft their own personal narratives in the new language. Furthermore, stories can help develop learners' linguistic knowledge centres and widen their background knowledge, as well.

When selecting titles for the language class, it will be good to keep in mind Vandergrift's and Goforth's earlier cited notions about good children's literature. It will be also very useful to keep in mind the cautionary note of C. S. Lewis, the author of *The Chronicles of Narnia*, who argues that 'a children's story which is enjoyed only by children is a bad children's story' (Lewis 1963: 460). It is, indeed, a hallmark of good children's story that readers of all ages will find it interesting, amusing, sad or meaningful in some way.

Recommendations for Practice

Teachers

- Whenever possible, supplement the coursebook with children's literature and read the stories to children.
- If the coursebook includes stories that are told in the present tense, reword them using the past tense forms and retell the story a number of times. Ask questions that call for the past tense verb: 'Where did Goldilocks go? She went ….' Model the correct past tense form and provide assistance until children pick it up.
- Whether authentic children's story or a retold version of a coursebook story, invite children to retell the story in their own words. As children offer their ideas, write their sentences on the board. When children are satisfied that they have all the important ideas included, they can copy their version in their copybooks. Then, invite children to write a new story, using their version of the original as a template.
- If possible, obtain copies of high-quality storybooks, such as those mentioned in this chapter, and read them to the class using some of the approaches teachers in this volume demonstrate. Inexpensive paperback copies of popular children's book are readily available on the internet.

Materials Developers

- As much as possible, incorporate natural sounding narrative texts – both fiction and interesting non-fiction – into TEYL and TEVYL coursebooks. Draw on these texts to develop relevant vocabulary and language-practice activities.
- In the teacher's guide, provide suggestions on how to use the non-narrative texts to generate narrative discourse and texts.

3

Meeting the Challenge of English-Medium Instruction with Stories

'Reeling, Writhing, of course, to begin with', the Mock Turtle replied; 'and then the different branches of Arithmetic – Ambition, Distraction, Uglification, and Derison.

Lewis Carroll – Alice's Adventures in Wonderland

Given that one purpose of this volume is to examine how Arabic-speaking children can develop sufficient English-language skills to manage EMI in subject matter classes, it is pertinent to allocate some time to discuss academic literacy and how it develops. If students are to be successful in school subjects taught in English, mastering interpersonal communication, or even basic literacy, is not sufficient. Because language underpins the whole academic curriculum, children must develop also competence in the language needed to access different school subjects successfully. The term 'academic L2 literacy' is used here to refer to such competence. To be 'literate' in something, according to *Merriam-Webster's Collegiate Dictionary* (1994: 680), means, among other things, 'having knowledge or competence' in something, while 'competence' refers to 'knowledge that enables a person to speak and understand language' (ibid: 234). Therefore, to be academically literate means to have knowledge of and be able to speak and understand the language associated with school subjects, that is, academic discourse. Students must not only be able to read subject matter texts but also be able to express their knowledge in classroom discussions and written exams. In other words, they need to develop competency in the language of academic discourse.

Skills of General Academic Literacy

Much has been written about students developing academic literacy, and much of the related research has focused on immigrant children's performance in subject matter classes and performance of foreign students in tertiary education in English-speaking countries. Much less has been written about children's learning in EMI schools in countries where English is not the mainstream language. This can pose a problem for young learners' academic progress in EMI subjects. Academic language includes both general and subject-specific language. Some of the general language functions required for subject matter learning include the ability to ask questions, understand written texts and written instructions for tasks, and familiarity with general academic register. Skills such as analysing, reflecting, examining different viewpoints critically and justifying one's opinions are part of academic language functions and should be learned early on. In primary school classes, children stories offer many opportunities for these skills to develop as long as the teacher takes advantage of them. Students must also be able to communicate their learning and understanding of concepts and processes during teacher–student exchanges. This requires considerable skill, both linguistic and cognitive. Linguistic skills are required if they are to demonstrate their cognitive abilities such as classifying, comparing, sequencing, evaluating, hypothesizing, inferring, predicting and generalizing ideas. Many of these language skills can be fostered within story-based instruction, as illustrated in Table 3.1.

To participate successfully in the classroom discourse in subject matter classes, students must have certain pragmatic and interactional skills, such as an understanding of the 'ground rules' of classroom discourse in both teacher-fronted and group work situations (Cameron et al. 1996: 226). This is not relevant in monocultural primary school classes, where both teachers and students come from the same cultural background and have similar modes of communication, as well as shared expectations about classroom discourse. However, it becomes very important where native English-speaking teachers from cultural backgrounds different from that of local culture are brought to schools and colleges to teach either language or other subject matter in English. Emerging research suggests this to be a problem in the Arabian Gulf (e.g. Al-Bakri 2013; Belhiah and Elhami 2015; Diallo 2014; Jarrah 2020). Foreign teachers should familiarize themselves with the local culture and customs and perhaps observe their local colleagues working with students. This is not to say that new ways of teaching or thinking should be avoided, but it needs to be

Table 3.1 Activating Academic Language Functions with Stories

Language Functions	Sample Story Questions and Tasks
Seek information	• Answer factual questions: What did Goldilocks break in the bears' house? • Write three questions about *The Ugly Duckling* for your partner to answer.
Inform	• Describe the setting and characters in *Mufaro's Beautiful Daughters*. • Tell who the main characters are in *Cinderella*, and what the key events were.
Compare	• Compare *Zeke Pippin* and *Amazing Bone*. • Explain how *Stone Soup* is similar to *How Rabbit Got Its Short Tail*.
Order	• Arrange the pictures/jumbled sentences in order to tell the story of *The Gingerbread Man*. • Tell what the caterpillar in *The Very Hungry Caterpillar* ate first. What did it eat next? • In *Alexander and the Terrible, Horrible, No Good, Very Bad Day*, what was the first thing that went wrong for Alexander? What was the next one? What was the last thing that went wrong before things got better?
Classify	• Group given stories into fables and trickster tales. • Explain why *Stone Soup* is a trickster tale and *The Lion and the Mouse* is not.
Analyse	• Fill in the plot profile for *Snow White*. • How does the Grouchy Ladybug change at the end of the story?
Infer	• What do you think will happen when the rabbit puts its tail in the pond? What makes you think that? What do you think will happen next? • Why do you think Maddie and the other girls did not try to stop Peggy from bullying Wanda in *The Hundred Dresses*? What makes you think that?
Justify/persuade	• Do you think it was right or wrong that Cinderella's stepmother and stepsisters were not punished at the end? Why? (In the original they face cruel punishments.)
Solve problem	• How did Mrs Haktak's magic pot work in *Two of Everything*? • Give Alexander some advice on how he could avoid the problem with his money.
Synthesize	• Write a new *Goldilocks* story by changing the setting, characters, objects and the ending. • Summarize the story *Harry and the Terrible Whatzit*.
Evaluate	• What do you think about Snow White's decisions to go into the house in the woods? Justify. • Would it be more important for Cornelius (in *Cornelius*) to behave like the other crocodiles or to imitate others? Justify.

(*continued*)

Table 3.1 Continued

Language Functions	Sample Story Questions and Tasks
Predicting outcomes	• What do you think will happen when Fish in *Fish Is Fish* gets out of water? Why? • What do you think *Cornelius* will see next? What makes you think that?
Hypothesizing	• If Wanda had mentioned to the other girls that her 'dresses' were drawing, do you think the girls' attitude would have changed? Explain. • If the drought in *Stone Soup* continues, and people will go hungry, will the rich man share his food with the villagers later on? Explain.

done in ways that enable children to remain in their own 'persona' during language practice. Role-play and dramatization of stories is another matter, and most children easily and enthusiastically engage in these activities.

Students should also be able to understand and be able to express different points of view; know what kind of language is used to express a differing viewpoint or to evaluate different viewpoints proposed by peers. Such language can be incorporated into young learner language classes without major difficulty with stories or other content that lend themselves to discussion about different opinions; for example, 'Do you agree with X that …?' 'Why do you disagree with her?' 'Can you explain why you disagree?' and so on.

One might, perhaps rightfully, argue that in monolingual subject matter EMI classes, some of these skills could be demonstrated in students' L1. However, this will do a disservice not only to students who need to be able to apply this proficiency in official and/or standardized examinations but also to students who wish to pursue tertiary education in colleges or universities where English is the language of instruction and where L1 clarifications or explanations might not be readily available.

Many primary school subject matter teachers view as effective responders students who 'speak clearly, answer questions correctly, and volunteer frequently', and also ask clarifying questions and who offer answers that are 'full, with more explanation, definition, and description' (Schleppegrell and Simich-Dudgeon 1996: 275, 281). When Solomon and Rhodes (1995: 5) investigated the quality and nature of academic language in two grade-five classrooms in a bilingual school in Washington, DC, teachers identified specific stylistic registers with which they expected students to be familiar, and the choice of a stylistic register was task-specific; for example, retelling of events was expected to follow chronological order and responses to written questions to be phrased in complete sentences. Informal interviews with Lebanese English teachers suggest many of them have similar expectations, particularly when it comes to answering questions in complete sentences. One can safely assume that secondary- and tertiary-level teachers would expect no less comprehensive and detailed responses from the learners. A quick overview of the scope and sequence in three young learner courses published in 2020 reveals little, if any, language necessary to negotiate school subjects such as mathematics, sciences or social science, for example.

It has been argued that classroom interaction opportunities are particularly important, if not critical, for second language learners who need to learn language conventions that will facilitate their participation in academic discourse in the new language (Faltis and Hudelson 1998; Hall 2000; Tharp and Gallimore 1991; Verplaetse 1998). This raises the question to what extent primary school language teaching materials generate opportunities for interactions and the kind of communication associated with subject matter learning and academic discourse.

Discipline-Specific Language Skills

Another problem area young ELLs face in different academic subjects is the discipline-specific jargon each subject matter has. Mathematics and sciences are of particular concern because of the language associated with them and because FLAPPS students must often study these subjects in English from the onset of schooling even if other subjects are taught in L1. This is the case in Lebanon, for example, where students must pass these subjects in English or French in the national examination at the end of year nine if they are to proceed to secondary school and the matriculation examination at the end of year twelve that will determine whether they are eligible to apply for tertiary education. Research in some Arab countries where EMI is practised suggests that students are not achieving expected results, doing poorly in international tests such as Trends in Mathematics and Science Standards (TIMSS) (see Mullis et al. 2016).

Mathematics

Development of mathematical ability is linked to command of mathematical language, argues Anstrom (1997: 12), and the National Council of Teachers of Mathematics (1991) in the United States notes that limited language proficiency can, in fact, present a significant obstacle to mathematics learning. This is because several aspects of mathematics learning require a considerable level of language proficiency to be understood and manipulated. Take vocabulary as an example; in addition to its own highly specialized vocabulary (quotient, divisor, denominator, minuend, etc.), mathematics uses everyday vocabulary with new meanings (odd, even, table, column, product, volume, etc.). Similarly problematic appear to be syntactic features, such as comparatives, logical connectors, use of passive voice and a variety of prepositions (Spanos et al. 2013). The language needed to use to express hypotheticals, or probabilities and possibilities can also be problematic.

Some of the above language features do not appear in typical TEYL courses until upper primary levels in grades five or six and above. One example is conditionals, which often appear in lower primary mathematics books:

> … How many milliliters of water <u>would be</u> in the jug if it were completely full?
>
> … <u>If this</u> pattern <u>continued</u>, how many people attended the last class?
>
> …What sandwich and drink combinations <u>could</u> Hani <u>have</u> ordered?

An examination of the scope and sequence of one widely marketed international young learner course reveals that in level four, simple present and present progressive are featured, but simple past tense is only introduced at the end of the last unit. Level-five language objectives in the same course are still limited to simple present and past, with two units addressing future tense and only one passive voice modal 'could' is introduced in the last unit of the book. Level six introduces perfect tense and passive voice in simple past toward the end of the book. This is, of course fully understandable and appropriate where interpersonal communications skills are the goal, but less so where academic language proficiency is expected. Third and fourth graders facing the above-cited math problems would not have been exposed to the language required to work through the problems. One can only imagine how much more difficulties students might face when they reach grade five and six mathematics classes.

Research suggests that children's stories with mathematics concepts can facilitate the development of mathematical understanding and the associated language. For example, children's stories presenting mathematical concepts and what Freidman (1997) calls 'math morals' (e.g. exponential growth is rapid; incomplete information can be inaccurate) can be useful in the English-language class. Let us look at how some stories and appropriate follow-up activities can be used to reinforce mathematics language and concepts. The first example is from Lily's fourth-grade class where children have read Gerige's *Three Hat Day*, and their task is to work in groups and use the story concept to write new math problems for their peers. Here is an example from one group:

> RR. Pottle the Fourth had seven pairs of shoes of all kind. When she wanted to be happy, she always had two different shoes on. How many days she can be happy before she must start from the beginning?

Here is another example from the same class:

> RR. Pottle had lots of shoes. She had blue Nikes, pink ballet shoes, black and brown rainboots, silvery ballerinas, green beach shoes and Hello Kitty slippers. When she was sad, she put on two different shoes. One time she was very sad for a week. So she put a Hello Kitty slipper and Nike. How many times can she put on Hello Kitty slipper in one week?

How Big Is a Foot (Myller 1990) is an amusing story that illustrates the importance of standard units of measurement and *Anno's Magic Seeds* (Anno 1995) illustrates the speed of exponential growth in a child-friendly context. It lends itself well to activities where children can use manipulatives or drawings of objects to gain an understanding of the speed at which the growth occurs. *The Doorbell Rang* (Hutchins 1986) has been used by many teachers to introduce the concept and vocabulary of division. A second-grade math teacher, Amal, in an EMI school in Lebanon reported using the story every year with her second graders, and Ghosn (2012, 2013) shows how two English teachers approach the same story in very different ways. *Spaghetti and Meatballs for All!* (Burns 1997) is an amusing story that explores the perimeter of the area as a family is trying to ensure that all their guests will have a seat.

Sciences

National Science Teachers Association (1991) has identified functions of scientific academic language to include, among others, formulating hypotheses, proposing alternative solutions, describing, classifying, making inferences, interpreting data, predicting and generalizing. Just as mathematics, science also assigns unique meanings to common everyday words (e.g. table, mass, energy and force). Science class discourse is also characterized by use of the passive voice and long noun phrases, as Lemke (1990) has pointed out. Like in mathematics, this may pose obstacles for learning as students may develop erroneous conceptualizations because of language limitations or may lack the ability to express their understanding concisely, whether orally or in writing. The following excerpt is from an American third-grade science book used by many schools in Lebanon (emphases denote structures not typically found in level-two and level-three TEYL courses):

> Fuels release energy that *can be changed* into electricity. Electricity is a form of energy that people *make by using* kinds of *energy found* in nature (…) Energy that comes into our homes as electricity *can be used* to light lamps, run computers, or cook popcorn. (Harcourt Science: F7 2002)

However, typical TEYL coursebooks do not prepare children for this type of language in grade three or even four as discussed above in connection of mathematics.

Carle's *The Very Hungry Caterpillar*, Lionni's *Fish Is Fish* and Andersen's classic *Ugly Duckling* illustrate animal life cycles while being also highly entertaining and even thought-provoking. There are plenty of similar titles available, but one just needs to make sure the facts are accurate even when the goal is language. For example, a spider should not be represented with an illustration or a model as having six legs, as one KG teacher was observed to do. When her attention was drawn to the mistake, she noted, 'But we are just teaching language and not science.' However, language teachers do not 'only' teach language, they must always also present correct information to children.

Social Studies

Of lesser concern in the MENA region – as in many other regions – is the language associated with social studies since this subject is often taught in the national language. However, in many international schools, the social studies subjects are taught in English. As mathematics and sciences, social science has its own jargon, which include expressions useful in other contexts as well. For example, typical language functions associated with history classes are explaining, describing, defining, justifying, sequencing, comparing, contrasting and evaluating. History also involves time-specific language, cause-and-effect relationship signals, sequence words and specialized vocabulary (e.g. Short 1994). These are all potentially problematic for young ELLs. Other problematic issues in social studies taught in a foreign language, and particularly when using a foreign textbook, include possibly unfamiliar political and cultural concepts (such as 'liberal', 'suffrage' and 'abolition' in the North American texts).

An excellent series pertaining to history is the *If you ...* series that describes events in American history in a child-friendly way: *If You Sailed on the Mayflower* (McGovern 1969), *If You Traveled West in the Covered Wagon* (Levine 1993), *If you Lived with the Cherokee* (Roop and Roop 1998) and *If You Traveled on the Underground Railroad* (Levine 1993). The subjunctive mood is very clear in context and will be helpful, for example, in a science class: 'What if you planted the seed in clay? What do you think will happen?' Or in math: 'If you planted two more seeds than Jack planted the first time, how many seeds would you have the second year? What about the third?'

Developing Academic Second Language Proficiency

It is obvious from the above that tackling academic subject matter in L2 is not at all a simple process and might present considerable challenges to young learners. The language teaching textbook and the interactions its activities generate must prepare ELLs for the challenges of the academic subject matter texts that they will encounter in the content area classes.

Less-Than-Satisfactory Progress

The progress – or the lack thereof – of L2 learners in the United States has often been a highly political issue, and calls for multilingual education, sheltered ESL education, total immersion and other formats of instruction for immigrant population have often shaped funding. In the UK, the relatively low performance of immigrant students was also noted in the 1970s and 1980s. Both the Bullock Report (1975) and the Swann Report (1985) addressed the problem of adequate preparation of language-minority children for general curriculum studies. However, in the early twenty-first century, reports emerged suggesting that ELLs in Britain are catching up with their peers.

Research of the past forty years shows that development of academic second language proficiency can take anywhere from five to ten years in the target language context, that is, learners live in the target language culture and attend English-language classes, whether ESL classes, sheltered English classes or mainstream classes. It is much more complex than the interpersonal communication competence aimed at in typical TEYL courses. Cummins (1984: 4) argues that academic second language proficiency is 'socially grounded and could only develop within the matrix of human interaction', within which students can examine and interpret information, formulate and express argument, and utilize their higher order thinking skills. This suggests that the instructional materials and activities should provide plenty of opportunities for these skills to develop.

Cummins's BISC–CALP Model

Cummins (1984: 12) has conceptualized the basic interpersonal communication skill (BICS) and cognitive academic language proficiency (CALP) along two intersecting continua. On the BICS continuum, communication can range from highly context-embedded to context-reduced. Paralinguistic, situational cues and objects at hand contribute to building context, while context-reduced communication has fewer or none of these features. For example, discussing real objects in face-to-face communication where one can point to things or talk about texts with plenty of picture support is an example of context-embedded communication. Context-reduced communication, such as a telephone conversation or an academic lecture, relies heavily or exclusively on linguistic cues and where a shared reality cannot be assumed.

On the intersecting CALP continuum, the cognitive demands a given task places on the learner can range from undemanding to demanding. The level of demand depends on how much the learner can rely on 'automatized' linguistic tools or need to rely on 'non-automatized' linguistic tools (Cummins 1984: 12–13). For example, completing cloze exercises, grammar transformation exercises and reciting a list of irregular verbs from memory are cognitively much less demanding than comparing and contrasting given concepts or trying to prepare a persuasive presentation. According to Cummins, academic language will be at its most difficult level for second language learners when it requires them to complete cognitively demanding tasks in context-reduced situations. For example, compare the demands of writing paragraphs about your holiday trip with writing persuasive presentation about the importance of recycling.

Based on the Cummins model, the initial L2 input should be heavily context-embedded, making it more comprehensible to learners. For example, giving children pictures or objects to manipulate and talk about is more contextualized than dialogue practice, especially where the concepts provided as examples are culturally unfamiliar. In many TEYL courses, dialogue practice involves topics such as breakfast foods, leisure time activities and other seemingly 'contextualized' topics. However, what is considered 'common' in the United States or the UK may vastly differ from what is common, for example, in Morocco, Oman or Lebanon. Breakfasts and other foods are just one example. Even an immigrant child living in the UK might find some of the common UK foods unfamiliar. Gregory (1996) gives an example of the little Cantonese Tony, who was not used to toast and jam for breakfast and thus was confused when encountering the concept for the first time. Imagine if Tony and children in different other parts of the world would be expected to discuss their favourite breakfast food and the only options offered by their coursebook would be those with which only British or American children are familiar. (See Recommendations for practice for suggestions.)

Cummins goes further to suggest that the initial context-embedded language will facilitate development of L2 competence in eventual context-reduced communication. Assuming that the CALP model is valid, good young learner courses would begin with context-embedded comprehensible input that is not cognitively very challenging. The lesson tasks would then gradually proceed towards more context-reduced and cognitively more demanding as learners gradually develop automaticity.

The Prism Model

In a study involving of over 700,000 students in five large school districts in the United States, Thomas and Collier (1997) arrived at a slightly different conclusion from that of Cummins. They found that not only is the development of second language proficiency time-consuming, but that the development of academic language proficiency is also closely related to learners' level of their first language proficiency. They found that ESL students doing well in the upper grades had had an opportunity for cognitive and academic development both in their first language and the L2 at least through the primary school (Thomas and Collier 1997: 14).

Based on their investigations, Thomas and Collier developed another conceptual model that aims at explaining the development of second language skills for academic purposes. Their Prism Model recognizes the complex mixture of processes involved in the development of academic second language proficiency: L1 and L2 language development, academic development, cognitive development, and social and cultural processes or interactions in the learner's life.

Unlike Cummins's CALP construct, which focuses on skills, the Prism Model focuses on the processes. These processes, although existing separately, are interdependent; therefore, failure in one area may negatively influence the learner's overall development and growth (Collier 1995). The Prism Model reveals complex interdependent relationships between several interacting variables, and thus indicates an approach to research that would take into account this complexity. The aim of this volume is to examine the interdependence of language-teaching materials, teacher questions and feedback, student language production and achievement, and the role culture plays in the processes.

In FLAPPS context, the development and maintenance of learners' first language proficiency beyond aural/oral skills must be ensured for full first language literacy to be achieved, even if many school subjects are taught in English. This is of particular importance in the MENA region, where local spoken colloquial Arabic dialects differ significantly from the Modern Standard Arabic (MSA) that is the medium of all newsprint, official documents and court proceedings. Therefore, full first language literacy – MSA in this case – ought to be a key goal of language policies. One avenue to explore in the MENA region would be some form of bilingual education. For example, primary school students would benefit from Arabic language instruction in key school subjects, such as mathematics and science, either before EMI in these subjects, or by implementing Content and Language Integrated Learning (CLIL).

There is, however, some disagreement in the field about the role of L1 instruction in academic L2 achievement. The value of bilingual education has often been hotly debated in the United States. A 1997 review of benefits of bilingual education by the National Academy of Sciences found no negative effects in children not developing L1 literacy before beginning to read and write in L2 (August and Hakuta 1997). Following the report, the 'English for the Children' campaign resulted in California to eliminate bilingual education in 1998, but voters reversed the decision in 2016 (Garcia 2020). In Colorado, the same campaign in 2002 fought to eliminate bilingual education but was eventually defeated when both Latino immigrants and African Americans were convinced that English-only education would result in large numbers of children being illiterate (Padres Unidos 2002). If English-only education can be a problem where children are immersed in an English-speaking environment, then it may be a bigger problem where English is not the mainstream language. Research has shown that in the Arabian Gulf, for example, the increasing popularity of English-medium instruction has raised concerns about the Western instructional materials and pedagogies potentially hindering students' Arabic-language proficiency and even affecting the development of cultural identity (e.g. Belhiah and Elhami 2015; Diallo 2014).

Activating Academic Language Functions with Stories

In their *CALLA Handbook*, Uhl Chamot and O'Malley (1994: 42) identified eleven academic language functions, and Table 3.1 illustrates how these can be activated in story-based English lessons. It would behove the language teachers and subject matter teachers to get together to identify relevant language functions in a given subject to enable language teachers to select appropriate stories. Subject matter teachers might also supplement the coursebook with relevant storybooks to further reinforce these language functions.

Conclusions

Learning school subjects in a second language is a challenge for young second language learners. Yet, the demand of English-medium instruction is increasing, including in the MENA region, and student achievement is less than satisfactory. One reason may be found in instructional materials; the typical young learner courses with their structured syllabus and simplified language do not facilitate acquisition of academic language functions although many courses are content integrated. One way to prepare students for learning in English would be to use children's literature to activate academic language functions.

Recommendations for Practice

Teachers

- When the coursebook calls for dialogue practice about different objects, foods or even actions, whose aim is to practice polite questions, requests and responses, the suggested procedure can be modified as needed. For example, dialogues can be created around real objects or pictures (if they are part of target vocabulary). A good beginning example is the classic 'Go Fish' game played in pairs or small groups:
  o   Do you have [target object/activity]
  o   No, I'm sorry, I don't. Go fish. / Yes I have.

- As often as possible, engage students in conversations, such as you will see some teachers routinely do in later chapters. For example, if students are to practice some vocabulary or structures, rather than directly get them to the dialogue, present the vocabulary and then engage the class in a relevant 'conversation' as in the Recommendations for Practice in Chapter 1.
- *The Tiny Seed* (Carle 1987), and *Carrot Seed* both illustrate how seed grow. In a language class, this could be followed by a simple project of children planting a few tomato seeds and placing them in different locations in the classroom. Children can be encouraged to hypothesize whether all the seeds would sprout at the same time, and when they do sprout, would there be any difference in the sprouts in different locations, etc. This does not need to take much time from the language curriculum since children will be using English and be introduced to relevant vocabulary and expressions in context ('I think the seeds will …'; 'If we put the … I think…'; 'What do think will happen if …?'). Children could keep personal observation diary of their plant's growth. Alternatively, few minutes from the class time every few days could be used for a collective journal with the teacher taking children's dictations.

Materials Developers

- For dialogue practice, provide relevant reproducible pictures that will facilitate games such as 'Go Fish'. This will save teachers' time.
- Where math and sciences are taught in English, incorporate vocabulary and language most commonly needed in these subjects. A good idea would be to include some short stories with follow-up math activities in a way that they could be duplicated and shared with math and science teachers.
- Where social studies (e.g. history, geography, government) are taught in L2, one option would be to include excerpts from children's books that depict relevant issues in current time as well as in history. Vocabulary and syntax typically in social studies can be presented in a story set in a target language or an ancient culture.

Part 2
Insights from Classroom Research

4

Teacher Questions versus Learner Engagement

'What is the use of repeating all that stuff', the Mock Turtle interrupted, 'if you don't explain it as you go on?'
Lewis Carroll – *Alice's Adventures in Wonderland*

Teacher Questioning

Cline (2021: n.p.) suggests that asking questions is 'perhaps the most powerful tool' teachers have in their possession and that 'questions-asking serves many functions that makes it the stock in trade of the skillful teacher'. Teacher questioning is, indeed, one of the primary means of generating learner output in the classroom, and a language classroom is not different in that sense. Teacher questions typically form the first stage of what is often referred to as initiation-response-feedback (IRF) sequence: teacher initiates with a question, students respond to it and teacher evaluates the response. Questions can also inform the teacher about what learners know or do not know, their answers serving as an important determiner for instruction that follows. Since the 1960s, teacher questions have been classified in several different ways and are argued to generate different learner output. For example, Long and Sato (1983) distinguish between 'display questions' and 'referential questions'. Display questions are questions to which the teacher has an answer in mind, while referential questions aim to elicit information the teacher does not have.

The following fifth-grade teacher questions about simplified excerpt from *Moby Dick* illustrate the two types: 'The whale Moby Dick, what did he do?' 'What do you think about Captain Ahab wanting to kill the whale?' The first one is an example of a display question as the teacher is clearly checking students' comprehension of a story and has a specific answer in mind ('Moby Dick shook the boat'). The second question is a referential question to which the teacher does not have any obvious predetermined answer in mind but is asking for students' personal opinions.

Barnes's early classification of teacher questions distinguishes between factual questions and reasoning questions, the former beginning with 'who', 'what', 'when' and 'where' and the latter beginning with 'how' and 'why' (Barnes, Britton and Rosen 1969). In Barnes's classification, both factual and reasoning questions could be either closed or open, the former limiting the response options and thus student output. The first question in the above example represents a factual, closed question while the second represents an open reasoning question, the answer not being implied based on teacher feedback to student questions.

The following two examples further clarify Barnes's classification. The first one is an example of an open factual question while the second represents a closed reasoning question to which the teacher knows the answer but which requires the student to engage in reasoning: 'Do you like to read stories?' 'Why did Captain Ahab chase the whale?' The first one is also an example of an open factual question while the second clearly represents a closed reasoning question. Although the teacher knows the answer, the question might require students to engage in some reasoning, depending on how much explicit information about Ahab's reasons is given in the simplified student text.

Teacher questions can also be classified based on the cognitive demand they place on the learner. Smith (cited in Orlich et al. 1994) classifies teacher questions as convergent and divergent, and Shrable and Minnis (1974) differentiate between data recall, data application and data processing. Both divergent and data application and processing questions are more demanding than convergent and data recall questions. The first question about *The Black Stallion* is a convergent, data recall question, requiring students only to remember facts from the story, while the second is divergent, data processing question that calls for analytical thinking: 'How many times did Alec try to ride the horse?' 'How would you describe Alec's character? Explain.'

Classifying Teacher Questions

Classifying teacher questions is not straightforward, however. For example, in her observations of Hong Kong language classrooms, Tsui (1995) noted several instances where language teacher questions appeared on the surface to be of reasoning or referential type, yet on closer inspection turned out to be either factual or display questions. The following examples from transcripts collected from two different fifth-grade classes help illustrate the difficulty:

T: Why would Tom not want to paint the fence?
S: He like to play.
T: He would like to play, yes, but what else?
S: The other boys will laugh.
T: Yes, the other boys would laugh at him. (Ghosn 2001: 42)

Although the question seems on the surface to be a reasoning question, the teacher was clearly trying to elicit the answer indicated in the teacher's guide. The following question about personal information also seems to be referential, but the teacher feedback reveals something else:

T: Do you have any aunts?
S: No.
T: You have no aunts? ... How come? What about your aunt Zeinab? (Ghosn 2001: 43)

The question is, after all, a display question as the teacher clearly knows the student's family situation and is asking the question to check whether the student understands the word 'aunt'.

'What do you think Captain Ahab should do?' is an example of an open factual question as Barnes defines them, as it begins with 'what'. However, despite the 'what', it is a reasoning question as the response requires some, perhaps even quite sophisticated, thinking.

Although teacher questions have been classified in different ways, they share some common features and can be characterized along two intersecting continua as shown in Figure 4.1. Display questions, which aim to get students to demonstrate knowledge already known to the teacher, can range from those requiring only data recall to those requiring data processing. Referential questions, which aim to get students to share knowledge that the teacher does not have, can also range from those requiring only data recall to those that require data processing. Questions falling in the two bottom quadrants are more demanding than those falling in the two top quadrants. Table 4.1 helps illustrate the differences.

Note that it is impossible to place the first three questions along the continua in Figure 4.1 without knowing the context where they are asked, or how they were answered and how the answer was received by the one asking

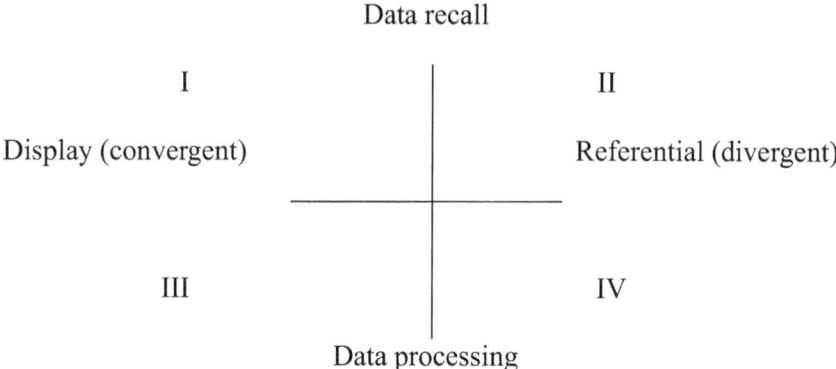

Figure 4.1 Continua of teacher questions
Source: Ghosn (2001).

Table 4.1 Examples of Questions

	Question	Type
1	Where is the ball?	Display/Data Processing
2	Who helped Cinderella to go to the party?	Display/Data Recall
3	How do you say that in the past tense?	Display/Data Processing
4	What did you find funny in the story?	Referential/Data Processing
5	Where did you go on holiday?	Referential/Data Recall

the question. Assuming a classroom context, it is likely that the teacher wants Zeina to show her ability to tell time in English; the teacher knows who assisted Cinderella; and the teacher wants to find out whether the student knows the required past tense form. These assumptions would conform to the suggested types of question. However, first question might well be also referential if we assume that the teacher does not know where the ball is, as would the second question if the teacher is not familiar with the story. If the questions are asked in a context outside the classroom, the categories would need to be revised. Even the question about the past tense takes on a different function as genuine information seeking if we assume a younger sibling and older sibling interaction, or a child–parent interaction. The examples illustrate the difficulty of classifying questions out of context, and show that, in the classroom context, accurate classification necessitates examination of both student responses and the subsequent teacher feedback.

Teacher Questions and Learner Output

Extensive research has revealed that teachers tend to ask more closed, display questions than more demanding higher order questions (e.g. Lynch 1991; Yang 2010). Little of this research has been conducted in the Middle East but the findings resonate with this research. For example, in the observations of Iranian English-language teachers, Farahian and Rezaee (2012) found that out of the 160 teacher questions recorded during five lessons, 90 per cent were closed display questions. Shomoossi's (2004) observations of five university EFL teachers in Iran reflects the same ratio; out of a total of 1,628 observed questions 1,335 were display questions and only less than a fifth were referential questions. Similar findings resulted from observations of six primary school English-language teachers in Lebanon (Ghosn 2001) examined here. During three 50-minute lessons recorded in six teachers' classes, teachers asked a total of 358 questions, over half of which were data recall questions and only slightly more than a fifth referential questions. The majority of the referential questions were posed by just two teachers. The data also showed that teachers differed significantly in their questioning strategies. While one teacher repeated the same question several times to different students, another posed a question and invited answers from several students before providing feedback. The latter strategy will give students time to reflect on the question, which is important, especially for students who want to give some thought to their answer. Tanya frequently asked students to repeat another student's answer, as in the following:

T: How many times a week do you wash the dishes, Zeinab?
S1: I wash the dishes once a week.
T: Ramzy, how many times a week does she wash the dishes?
S2: Once a week.

Teacher questions have a significant influence on learner engagement. Referential, divergent and data processing questions have been argued to generate more complex responses from students than display questions (e.g. Brock 1986; Kubota 1989), while cognitively higher-level questions may also increase the length and syntactic complexity of student output (e.g. Long and Sato 1983). Yet, research shows that teachers ask more simple display, data recall and convergent questions than open-ended, cognitively more demanding questions (Gallagher 1965; Sirotnik 1983). Not surprisingly perhaps, there seems to be a strong relationship between the cognitive level of teacher questions and the length and syntactic complexity of learner responses. After all, it will be hard to answer a cognitively demanding question with two or three words. For example, to answer a question 'Why is this summary better than the others?', students will first need to process the question and then explain their reasoning in English. Although 'How did the principal know that the roads were slippery?' is a recall question, it also needs more than one or two words. This is how students in Gloria's class responded to these questions:

T: Why is [that] summary better than the others? [pointing to a student summary suggestion on the board].
S: Because it is about (xxx) the main idea.
T: How did the principal know that the roads were slippery?
S: The driver (xxx) called the principal (xxx).

Very often teachers' guides for textbooks suggest questions to be asked. Let us take two examples. The first set of questions are provided in the teacher's guide for an excerpt from Walter Farley's *The Black Stallion* in a level-four book which many EMI schools used (prior to the late 2019 currency crash):

1. How did the horse and Alec help each other to get to the island?
2. What did Alec do to stay alive on the island?
3. What part of the story did you think was the scariest?
4. What was the first clue the author gave you that the Black was beginning to trust Alec?
5. Why did the ship come to the island?
6. How was Alec's kindness towards the stallion unexpectedly rewarded?
(Cullinan et al. 1989, quoted in Ghosn 2001: 201).

Although four of the questions are data recall questions, all require more than one or two words to answer. One is a referential question about students' personal opinions, and one is a reasoning question. While the last question is a recall question, it cannot be answered with one or two words.

Contrast the above questions with those provided for Tom's fence painting exercise from Mark Twain's *Tom Sawyer* in a level-five of an ESL course used in the class observed in this study, as well as in many other EMI schools in Lebanon:

1. What do you think whitewashing means?
2. Did Tom want to do the work?
3. Why not?

4. Who was the first person to come along?
5. What did Ben have?
6. Did Tom's plan work?
7. Where was Ben going?
8. What does Ben want to do?
9. Did Tom let him first?
10. Was Ben the only one who fell for Tom's tricks?
11. Name some of the things that boys gave him.
12. What great law of human nature did Tom discover?
13. What does that law mean?
14. How many boys do you think helped Tom whitewash the fence?
15. Why did they stop whitewashing the fence? (Walker 1996, quoted in Ghosn 2001: 202)

Of the fifteen questions, ten can be answered with one word and one with the names of boys. Research shows that when a question can be answered with one or two words, that is what most students do. Considering that children in both schools using the above books have been learning English since kindergarten six to seven hours a week and also math and science in English, the second set of questions seems overly simplistic and perhaps not very interesting for learners. In contrast, the first set of questions encourages students to construct their answers so that their meaning is clear, which may, as Shomoossi (2004, citing Brock 1986) notes, make learners focus on the language required for meaning to be conveyed.

Özcan's (2010) study in Turkey suggests that referential questions encourage longer learner responses than display questions. She also notes that less proficient students were more responsive to referential questions. This resonates with Shomoossi's (2004) findings in Iran that show referential questions producing more classroom interaction than display questions at a statistically significant level. We will see more of this in the next chapter on classroom discourse. It would be interesting to investigate to what extent hierarchical teachers look for one correct answer, the one in the book, for example, and to what extent egalitarian teachers accept diverse viewpoints and how they deal with responses that are not correct.

Mehan (1979) pointed out that turn-allocation strategies also influence classroom discourse. Teachers can allocate turns to individual learners or to the class as a whole to answer chorally. When individual learners are called on, they are 'put in a spot' and will need to respond whether they know the answer or not. Depending on the cultural context, this might place a student at a risk of 'losing face' or possibly being subjected to peer ridicule. In both cases, learner motivation to engage is at risk. When Erickson and Mohatt (1977) observed Native American classrooms, they found that Native American teachers rarely called on individual students but posed questions to allow for voluntary as well as group responses. Their practice was more aligned with the Native American cultural patterns that emphasize group effort. Middle Eastern cultures tend to be also more collectivist than individualistic, suggesting that allocating turns to groups might encourage all students to participate. Even a student who does not initially know the correct answer can answer on behalf of the group.

Teacher Feedback

Teacher feedback to students is argued to be 'the lynch pins of a lesson' (Brown and Wragg 1993: 22) because they determine the course of the lesson. Good feedback, according to Boud, is 'given without personal judgment or opinion, given based on the facts, always neutral and objective, constructive and focus on the future' (Boud 2002: 7). Teacher feedback can take many different forms; it can be positive or negative, with or without incorporating learner response in some way, and ignoring can be also one form of feedback, depending on how the teacher proceeds. The evaluative character of teacher feedback distinguishes question-interaction exchanges that take place in classrooms from everyday situations outside the classroom as Mehan's classic examples illustrate:

Speaker 1: What time is it, Denise?
Speaker 2: 2:30
Speaker 1: Thank you, Denise.
Speaker 1: What time is it, Denise?
Speaker 2: 2:30
Speaker 1: Very good, Denise. (285)

It is immediately clear that the second exchange takes place in the classroom, while the first could happen between two friends, between parent and child, husband and wide and the like. (In the naturalistic situation, the first speaker would often begin with the name of the other person as in 'Denise, what time is it?')

In a language class, correction of student errors is a fairly frequent form of feedback, but its influence is not clear although studies indicate that explicit corrective feedback has some benefits (Carroll and Swain 1993; Chaudron 1988; Lyster 1998; Lyster and Ranta 1997). Lack of attention to form has been suggested as one of the reasons for the frequency of accuracy errors observed in immersion students' output even after years of study (Chaudron 1988). Clarification requests, metalinguistic feedback and repetition have been shown to result in more frequent learner uptake than explicit correction or recasts which provide expansion or implicit correction (Lyster and Ranta 1997). Although considerable research has been conducted on error treatment, there is little empirical evidence to support any one type of error treatment as superior, as results have been inconclusive (Ellis 1994).

Conclusions

Teacher questions are an inherent part of classroom discourse and aim to elicit student output while helping teachers determine students' knowledge of lesson content. Teacher questions can be classified in different ways depending on the linguistic and cognitive demand they place on the learner. Research shows that when teachers ask closed data recall questions, student responses tend to be shorter than when teachers ask open or cognitively more demanding questions. However, not all teacher questions can be classified unless teacher feedback to student responses is also examined. Teacher questioning strategies also differ and may influence student responses and how much students engage. In the next chapter we will see how teacher feedback influences learner participation.

Recommendations for Practice

Teachers

- Plan questions in advance to make sure all levels are covered, such as recall questions, questions requiring information/language processing, and questions calling for students' personal responses (e.g. What do you think will happen? Do you agree with Darine's answer and why or why not? Have you ever …?). If the questions in the coursebook are limited to recall questions, try to add more higher-level questions that will require summarizing, synthesizing or evaluating information.

- In dialogue practice, add questions to extend the opportunities for engagement. Let us take as an example the dialogue exercise about favourite seasons we saw in Rima's class in Chapter 1. When the student reads the question from the book 'What do you do in the fall?' and the other student replies, 'Fall I go bike', instead of correcting the language error, the teacher could say 'Stephan likes to go biking in the fall. Who else likes to go bike riding?' [student answer] 'Why do you like bike riding? What makes you like bike riding?'

 The following exercise could also be modified:

 S1: *My favourite season is winter*
 S2: Why do you like winter?
 S1: Because it's cold.
 T: Because it's cold or you <u>like to play in the snow</u>? [underlined is suggestion in the book]

Instead, the teacher could say 'You like it because it's cold. What do you like to do when it's cold?' 'Who else likes cold weather?' and so on.

Materials Developers

- When developing 'global' coursebooks that are used in different countries around the world, provide teachers with some guidance as to how they can modify dialogue practice to suit the local conditions if topics are unfamiliar to children.
- Provide teachers also guidance on how to extend the discourse so that students will have more opportunities to engage in genuine discourse.

5

Classroom Discourse and the Role of Teaching Materials

'Would you tell me, please,' said Alice, 'what it means?'
Lewis Carroll – *Through the Looking Glass*

There are numerous theories about second language learning, but a rich body of literature indicates that language learning best happens within a context of negotiated interactions. Research on academic second language literacy is equally rich, and interactions are argued to be particularly important for students who need to learn school subjects in English.[1] Extensive classroom interactions research over decades shows the process to follow a rather predictable IRF sequence, regardless of the subject matter. The following is an example of a typical IRF sequence:

T: What's the weather like, Rania?
S: Sunny
T: Full sentence, please, the weather …
S: The weather is sunny
T: Right, the weather is sunny.

Teacher asks a question, student responds, teacher gives feedback and student modify the answer, which teacher then approves. While learner responses to teacher questions have been studied extensively, very little has been written on what role, if any, instructional texts and activities play in generating classroom discourse. Martin has argued that 'the instructional practices around texts are orchestrated by the teacher, but the unique social environment of the classroom is jointly constructed by the teacher, students and the texts' (Martin 1999: 11). Very little has been also written about how students react to teacher feedback. This chapter explores the construction of the social environment and subsequent discourse in Lebanese primary school classrooms. Lessons of six teachers, whose questioning strategies were explored in the previous chapter, Gloria, Maya, Houda, Joanna, Sarah and Tanya, were observed in their fifth-grade classes using a systematic observation schedule over three 50-minute lesson periods each. After the findings, further observations were carried out in more classes to examine if similar patterns could be noted at different grade levels.

Observed Teacher–Student Exchanges

Transcripts from the six classes revealed three basic types of exchanges between teachers and students and were identified as follows: Basic Exchanges (BEs), negotiated exchanges (NEs) and direct teaching (DT). BEs consisted of one IRF turn of a teacher question or initiation, student response and teacher evaluation of the response. NEs consisted of initiation, response and one or more negotiations and/or feedback turns. The NEs could be further categorized into three types identified in previous negotiation research: negotiation of meaning (NEm), negotiation of topic (NEt), and negotiation of form (NEf). NEm and NEt at times involved teacher scaffolding feedback, while NEf exchanges rarely contained any scaffolding attempts, consisting primarily of error repair or other type of rejecting feedback.

Interestingly, the most instances of NEm and NEt occurred when lessons were about a story or other interesting content, including language usage or students' personal experiences. In contrast, NEf tended to dominate during the typical language practice activities. The NEm and NEt enabled the discourse to flow, whereas NEf were typically brief, often consisting only of three-step BE. DT moves consisted of teacher explanations and lesson-related instructions, with some DT moves including not only scaffolding but also student-initiated questions. (We will look at scaffolding more closely in Chapter 13.) The instructional texts and other lesson content clearly influenced the IRF sequence, determining student output to a large extent. Episodes in Tables 5.1–5.4 illustrate the exchanges identified in the observed classes. (Square brackets identify exchange sequences.) The first episode is from Tanya's class.

In the next episode, this one from Maya's class, there are examples of DT, a BE, and student-initiated NEt. Within this exchange, there is also DT and

Table 5.1 Basic Exchanges with Teacher Negotiation of Form

BE	T:	Where, where were they camping?
	S1:	Near Lake Wenda.
	T:	Near the lake, Right.
NEf	T:	What was the scary experience?
	S2:	A bear it scare them
	T:	A bear scare?
	S2:	Scared them
	T:	A bear scared them.
NEf	T:	Look at the picture here on page 34. What is the bear doing?
	S1:	He take
	T:	He take?
	S1:	It takes ((glasses))
	T:	The bear is taking the binoculars. [to another student]/What is the bear doing? (Ghosn 2001:198)

Table 5.2 Three Types of Exchanges

	S1:	[reading] *The gods talked among themselves and decided to leave the boy. The happy couple agreed that this boy should see a land of peace and*
	S2:	And people who meet under it should exchange kisses
DT	T:	So I told you the mistletoe is used as a Christmas decoration, and I told you that when two people meet under mistletoe should kiss each other.
BE	T:	Now they tell us here. Where did they get this habit [*sic*] from?
	S3:	They said here that in Norse legends.
NE*t*	S4:	Miss!
	T:	Yes, Milad.
	S4:	Miss, how can they bring him back to life?
	T:	This is a legend. I'm telling you that
DT	T:	Now a legend first, a legend is a story that is told from before. And it's not true.
NE*m*	S4:	Life fantasy?
	T:	It's like fantasy, yes. They use magic. (Ghosn 2001: 196)

another student-initiated negotiation of meaning, followed by a response from the teacher. In the first episode, Maya's students are reading about the legend of mistletoe.

Episodes in Tables 5.3 and 5.4 illustrate exchanges when language is the topic of discourse. Note how both teachers' responses to student questions generate

Table 5.3 About Prefixes and Suffixes

	S1:	Miss, can we put two prefixes on one word?
NE*t*	T:	For one word two prefixes?
	S1:	[nods]
	T:	You can add one prefix and one suffix.
	S2:	Like unbelievable?
	T:	Unbelievable, yes
NE*t*	S3:	Miss, misunderstanding?
DT	T:	Yes, misunderstanding is another word, yes. (xxx) you make a compound word.. a compound word is a word that is made two words. Classroom is one such word it's made of class and room
	S4:	Miss, trashcan?
DT	T:	Trashcan, yes, trashcan. We don't change the spelling of these words, OK? When you add something to a root word, sometimes you change the spelling of the root word, like I showed you here about suffixes, believable, but in compound words
	S5:	Snowman?
	T:	[nods]
	S4:	Miss, can we put names?
NE*t*	T:	Names?
	S4:	Like Superman
	T:	Uh, yes, yes, Superman, they call him that because he is a man that is very strong. (Ghosn 2001:168)

more questions and input from other students. The following exchange was observed in Maya's class (Table 5.3).

One instance of student initiation of meaning and form was observed in Joanna's class during a preposition exercise where a tree house was mentioned:

T: So, where were they?
S: Miss, in the wooden house.
T: Wooden house, yeah, but it's a tree house.
S: We can't say 'are in the house on the tree'?

Practicing Language

The above type of negotiation was not observed in classes students were practicing dialogues and doing other-language practice exercises typical in TEYL courses. We already saw two examples in Chapter 1 of this conversation practice. The aim

Table 5.4 Figuring Out Vocabulary and Negotiation of Meaning

Here, Gloria's students take turns reading parts of a story aloud.

	T:	They were preparing breakfast, then what did they do?
	S1:	*They put on some warm clothes*, Miss, what we mean by 'scarf'?
NE*m*	T:	Scarf, what's a scarf. Do you know? Rami.
	S2:	They, they put it [demonstrates how a scarf is wrapped around the neck]
	T:	Uhuh. I think it's ((scarf)). OK. And they put on coats [some students pantomime putting on coats] and boots.
	S3:	And mittens, Miss.
	T:	What are mittens? Gilbert?
	S3:	Gloves without fingers.
NE*m*	T:	They don't cover your fingers, they are like this cut? [points to her fingers; student nods]
	Ss:	Gloves!
	S2:	No, the ones that comes (xxx) two pieces like here [points]
	T:	But what Gilbert means it doesn't cover the fingers. If they were going to play in the snow?
		[several students talking simultaneously about mittens having to cover the whole hand if children were going to play in the snow]
DT	T:	Right, mittens are like what Rami said. They cover the fingers. OK. Go ahead. (Ghosn 2004: 120)

of these activities is to get students to practice target vocabulary, expressions or grammatical structures in prepared dialogues. However, these activities are often not realized in the intended ways and may result what can best be described as artificial 'pseudo-communication' (Ghosn 2001: 152). Episodes 5.1 and 5.2 illustrate this artificiality. In the first episode in Houda's class, students are expected to practice congratulations. (Text in italics denotes student reading from the book.)

Episode 5.1 Congratulations!

T:	Now, we need two students to come up here to practice the conversation. Who will come up here? Rana and who else? Zeina? Now Rana, you congratulate her and she will thank you, OK?
S1:	Congra-conga [cannot continue]
T:	Congratulations
S1:	(congratulations) [attempt not transcribable]
T:	Congratulations. Come on, you can say it.

S1:	Congratulations [not clear]. *You were terrific.*[reads from the book]
S2:	*Thank you. I can't believe it.*
T:	Excellent. Now, Ibtissam and Gibran OK.
S3:	*You were fantastic*
S4:	*Thanks a lot*
T:	You were fantastic! Very good. (Ghosn 2003a: 9–10)

In the following episode students are practicing expressions of surprise and amazement. The book provides four dialogue samples and a word bank of sample expressions. Houda brought student pairs with their books up to the front of the class to perform the task.

Episode 5.2 Surprise and Amazement

T:	OK. Now we will practice this conversation. Zeina and Anissa, please.
S1:	*Hey, we won two tickets to the rock concert!*
S2:	*I don't*
T:	No, don't read the same, use words from the bank.
S2:	*You can't mean it!*
T:	Good. Now Hanadi and Rania.
S3:	*That's*
T:	Hanadi, you are not reading the answer. Rania should read the answer.
S3:	*A night on mers.*
T:	Mercury
S3:	*on Mercury is the same time as three months on Earth.*
S4:	*That's aston-aston*
T:	asto-ni-shing
S4:	*stonishing*
T:	OK, now Batul and Raghida. And use the data bank, please.
S5:	*Isn't he a great singer?*
S6:	[reads from the word bank] *That's unbelievable.*
T:	Raghida, you cannot say 'that's unbelievable' when she said 'Isn't he a great singer'. You must say something that agrees with what he said.
S6:	*No way.*
T:	Wait, no [laughs], I see, so you don't think so. OK. (Ghosn 2004: 114)

The exchange has a distinct drill flavour, and it appear that S6 either does not understand the comment or does not know which of the available options would be appropriate. Throughout teacher attention is firmly on the accuracy of form.

In the next episode, the aim of Tanya's lesson is for students to prepare a bar graph about family members of the students (sisters, brothers, aunts and uncles). First students are supposed to interview their peers about the family members and then the class will compile a bar graph of them.

Episode 5.3 Talk about Family Members

T: Who has not aunts? OK
Yes. Each of you will ask his partner and you'll write the number here. And then we'll do them straight on the board. OK.

S1: Miss, we only have one question?

T: Start asking each other questions, 'Do you have any sisters?' [to S1] Ask him 'Do you have any sisters?' How many sisters?

S2: ((two))

T: [to S1] How many sisters? [to S2] Do you have two sisters? [to S1] Write number 2.

T: [S2] Now you ask him. [To S1] Now he will ask you, 'Do you have any sisters?' He is going to ask you.

S2: Do you have any sisters?

T: Do you have any sisters?

S1: No

T: No what?

S1: No, I don't have any sisters.

T: You don't have any sisters. So, what do you write here? Zero, write here.
[…]

S3: Do you have any sisters?

T: How many sisters have you got?

S4: Four sisters. [to S3] So you write four. Who is the youngest? Who is the smallest?

S4: Two

T: Two are the smallest? Two are twins?

S4: Eh? [signals not understanding]

T: ((twins)) are they twins?

S4: No

T: So who is the youngest?

Ss: ((he's the youngest!)) [referring to S4]

The lesson went on in the same manner throughout the observation. The observer's impression was that many students did understand neither the meaning of the words needed for the 'conversation' nor the expected process. As Cameron (2001: 6) has pointed out, 'the course book dialogue is a rather strange invention', indeed.

Rima, whose students were talking about weather and seasons in Chapter 1, was also observed using this same approach in a grade four class during a task where students were practicing expression of likes and dislikes. When asked why she would not have the whole class engage in pair practice, which she could monitor by circulating among children, she responded:

> I tried it the way they say in the teacher's book to put them in pairs to practice. But it did not work because I could not hear all of them. … I'm sure they got some of the things wrong. So I changed. (Interview notes)

During these lessons teacher-fronted, textbook-bound discourse appeared to be a standard feature. Student-initiated negotiations and questions were observed frequently during story lessons, but rarely in the language practice lessons.

Talking about Stories

Genuine interactive, narrative discourse was observed during lessons where stories were the topic. In the first episode, Gloria is asking questions about Paul Revere, who was featured in a story her class had read.

Episode 5.4 About Paul Revere

T: Who can tell me something about Paul Revere? Who can give me some descriptive words? Joe?
S1: He was patient.
T: He was patient. Why do you think he was patient? What made you think that?
S1: Because when he go to prison, when he went to prison, he was patient. Yes, Natalie?
S2: When the officers caught him, he did not try to run away. He was patient. Maybe said to himself 'I will be patient and take time. I make a plan to escape'.
T: Right, he was patient, he was going to take time. OK.

Episode 5.5 was observed in Lily's fourth-grade class, where students were discussing *Children Who Hugged the Mountain* (Ghosn 1999a) that features a group of resourceful children taking action to protect a mountain from being quarried. The underlined

Episode 5.5 Characters' Motivations

T: So, the children decided to protect the mountain. Why?
S1: Miss, they love the mountain.
S2: Also because they think the mountain important. There is the prehistoric ((cave))!
S3: Also the nest of the ((owl)) owl, Miss.
T: Yes, you are right. Why was Mr. An-Nazar so angry with the children who were protecting the mountain?
S4: Miss, he very ((greedy)) and want to make money. Nothing else he cares only about money. He don't think mountain is anything ((important)).

The following transcript extract demonstrates how even a simplified story can generate connected interactive discourse, provided the teacher keeps the focus of interactions on the meaning as opposed to form. Here Houda's grade-five girls are discussing *Moby Dick*, a highly simplified excerpt from Melville's classic in their ESL book:

Episode 5.6 About Moby Dick

T: Please, the others are going to listen and see now if the answers are similar or not similar. Who can tell what happened? Did the sailors succeed?
S1: They did not succeed, they did not succeed because the whale didn't give them a chance because SHOKE, he shake the boat with his mouth.
T: So he didn't give them a chance. You mean that he didn't-e- give them a chance [writes the answer on the board] In other words, the whale, or Moby Dick was
Ss: Surprise!
T: A surprise, excellent. He surprised them. Fadia ((go ahead))
S2: They didn't succeed because the whale surprised them and he he take took and he take the small boat and swam away.
T: Aha, he moved the small boat. You mean that he shook-e- the boat?
S3: He pushed the boat.
T: OK, thank you [writes the answer on the board]
S4: (xxx) Moby Dick is like the answer of Ninar but some words were different.

T:	Were a little different, a little different, OK. She said here that the whale shook the boat. Wait, do you think they are the same, the same answers?
Ss:	No!
T:	What is the difference? (Ghosn 2017: 224)

The discourse is quite different from that observed during the dialogue practice. It is interactive and connected, and students are clearly actively listening to each other's responses. Note how Houda at the end of the episode invites students to compare different answers thus activating one important academic language function. The level of student enthusiasm was evident to the observer, as students were eagerly bidding for turns. Teacher's focus on meaning and validation of student responses maintained student motivation to keep engaging. Student engagement in this session was very different from the one where Houda's students practiced congratulations. In Houda's case, it appears the instructional materials and related activities resulted in different teacher approaches at least in these two lessons, as well as in the lesson where her students were talking about Tom Sawyer's fence paining in Episode 5.4. At the time of the observation, students had read the story during the previous class session and were now using the illustrations to retell it.

Episode 5.7 Talking about a Story

T:	This is her suggestion and she is-e-free, she is free and she is also free to think as she wishes. OK. [unintelligible] We go now to Batul. Let us listen to Batul's suggestion about the first picture.
S1:	Tom Sawyer said for her 'oh, you are you are painting'
T:	Painting
S1:	Painting and I'm and I eating and playing
T:	Yes, I am free, you are busy. I am eating I'm not working free to go whatever where ever I like and you are here to whitewash. We'll see. Sabine
S2:	I think, I think so that that Tom saw the apple, so he said for his Ben
T:	To his friend, yes
S2:	Friend Ben that (xxx) can you give me the apple and I will let you to to to wash the
Ss:	Wash! Wash! [several students calling out answers]
T:	Wait, wait, listen, yes. She is saying something important and the others, shh.
S2:	and I will let you

T:	Have a turn
S2:	Have a turn to paint.
T:	To paint. Maybe, maybe. Very good. Gibran
S3:	The boy are fighting who want to paint
T:	Yes
S3:	Eh, second the Ben gowed and have an
T:	Has gotten an idea, yes
S3:	Yes [unintelligible] an apple and he go for his friend Tom
T:	Yes
S3:	He said for him, you isn't
T:	Yes, you aren't what?
S3:	Do you want to eat? Tom said yes. He taked the apple and he he start eating
T:	Ah, he started eating. (Ghosn 2001: 173–4)

Although Houda could have interrupted the students less often, most of the interruptions were approving and extending the responses, encouraging students to continue. The videotape shows students eagerly bidding for turns.

None of the students in the communicatively oriented practice lessons were observed generating the above kind of connected narrative or considering characters' feelings or motivations. This was probably partly due to the type of simplified texts children were taught with that did not promote connected narrative discourse and may have had little content inviting thinking and discussion about motivations and states of mind of others.

Personal Narratives Prompted by Stories

In some of the story-based classes, lesson content generated plenty of personal narratives. In the following lesson excerpt, Maya's students are working on a reading selection involving rock climbing when a student initiated an account of his personal climbing experience.

Episode 5.8 About Rock Climbing

S1:	Is it exciting?
T:	It's exciting. It seems exciting but it's risky.
S2:	Miss, one day I climbed, one day I climbed in the [activity centre with a climbing wall] it was fun

T:	Yes, so it was fun but was it scary?
S2:	Yes
T:	Yes? You were tied to a rope?
S3:	Miss, he was talking about a parachute? It has a [unintelligible] It has a (xxx) and he does like this [waves arms indicating a gliding motion]
Ss:	Yes! I've seen it!

This exchange stimulated other students to talk about their climbing experiences:

S4:	Near our house there is uh there is some rocks I climb, climbed. I teach all my friends to climb those rocks.
T:	You climb those rocks? Are they very high?
S4:	No, they are like this [moving hand up and down]
T:	Small hill or something?
S4:	Yes, Miss.
S5:	Me and brother, the little hill was slippy
T:	Slippery?
S5:	Yes. We climbed it and we went down rolling.
T:	Was it fun?
S5:	Yes, Miss.
T:	OK. Yes, last one
S6:	Miss once I was climbing (xxx) with my two best friends to the snow
T:	Was it high, the snow?
S6:	Miss, till here [motions to chest level]

After the exchange, the teacher returned to the lesson content. Maya stood out from the other teachers as one who was observed during each session to give some time to students to talk about their personal experiences. The following episode was observed after her students had read a story about Halloween just days prior to *Eid el-Barbara*, a local feast where children dress up and collect sweets. On Monday, following the holiday, Maya asked students to tell what they did over the weekend. The underlined words/phrases suggest children's ability to think about the feelings and motivations of others in Episode 5.9.

Episode 5.9 Trick-or-Treating

S1:	Yesterday I made a trick with my friend, Miss.
T:	Yea? What did you do?
S1:	We were going to a house, and Miss I told her not to open (xxx)
T:	Open what?

S1: Not open [turn on] ((the flashlight)) so he will not see us.
T: OK. You did not turn on the flashlight.
S1: When we went there, Miss, he open the door and <u>I scare him</u> and he fell on the ground!
T: What did you dress as?
S1: Dracula, Miss. So <u>he thought I was Dracula</u>!

Several other students then shared their own weekend activities. During all observed lessons, both Maya's and Gloria's students engaged in negotiations of meaning and topic. Yet, both teachers were able to complete the planned activities. Because students were actively engaged in the tasks or conversations, they did not need to spend time disciplining students or trying to get them back on task. In classes where students were practicing dialogues or filling in blanks from a word bank, students did not initiate any interactions about any personal experiences, and only two instances of student-initiated negotiation was observed in Joanna's class.

Reading the Mind of Others

During story-based lessons, many students were observed discussing feelings and state of mind of others, as shown in the below exchange from Lily's class. The following student-initiated exchange was observed in Violet's sixth-grade class, where students had read *The Hundred Penny Box* (Mathis 1975). One student volunteered that his grandfather is old and also forgets things and confuses his name with those of his brothers. Another student commented on that:

S1: Miss, he said his grandfather forgets their names because he is old. I think he forgets them because they are so many boys! [laughter]
S2: I think <u>may be he ((does it on purpose))</u> to ((tease them)), Miss.
T: Oh? Why would he do that?
S2: They always run and make noise and he <u>want watch television</u>.

Similarly, the same group was able to discuss the feelings and thoughts of characters when talking about *The Hundred Dresses* (Estes [1940] 1973). In Bassima's sixth-grade class, students were discussing *The Dragonfly Surprise* (Ghosn 1999b) set in the Lebanese context and featuring some prejudice based on socio-economic class. (Chapter 12 shows some fifth-grade students' written responses to the same story.)

Episode 5.10 Expressing Viewpoints

T: What do you think about Heba's behaviour? [Heba cheated to help her friend without the friend's knowledge but revealed her reasons at the end of the story.]

S1: Miss, I think Heba she is a good friend. It was very wrong for Miss Randa to not let Mallika put her dragonfly in the contest.

S2: I think Miss Randa is not a nice person. She should not be mean to Mallika ((just because she is the daughter of a maid)). She must show respect.

S3: But it is ((forbidden)) to steal. She stoled the dragonfly from Mallika. It is also wrong that she put it with her name. She's ((a liar)).

T: So, Rana thinks Heba was a good friend but Hani thinks Heba must not steal and lie. What about others?

S1: But Miss, Heba she <u>wants to help</u> her friend. <u>She loves</u> Mallika. We must help our friends.

S3: But it is wrong what she did!

S4: Yes, but we must help others. Also sometime you must lie!

T: So you think sometimes you must lie? Tell me when?

S4: Well, me for example, my friend cut her hair [had a haircut] and it looks funny. When she ask me if I like it, I must say yes I like it. If I say it looks funny <u>she will be very sad</u>. So I must lie.

The discussion would have gone on, but Bassima cut it short and told the students to talk about the issue with their parents. Students in both classes, as well as in Lily's, were clearly able to 'reason about mental states of other people' (Pearson and deVilliers 2018: 12). In Houda's class during story discussions, students were able to say how they would feel if they were one of the characters, but none were able to answer referential questions about captain Ahab's or Tom Sawyer's thoughts, feelings or plans. When they were expected to narrate the story, they were able to do so only with considerable prompting from the teacher.

Teacher Feedback and Classroom Discourse

Data from the transcripts indicate that teachers differed not only in their questioning strategies but also in the type of feedback they provided. The data suggests that these differences were, to some extent, associated with the lesson content, and different teacher feedback resulted in significantly different interactions and had an influence on student output, participation and genuine student engagement. Reading-focused lessons and language arts lessons generated negotiated exchanges of meaning and topic (NE*m*, NE*t*) and longer DT moves, with some also involving negotiation of form (NE*f*). The same was observed during exchanges related to students' personal experiences. The negotiated exchanges often built into what Hoey (1991) calls 'exchange complexes', which involved negotiation of meaning and extending, bridging and scaffolding teacher feedback.

Although Gloria was not observed entertaining any personal experience initiation from students, her students were similarly engaged and her lessons moved on smoothly. In contrast, Rima and Tanya demonstrated a very hierarchical approach to their lessons while Joanna, Lily, Violet and Roula exhibited more egalitarian approaches. However, Joanna was somewhat constrained by the communicatively oriented language practice although she made attempts to engage her students in more interactive discourse. Sarah's approach in her immersion class was very different from the others, and we will return to her class in Chapter 13.

Conclusions

Although it might be easy to point to the coursebook topics and activities as the sole culprit for the discourse observed, there is also the individual teacher factor. Recall Joanna from Chapter 1. She was able to make a potentially tedious and meaningless practice into a motivating and participatory activity as most likely intended by the coursebook authors, and her class enthusiastically worked on the restaurant dialogue activity. In contrast, Rima, Tanya and Houda were not able to accomplish this. Houda only managed to engage her students more during the lessons dealing with stories.

The classroom episodes clearly suggest that stories or other interesting content generates more engaged, genuine discourse than language-practice dialogues. Stories, because of their universal appeal, offer an ideal medium for language teaching, not only because of their rich language but because they are more 'culture-friendly' than the dialogue practice. Regardless of the teacher's cultural orientation, stories naturally lead them to ask questions, whether factual or inferential, and students eagerly respond. The resulting discourse is both natural and meaningful to children. Allowing students time to link the new information to their own lives and encouraging student initiations also keep the flow of discourse natural, and more students are actively participating. Cognitively more demanding activities, such as reading comprehension and language arts lessons, focused teacher and student attention on meaning than form, resulting in more student output and more opportunities for negotiation. This, in turn, contributed to the development of connected, interactive discourse in the classrooms observed. In contrast, artificially contextualized language-practice dialogues focused teacher attention of form rather than communication of meaning. In addition, many of the culturally unfamiliar concepts further contributed to a discourse where teacher attention remained on form, with students reciting from the book as opposed to genuinely communicating. The focus on form and accuracy resulted also in more rejecting teacher feedback. However, observations also reveal the crucial 'conductor' role the teacher plays in classroom discourse. However, the difference between coursebook dialogues and genuine conversation – whether about topics or language itself – is that in the former often remains a mechanical drill, whereas in the latter the interlocutors engage in real exchanging meaningful ideas. Evelyn Hatch (1978: 404) has argued that English-language learners 'learn how to do conversation, how to interact verbally, and out of this interaction syntactic structures are developed'. The following chapter presents some evidence that supports her argument.

Recommendations for Practice

Teachers

- Invite students to link the coursebook materials, whether stories, informative selections or dialogues, to their lives and personal experiences whenever possible. Allow some time for students to share their ideas. This will also be a good opportunity to extend questions to the other students. This demonstrates that you are really listening and valuing the student contribution.
- Try to use the scaffolding approaches modelled by Maya and Gloria in their classes.
- Acknowledge and validate student responses even when they contain grammatical errors. Recast the erroneous response into correct English. For example, when student says 'My mother she make cookies yesterday,' respond 'Oh. Your mother made cookies yesterday. Did you all hear? Hani's mother made cookies. Who likes cookies?'

- When student's meaning is not clear, engage in negotiation strategies, such as 'I am not sure what you mean,' 'Do you mean …?'

Materials Developers

- Provide guidance to teachers on how to adapt dialogue practice if concepts or topics are unfamiliar to students.
- Use interesting and/or amusing stories as a starting point for lessons and draw dialogue content from the stories using vocabulary and structures featured in the stories.

6

Influence of Instructional Materials on Reading Comprehension

'And what is the use of a book,' thought Alice, 'without pictures or conversation?'

Lewis Carroll – *Alice's Adventures in Wonderland*

Which of the following texts might young English-language learners find more interesting?

The first text is from a typical TEYL book. Illustrations are indicated in brackets.

[A grocer to a boy] 'Please don't take the fruit.'

[A woman to the grocer] 'A banana and some cherries, please.'

[The grocer to the customer] 'Please take a plate.'

[A girl to the grocer] 'Sorry, six apples, please.'

[The grocer to the girl] 'Here you go. Six apples … and a cake!'

[The girl] 'Oh. Thank you.' (Cant and Charrington 2014: 9)

The second excerpt is from a book intended for beginning readers.

Pete wants to look cool. He asks everyone 'What should I wear?'

'Wear your yellow shirt,' his mom says. 'It's my favorite.' So Pete does.

'Wear your red shirt', Pete's friend Marty says. 'It's my favorite.'

So Pete does …

[And so it goes … until after trying on a variety of clothing items from cowboy boots, striped neck-ties to polka-dot socks Pete decides to wear his own favorite clothes]

Pete says, 'Now I am COOL!' (Dean and Dean 2014: 1–13)

The first text is from *Next Move*, level 2 and the second from *Too Cool for School* from the *Pete the Cat* picture book series, which reads at low first-grade level. The humorous story of Pete's outfit dilemma is loaded with repetitious phrases that young learners can easily pick up (video available at www.youtube.com/watch?v=AucIEFdWHjc). Classroom vignettes in Chapters 1 and 3 indicate what type of discourse the two texts might generate. For the first dialogue to provide real contextual practice, students would need to have the actual objects, realistic replicas or picture cards to manipulate in order for the dialogue practice to make sense. For the second text, the illustrations can generate authentic dialogue without any additional materials. Pictures of additional different clothing items would provide more practice.

For many young English learners, the teacher and the textbook are the only sources of the target language, determining the quantity and quality of the language learners can be expected to acquire. Although in many cases, young learners may be exposed to some environmental print in English, the expected learner engagement in the classroom is largely determined by the teacher and the language teaching texts and related activities, particularly where English is not the mainstream community language.

Language Teaching Texts

Extensive research from around the world indicates that story-reading approach to teaching English to young learners facilitates acquisition of all four language skills. Yet, the 'global' coursebooks produced in the UK and United States, and which dominate the world's TEYL market, do not typically include 'stories' as defined by Oxford Languages: story is 'an account of imaginary or real people and events told for entertainment' or 'an account of past events in someone's life or in the development of something'. The brief 'stories' in typical TEYL courses are, in fact, scripts told in the present tense, often with little or no clear plot. For example, *Hip, Hip, Hooray!* (Eisele et al. 2019) is marketed as 'classic stories'. However, a highly simplified rendition of the classic *Jack and the Beanstalk*, for example, is presented as a 'story' but it is a dialogue in the present tense rather than a narrative:

The woman takes Jack inside the castle. She tells him about the giant.

Jack: What's the giant doing?
Woman: He's sleeping.

Jack:	What's he like?
Woman:	Oh, he is very mean.

(Eisele et al. 2019: 44)

Other courses also often identify such dialogues as 'stories'.

Despite the research supporting story-based instruction, many schools in the Arab world adopt either 'global' ESL/EFL coursebooks or 'glocal' coursebooks. The latter are courses developed by international publishers for specific local markets but structured similarly to global ESL books, albeit incorporating local customs, names and the like. Some adopt American reading anthologies intended for native English speakers, as is the case in Kuwait, some schools in United Arab Emirates and most private EMI schools in Lebanon (Bacha, Ghosn and McBeath 2008: 282). In some cases, locally authored courses are used and these may or may not imitate global coursebooks in the structure of the syllabus. One such example is *Let's Learn Together* (Ghaleb et al. 1998–2000), a three-level course for ages six to eight produced by the Ministry of Education in Lebanon. The series, intended for public schools where English is taught as the first foreign language, is a hybrid between communicative ESL and reading-based L1 approach somewhat similar to those adopted by private EMI schools in the country. However, little research has been carried out in the Arab world about the influence of these different materials on young children's language learning. One exception is Ghosn's (2001) retrospective study in six schools from which some of the examples in this volume are drawn. The limited research is understandable considering the relatively recent emergence of TEYL in the region's lower primary schools. This chapter explores the influence of instructional texts and strategies on children's reading comprehension, summarizing data collected from nine schools: retrospective data from seven schools, experimental data from one school and an action research project data from another. The findings point to the benefit of story-based, reading-focused instruction on children's reading development.

Reading in a Second Language

What is reading? When I have asked teachers this question, typical responses included 'comprehension', 'decoding' and 'getting the meaning from a text', or something similar. Needless to say, comprehension, that is, to get the meaning from a text, requires decoding, but it is not sufficient. Let us take the following example from Lewis Carroll's poem *Jabberwocky* in *Through the Looking Glass*:

> T was brillig, and the slithy toves did gyre and gimble in the wabe;
> All mimsy were the borogoves, and the mome raths outgrabe.

Many readers might hesitate with decoding some of the words, let alone making sense of the meaning. Yet, the following 'comprehension' questions can be generated from the text and easily answered from the text as well: 'What was it like in the wabe?' 'How were the borogoves?' 'What did the mome raths do?' I have seen teachers in many classrooms asking such 'comprehension' questions about texts and their students reading the answers directly from the book, whether they understood the answer or not. Although decoding of vocabulary is essential, it is not sufficient, as the following often used example illustrates:

> A newspaper is better than a magazine. The beach is better than a crowded street. First, running is better than walking. Birds seldom get in the way. A rock makes a good anchor. Rain, however, will make everything soggy, and you will have to start all over again.

While the vocabulary is quite familiar and easy to decode, it is difficult to say what the passage is about. The problem is the context, or rather, the lack thereof. For a reader who has experience in making and flying kites the passage will be easy to understand. This illustrates the importance of background knowledge. While English vocabulary and decoding are challenging enough for young learners, background knowledge is even more so, because it involves so much. It involves not only knowledge about language, for example, letters, sounds, grammar, coherence and cohesion, but also knowledge about other types of texts and their structures and functions, as well as knowledge about the world.

Reading is considered one of the single most important sources of vocabulary and new knowledge, and it is especially important for students having to access academic subjects in the new language. It is also very important for students aiming for tertiary education in EMI colleges and universities. Yet large-scale studies in the United States have shown that although most American fourth-grade students can recognize the vocabulary in their grade-level coursebooks, two-thirds do it so slowly that it impedes their comprehension (Hiebert and Fisher 2005). It is therefore clear that young second language learners will face significant challenges when learning to read subject matter texts in English. Not only must children be able to decode the words in their coursebooks but must also be able to connect the words to concepts for which they may not yet have labels even in their L1.

Arabic-speaking children face some additional challenges, because Arabic uses a different alphabet system and a different reading directionality. (The same is true for Chinese and Japanese learners of English, for example.) If children have already learned to read Arabic, the Arabic reading may have shaped their neural pathways, which may be very different from the pathways used when reading in English, as Wolf (2007) found to be the case with Chinese English learners. One must also ask what happens when young Arabic-speaking children are trying to learn to read Arabic and English at the same time, which is the case with Kindergarten-age children in EMI schools and the numerous international English immersion schools in the MENA region.

Typically, TEYL courses are heavily aural/oral focused, with little, if any, explicit instruction in reading strategies indicated either in the student books or in teachers' guides. While oral English proficiency does play a role in reading development (August 2003), it can take children four to seven years to develop English reading proficiency (Hakuta, Butler and Witt 2000). If EMI begins in lower primary school, it poses a serious challenge for young language learners, making reading subject matter texts in English a serious challenge. If young native English speakers need more than four years to make sense of their grade-level texts, young ELLs can be expected to take at least as long and possible much longer. At the same time, there is the concern that early EMI might deprive children of developing academic language competence in their L1, which, in turn, may hinder the development of subject matter concepts in L1.

Reading research indicates that young English-language learners are both eager and capable of developing their literacy skills simultaneously with their development of oral language (Gregory 1996), given the right methodology and appropriate support. Araujo's (2002) year-long case study of a five-year-old ESL learner in a US kindergarten further suggests that young learners can advance their literacy knowledge beyond their oral language, and that knowledge of print can help their oral language development by enabling them to revise their 'hypothesis about how oral language works' (172). Chiappe, Siegel and Wade-Woolley (2002) and Lesaux and Siegel (2003) found that some young second language learners can learn to read as well as their native English-speaking peers, even outperforming them in some skills. However, without knowing something about the learners' background, one cannot assume that something in the classroom facilitated the learning. It is possible that factors outside school were behind their achievement. Some young ELLs may well be exposed at home to a richer language environment than some of their English-speaking peers, giving them an advantage for second language literacy as well.

Reading Comprehension after Six Years of English

To assess young Lebanese ELLs' vocabulary and reading skills after six years of formal English instruction, retrospective data were collected from 220 fifth-grade children in seven schools. Six of the classes were taught by Maya, Gloria and Sarah, who used a native speaker reading series, and Rima, Houda, Tanya and Bassima who used an American content-integrated ESL course. (We met the first six in Chapter 4 about teacher questions.) Students in the seven schools came from middle class and lower middle class and were taught math and science in English. Sarah's school is an exception being an English-immersion school, offering International Baccalaureate option and catering primarily to upper socioeconomic classes. With the exception of the immersion school that has several native English-speaking teachers, the teachers in the other schools are primarily native speakers of Arabic and, in some cases, Armenian.

TORC-3 Test of Reading Comprehension (Brown, Hammill and Wiederholt 1995), which was used to collect data, comprises subtests for general vocabulary, syntactic awareness, and reading comprehension measured through paragraph reading and sentence sequencing of short narratives. It also has subtests for subject matter, but these findings will be discussed in the chapter on vocabulary. In addition to mean scores, scores can also be converted to grade-equivalent scores from grade <2.2 to 12 as compared to the normative sample that included both native English speakers and ELLs. In the grammar subtest, students are required to identify two out of five sentences that mean almost the same thing. In paragraph reading subtest, students need to pick a sentence out of four options that best answers a given question about the paragraph. In the sentence-sequencing subtest, students must order five sentences in a sequence that produces a logical course of events. In the following schoolwork directions task, students must read the instructions for how to mark the correct answer either by underlining or circling the correct answer or by crossing out one that does not belong.

Significant differences emerged between the classes. Gloria's, Maya's and Sarah's students in the reading series classes scored statistically significantly higher than their peers in the four ESL course classes in general reading comprehension, syntactic similarities, paragraph reading and sentence sequencing. More specifically, the children scored significantly higher than their ESL course peers in understanding passive voice sentences, relative clauses and making inferences. However, Gloria's and Maya's students significantly outperformed Sarah's immersion students, whereas the differences between the ESL course classes did not reach statistical significance. Grade-level equivalences ranged from low second grade to fourth grade in the ESL classes and from high third grade level to high sixth grade in the reading series classes. Such diversity or reading abilities in one class poses a problem for the teacher: how to ensure that the lower-level readers will catch up while not demotivating the more advanced leaners with too simple texts?

Interestingly, the subtest of Reading Schoolwork Directions proved problematic for great many of the children in all seven schools, with grade equivalences ranging from low second grade in Rima's class to low fourth grade in Gloria's and Maya's classes. The test aims to check whether children understand directions, but despite given examples, children focused mainly on getting the content correct, ignoring how they were supposed to signal the correct answer. For example, in an item 'Put a *V* beside each word that names an animal', many children circled or underlined the target words, thus failing the item.

Reading Comprehension with the Help of Stories

Findings from an experimental study resonate with the above findings. Forty-eight children (ages nine and a half to eleven) in Bassima's school participated in a random-grouping study, forty-eight in post-test-only condition and another forty-nine in a pretest–post-test condition. A story-based fifty-minute intervention was implemented in the experimental classes once a week for fifteen weeks while the control classes worked on the lessons in their content-integrated ESL book. Once a week, children in grade five selected short illustrated books to read from a selection, and after reading, they chose a written reader response task from a given set; choices ranged from adding something to the story to literary journal entries from characters' point of view to letters to or between characters.

Written responses were selected because it has been argued that writing can enhance young learners' L2 reading development (Hudelson 1984; Zamel 1992). In grade six, children were all assigned a same-chapter book to read at home during the week. At the end of the week, students met in small literature circles and were given discussion starters in case they had difficulty getting started with a discussion. For example, one of the literature circle starters for *Sarah, Plain and Tall* was 'What did you think when you read about Anna's and Caleb's father putting an ad in the paper to get a wife?' After ten to fifteen minutes of discussion, the teacher led a whole-class discussion. Discussions were selected because it has been argued that language learning best happens within the context of social interaction. At the end of the intervention, both groups were administered the *TORC-3 Test*. The same procedure was carried out with another group of forty-nine children as a pretest–post-test study, twenty-four in the experimental condition and twenty-five in the control condition. Both groups were administered the *TORC-3 Test* before and after the intervention. (The post-test-only condition was deemed necessary as *TORC-3* comes only in one form.)

In the pretest–post-test group, the control groups began with statistically higher means than their experimental group peers in all but general reading comprehension, where the difference was minimal. However, in the post-test, the experimental groups outperformed their control peers in general reading and overall reading with differences being statistically significant. The experimental group made significantly higher gains than their control peers in general reading comprehension (4.23 points vs. 2.53) and in overall reading comprehension (14.58 points vs. 6.29).

In the post-test-only group, the experimental group scored higher means in all subtests at statistically significant level, and the group that read stories silently and completed reader response tasks scored statistically higher means than the group that only discussed the stories. This suggests that students having to return to the story, first when deciding on the response tasks and again while working on the tasks, is more useful than simply reading the story, even when a discussion about the story follows. After all, when having to complete a written task students are actively engaged, whereas when sitting in a discussion circle they can easily 'tune out' and not participate actively. Both during reading and the reader response tasks, students were also able to ask their teacher questions, such as vocabulary they wanted to use but did not yet have in their productive repertoire. Since the reading-discussion group read the stories at home, they did not benefit from teacher assistance (but could have used, e.g. help from parent or use a dictionary).

A paired samples comparisons of girls' and boys' scores in the pretest–post-test group revealed that the experimental group's girls made statistically significant gains in overall reading comprehension, whereas the control group girls showed statistically significant gains only in general reading comprehension.

The experimental group boys made also statistically significant gains in general reading comprehension and in the overall reading, as compared to their control group peers.

The Following Schoolwork Directions subtest revealed similar surprising outcomes found in the retrospective study above, with grade-level equivalences ranging from low second- to mid-third-grade levels in both groups.

Levelled Books and Strategy Instruction

One way to meet the reading needs of all students in a diverse class is the approach described by Chaaya (2006). At the beginning of the school year, second-grade teacher Dima in an English immersion school faced a dilemma. Many children in the class had developed good verbal communication skills but varied considerably in their English literacy skills. At the beginning of the school year, children's reading levels in the class ranged from kindergarten to high third grade as assessed by Nelly and Smith's (2000) *PM Benchmark* records. The teacher decided to try instruction using levelled books and explicit reading strategy instruction because there was a considerable body of literature showing their effectiveness.

'Levelled books' refers to a collection of literally thousands of trade books ('real books'), classified into levels of difficulty from A to Z by Fountas and Pinnell (2002). The collection includes fiction, non-fiction and content area readings. See Table 6.1 for sample text excerpts for the different levels. Strategies are defined by Clay (1991: 328) as 'a network of unobservable in-the-head' operations that enable the reader to 'attend to information from different sources'. Strategies believed to help young ELLs especially include the use of picture cues to construct meaning; chunking words into decodable parts; making predictions; self-correcting; summarizing; thinking aloud; monitoring comprehension by asking questions; and making text-to-text, text-to-self and text-to world connections (Bergeron and Wolff 2002).

After the initial assessment of reading levels, children in the class were divided into groups of low, average and high readers based on their reading ability as measured by the *PM Benchmark*. Dina and her assistant teacher worked with small groups of four to six children of similar reading levels, using books at children's instructional level. These teacher-guided sessions, which lasted approximately twenty minutes, were divided into three phases. First, the teacher introduced a new book (or reviewed a previously read book), inviting children

Table 6.1 Sample Text Excerpts

Level D KG	Brown bear, brown bear, what do you see? I see a red bird looking at me. Red bird, red bird, what do you see? I see a yellow duck looking at me (*Brown Bear, Brown Bear*, Martin and Carle 1967: 1–3).
Level E Low grade 1	'Oh, lovely mud,' said the cow, and she jumped in. 'Oh, lovely mud,' said the pig, and he rolled in it. 'Oh, lovely mud,' said the duck, and she paddled in it (*Mrs. Wishy Washy*, Cowley 1999: 2–7).
Level I High grade 1	Here is Little Bear again. 'Oh,' said Mother Bear, 'do you want something?' 'I am cold,' said Little Bear. 'I want something to put on.' So Mother Bear made something again for Little Bear (*Little Bear*, Holmelund Minarik 1957: 16–17). Harry was a white dog with black spots who liked everything, except … getting a bath. So, one day, when he heard the water running in the tub, he took the scrubbing brush … and buried it in the backyard. Then he ran away from home (*Harry the Dirty Dog*, Zion [1956] 2002: 1).
Level M High grade 2	That's where! I quick ducked down and hided around the corner. Then I did some sneaky peeky spying on them. I saw Mrs. Picking out yucky blucky brocly. And stewie pewie tomatoes. And also the kind of vegetables named Sue Keeny. Except for then the strange man snatched Sue Keeny right out of her hands (*Junie P. Jones and some Sneaky Peeky Spying*, Park 1994: 36).
Level P High grade 3	There wasn't any Mr. Herdman. Everybody agreed that after Gladys was born, he just climbed on a freight train and left town, but some people said he waited year or two. 'Gladys probably bit him,' my friends Alice Wendleken said. 'Not if she was a baby?' (*The Best [Worst] School Year Ever*, Robinson 1996: 8)

to examine the cover and the illustrations and making predictions about the story. Then the teacher introduced and modelled the targeted reading strategy as in the following example:

> You can look at the illustrations in the book to predict, to guess, what a word might mean. Let's see … it says here Charlie 'really needed a new cloak'. If you look at the picture on this page, you can guess what a cloak might be. Look at Charlie. What can you see? (Chaaya and Ghosn 2010: 333)

As children began reading the book the teacher observed them closely, guiding individual children and their attempts to utilize some of the strategies. Reading was followed by a teacher-led discussion about the book. During these guided reading sessions, other children engaged in independent reading of books at their independent reading levels.

Using Nelly and Smith (2000) reading record kit, children's reading levels were assessed monthly, and when indicated by the assessment, children were

Table 6.2 Sample of Six Children's Progress

Child	September	November	February	April
High Girl	3.9	5	5	6
High Boy	2.9	3.9	4.8	5
Av. Girl	1.9	2.7	2.7	3.3
Av. Boy	1.9	2.9	4.3	4.3
Low Girl	1.5	1.8	2.2	2.7
Low Boy	1.4	1.7	1.8	2.4

moved to another group. See Chaaya and Ghosn (2010) for detailed description of the approach and calculations of reading accuracy levels. Table 6.2 shows the *PM Benchmark* scores and instructional reading levels of six children, two from the low reader group, two from the average reader group and two from the high reader group. By the end of April, the two highest readers had gained two full grade levels each, reading at sixth and fifth grade levels. The two average readers had gained 2.3 and 1.3 grade levels, with one of them now reading at low third-grade level and the other at low fourth-grade level. One of the lowest readers had gained one full grade level, reading at mid-second-grade level, while the other had progressed twelve levels, reading now at high second-grade level.

The two low readers' attitude about reading and perception of themselves as readers had changed significantly by April. At the beginning of the year, the low reading boy often cried during reading sessions or showed otherwise high frustration levels. He admitted that reading was difficult for him and that there were often big words he did not know how to read. However, in April, he stated that he was reading better and knew 'lot of words'. He said that the strategies he had learned were helping him read not only easy books but also harder ones. When at the beginning of the year he did not like the reading sessions, by mid-year he was asking when the reading time will be. Similarly, the low reading girl did not like to read, and often only looked at the illustrations in books. She did not see herself as a good reader because she could only read easy books. By spring, she saw herself as a good reader and liked to read. She said she liked to read because she now knew how to read even difficult words.

Conclusions

The findings from the three studies suggest that reading-focus language instruction can be beneficial for young learners, especially those who may need to access school subjects in English. Although some of the fifth graders in the first study were reading at or above grade level, as compared to their US peers, many others were struggling two or more years behind. Yet it seems that even children three years behind in their reading had managed to gain information from their mathematics and science books sufficiently well to reach grade five. However, post hoc interviews with some science and mathematics teachers confirmed Armstrong and Armbruster's (1991) findings; lower primary school children need to read very little in their textbooks apart from homework assignment problems. Rather, the lessons rely heavily on teacher explanations of the content and subsequent exercises, with some explanations in Arabic when necessary. The only exception to this was Sarah's school, where all subjects were taught in English, many of them by native English speakers.

While the retrospective study does not allow cause–effect conclusions to be drawn, the findings from the classroom experiment further point to the benefits of story reading, suggesting also that written reader responses to stories are more beneficial than reading and only talking about the stories. The progress of the six children in the action research is also noteworthy. Although the design of the study does not allow drawing of any cause–effect relationships, children's use of the taught strategies clearly helped them develop as readers, as they all stated when interviewed at the end of the school year. Appropriately levelled books can provide scaffolding for young second language learners' reading development, particularly in a class with diverse reading abilities. Findings from the three studies suggest that story-reading had a positive impact on children's reading comprehension.

Courses featuring plenty of quality children's literature and interesting school subject–related information can be rich in language. Children can encounter vocabulary and structures in multiple, meaningful and contextualized situations, which can help them acquire the new language faster. Reading and vocabulary acquisition are interdependent, one influencing the other. In the communicatively oriented ESL courses, children have fewer opportunities to repeat encounters with language in different meaningful contexts. Reading selections in these courses are typically brief and at the lower levels in highly simplified language. The most important difference between the two types of materials is perhaps the approach they take to instruction. The literature-rich materials, whether fiction or non-fiction, focus on meaning, while the ESL courses focus on interpersonal communication. The instructional approach, together with the amount of exposure to the type of language and opportunities to extended reading may be at the core of what the outcomes are likely to be.

Although communicative language competence is important, it is not enough to access school subjects in English, let alone manage academic discourse at tertiary level. One must ask how students scoring two to three years below grade level in their English reading will be able to cope with other school subjects taught in English in the upper levels. Not so well, it seems, if one examines the TIMSS results mentioned in the introduction. Not surprisingly, in the TIMSS, children at or above grade level in Lebanon were enrolled in private schools with annual tuition fees six to ten times the minimum monthly wages. The lowest percentage of at-grade-level students was found in public or subsidized schools with low tuition fees. Story-based, reading-focused instruction might be especially helpful for children from lower-income families where parents cannot support their children's foreign-language learning with tutors or other out-of-school help.

Recommendations for Practice

Teachers

- Whenever possible, select ESL courses that feature many interesting storylines. In the beginning levels, for example, each unit should have a story narrative that either introduces new language and structures or reinforces them.
- If storylines are in the present tense, as in the earlier mentioned story from *Hip, Hip, Hooray!* Level 3, extend the story and engage the children to talk about it. After students have read the story, ask questions that require the use of past tense, 'Where did the woman take Jack?' When children answer 'castle' or 'she take Jack ...', validate the answer by saying, 'Right. The woman took Jack to the castle. She took him to the castle.' Repeat with other sentences. Then invite students to retell the story using the picture clues. Again, validate response and model the use of past tense.
- If the coursebook does not include stories, supplement the coursebook with illustrated children's literature. There is no need for each student to have a copy of a story; you can read the story to the class using a dialogic approach during which you stop to invite younger children to point to pictures, and with older learners you can stop at key points to ask for predictions.

- Plan for oral and written follow-up activities for stories that will instantiate subject-specific language (comparison, cause-and-effect, hypothesizing, etc.) and incorporate work on tables, charts, graphs and the like.
- Where inexpensive paperback children's books are readily available, with a relatively small investment, the school can purchase a set of few titles that can be circulated among different classes. For example, a set of five to six titles representing different difficulty levels depending on the need of learners, or approximately forty to fifty titles. Used books are available at costs as low as a dollar per copy on the internet.
- Teachers can use the books as well as any reading selection on the coursebook to model reading strategies described above. They can assign books from the classroom collection for children to read at home, and children can be given a checklist of strategies to take home and refer to while reading.

Materials Developers

- When developing materials for FLAPPS contexts, include plenty of narrative stories and informational content that can introduce and activate subject-specific vocabulary and academic language functions outlined in Chapter 3.
- Consider approaches that will generate authentic discourse in addition to the common prepared dialogue practice.
- Include some explicit guidance on reading instruction in the teacher's guide.

7

Influence of Instructional Materials on Receptive and Productive Vocabulary

'The question is,' said Alice, 'whether you can make words mean different things?'

Lewis Carroll – *Alice in Wonderland*

A key feature in language learning is vocabulary. It enables learners not only to communicate but also to access written texts, which further increases their vocabulary acquisition and subsequently improves their ability to comprehend written texts. In other words, the more vocabulary learners acquire the more texts they can access, the more they can increase their vocabulary. In this chapter we will review what vocabulary knowledge entails, and examine young Arabic-speaking students' receptive vocabulary after six years of learning English and productive vocabulary assessed in a classroom-based experiment.

Challenge of English Vocabulary

Vocabulary learning presents a challenge to young second language learners and to their reading development in particular, because word knowledge means many different things, as researchers have pointed out. (For more detailed discussions, see Cameron 2001; Nagy and Scott 2000; Nation 1990; Zimmerman 2009.) First, there is conceptual knowledge, whether receptive or productive, which means to understand a word and be able to use it correctly. In English, polysemy can present a vocabulary challenge as some words can have two or more totally unrelated meanings; for example, 'crane' can refer to a bird, a machine or a movement of one's neck. This can be difficult for young ELLs. Then there is metalinguistic awareness, which involves morphological knowledge and helps us make sense about meanings of inflections and derivational affixes;

for example, to know that 'walk' becomes 'walked' in the past tense, but 'teach' becomes 'taught', and that the adjective 'helpful' becomes 'helpfulness' as a noun while 'difficult' becomes 'difficulty'. Grammatical knowledge enables us to understand the word's function in a sentence and use it in a grammatically correct way and understand that a word can serve in more than one function, such as 'record' (noun; verb) and 'counter' (noun; verb; adverb; adjective), for example.

Semantic knowledge implies the understanding of collocation, to understand what words usually go together or not. For example, we talk about the 'aroma' of fresh coffee and not 'perfume' of coffee, or 'a pretty woman' but not 'a pretty man'. It means also knowledge of how to use words metaphorically, as in 'Don't be such a chicken' or 'Ben is a real lightning on the court.' Semantic knowledge involves also knowledge of connotations, as some words have positive connotation while others imply negative qualities. For example, calling someone 'skinny' has a negative connotation while calling the person 'slim' has a positive one. Word knowledge implies also pragmatic knowledge, which means to know how to use a word correctly in real-world situations. For example, it might be quite appropriate to greet your friend as 'How's it going, mate?', but it will not be an acceptable greeting to one's teacher, the school principal or a doctor. Finally, phonological knowledge means to know how to pronounce a word or to recognize it in spoken and written language. Again, English language with its numerous exceptions to rules can be daunting. For example: Why does 'stove' not rhyme with 'love' or 'home' with 'come'? Why is letter 'c' pronounced as soft in 'circus' but hard in 'cat'? Why is 'gh' pronounced as 'f' in laugh, and why 'phone' begins with 'f'? and so on. The exceptions seem to be more numerous than the rules!

What might also be difficult for young learners is that in spoken language a group of words may sound as a single word, even for first language learners. For example, the phrase 'this is a ...' is often heard by children as 'thisisa' and consequently spelled like that in their writing. Another example is the familiar fairytale beginning 'once upon a time', which has been spelled by children in some of my research projects in more than a dozen different ways, either as single words, such as 'wansaponetim' or short phrases such as 'wansa ponatime'.

Finally, many English words may be somewhat contradictory, as Richard Lederer, the author of *Grazy English* (1989) points out: How come we drive in the parkway but park in the driveway? Why do musicians play at recitals, but actors recite their lines in plays? How can quicksand take us down slowly? Why do we call boxing rings square? (I highly recommend the book for all teachers of English.) Such complex word knowledge develops gradually over time, as children hear, see and use a given word. The more often a given word is encountered, the more likely it is learned, and Nation and Wang (1999) suggest that a minimum of ten encounters are necessary for likely acquisition.

The Challenge of Time

Examination of vocabulary in some popular young learner courses suggests that there might not be sufficient time for all the target vocabulary words to be encountered sufficiently many times for complex word knowledge to develop. For example, typical TEYL courses have six to ten thematic units to be covered within the academic year, which in the MENA region averages around thirty-six weeks, that is, around 180 days. This includes time for class tests as well as school-wide tests, which may vary in frequency from school to school. In Lebanon, for example, frequent tests are assigned even in primary school, sometimes as often as once a week to cover dictation, spelling, vocabulary, grammar, reading comprehension and compositions. Moving religious holidays happening during the school year may shorten schooldays, putting more pressure on teachers to cover the curriculum.

One widely marketed international TEYL course has ten units and 144 target vocabulary words in level four. Another popular course has eight thematic units and a total of 167 target words and expressions in level three. This suggests roughly five to six words per week, which may sound quite reasonable. However, two surveys indicate that in typical YL classes, English is allocated an average of two hours per week in Europe (Enever 2011) while worldwide averages range from thirty yearly hours to over a hundred hours (Rixon 2013), that is, around five weekly hours. In the latter group, there are five Arab countries: Jordan, Palestine, Qatar, UAE and Yemen. In the Lebanese English as the first foreign-language program (which was not included in Rixon's survey) children have forty-five- to fifty-minute English lessons from five to seven hours a week, depending on grade level. In English as the second foreign-language program, primary school students typically have one to two hours of English a week.

A question to ask is whether the time will allow sufficient repetition and recycling for all target words to be acquired by average learners, especially because one has to consider also coursebook language that is not the target but that needs to be attended to in order for learners to complete given tasks.

In addition, the expectation of both school principals and parents, at least in Lebanon, is often that teachers 'cover' the complete book, as many teachers have reported to me. My observations in numerous classrooms suggest that in a class of thirty-five to forty students, teachers are often rushing through the lessons and the instructional cycle consists primarily of teach-homework-test cycle, with little or no time left for the important guided and independent practice phases. Thus it is unlikely that students would be able to develop the kind of complex word knowledge described above within six years of primary school.

Contrary to Nation and Wang's above claim, Zimmerman (2009) argues that a word can be learned even with fewer encounters, provided it is salient within the context it occurs, and Elley (1997: 6) argues that 'much of our vocabulary development is a result of incidental learning from silent reading'. Both Zimmerman's and Elley's arguments are supported by research, most notably by Elley and colleagues' large-scale 'book flood' projects in different countries. They found that story reading had a positive influence on all four language skills, including vocabulary. Several small-scale experiments have come to the same conclusion.[1] However, in most TEYL courses reading selections are typically short and linked to accompanying exercises, and the saliency of the vocabulary is not always clear. For example, in a six-level course, the third-level book presents a lesson *Sally Climbs*. The unit begins by a mouse-like character pointing to two framed pictures, one of them showing the character in water and the other on roller skates. The character says 'Look! I can swim. Can you swim?' If children do not already know the word 'swim' or 'skate', it would not be clear to them which one of the pictures depicts swimming. In contrast, as we will see in Chapter 11, a word, such as 'butterfly' can be so salient that even when it appears only once within a picture book that children immediately picked up began using it in their free time activities. There are many children's picture books that feature repeated words and phrases. *Goldilocks*, *Gingerbread Man* and *The Farmer and the Beet* are just three examples.

Receptive Vocabulary

After Six Years of English

The retrospective study of six classes described in Chapter 6 collected data also on children's receptive vocabulary in subtests of general vocabulary, mathematics vocabulary, science vocabulary and social studies vocabulary of *TORC-3 Test of Reading Comprehension* (Brown et al. 1995). Similar data were collected from one additional school also from a fifth-grade class taught by Bassima. While social studies in all but the English-immersion school were taught in Arabic, mathematics and sciences were taught in English, beginning grade one. Four of the schools used a content-integrated ESL course taught by Rima, Houda, Tanya and Bassima, while the other three used a reading series. Two of the classes were taught by Gloria and Maya and the immersion class by Sarah. Reading books were assigned one grade level below the publisher-suggested level in Gloria's and Maya's classes and at grade level in Sarah's classes.

Not surprisingly, Gloria's, Maya's and Sarah's students in the reading series classes scored statistically significantly higher means in general vocabulary than their peers in the four ESL course classes. In the three subject matter vocabulary subtests, the grade equivalences in five of the classes were either above or slightly below fifth-grade level. The highest means were recorded in Maya's class, where the average was mid-seventh grade in math, low sixth grade in science vocabulary and end of grade four in social studies. Gloria's students came second with scores at end of grade five, mid-grade four and five, respectively. In social studies and science vocabulary, Bassima's and Houda's students reached low third-grade levels, only one grade level below their peers in the immersion school. Sarah's students' relatively low performance was unexpected since Sarah's students had been immersed in English all day long and were taught with the same reading series as Gloria's and Maya's students, and which included several science and social studies concepts and related vocabulary.

Although the ESL series used in the four schools contained some lessons related to math, science and social studies concepts, none of Rima's and Tanya's students were able to complete these subtests to reach a score convertible to low second-grade level, and Houda's students barely made it to <2.2 grade level. Bassima's students scored at mid- and high second-grade level. Since children, except for Sarah's immersion students, had studied social studies in Arabic, the low score in this subject vocabulary was not unusual, but the math and science vocabulary scores were unexpected since children had been taught both subjects in English since year one. Because subject matter instruction was outside the scope of the study, it is not possible to know how much of the low performance of the children was due to teachers possibly using Arabic to explain and clarify concepts, as already mentioned earlier. During my twenty-six years of teaching in an American university where English is the official language of instruction, I observed many times some faculty using Arabic in their classes when explaining new concepts.

After a Fifteen-Week Experiment

Receptive and productive vocabulary data were collected from students in grades five and six on general and subject matter vocabulary during a classroom experiment described in the previous chapter. Receptive vocabulary data were collected with *TORC-3 TEST*. The experimental groups participated in a fifteen-week intervention comprising story reading and follow-up activities once a week while their control peers work on their ESL coursebook activities.

In the *TORC-3 Test*, the experimental group began with a slightly higher mean in general vocabulary, whereas the control group began with higher means in the three subject matter subtests. None of the differences were statistically significant, however. In the post-test, the experimental group scored higher means in general vocabulary as well as in science and social studies vocabulary. While none of the differences were statistically significant, analyses of covariance revealed a statistical significance in mathematics, science and social studies vocabulary.

The experimental group also made significantly higher gains than their control peers in mathematics vocabulary (from 10.14 to 15.66 vs. 12.04 to 15.77), science vocabulary (from 4.79 to 8.28 vs. 6.83 to 7.27) and social studies vocabulary (from 8.87 to 10.26 vs. 9.50 to 9.59). A post hoc paired samples comparisons of girls' and boys' scores further revealed that the experimental group girls and boys made statistically significant gains in mathematics and science vocabulary as compared to their control group peers. The control group boys also made significant gains in the mathematics vocabulary, with their gains nearly identical to those of the experimental group. No significant gains were noted in science or social studies vocabulary between the two groups.

The control group began with statistically higher means than their experimental group peers in all *TORC-3* subject matter vocabulary subtests. However, in post-test, the experimental group outperformed their control peers in general vocabulary, social studies vocabulary and science vocabulary, with the difference being statistically significant. This study further supports the notion that reading and appropriate follow-up activities can have a beneficial influence on children's receptive vocabulary in subject matter.

Productive Vocabulary

During the fifteen-week story-based intervention, compositions were collected from ninety-eight children. A picture stimulus depicting a prehistoric scene of a group of people battling mammoths from *TOWL-3 Test of Written Language* (Hammill and Larsen 1996) was used to generate compositions in the pretest and a picture from the same test depicting a futuristic space scene with astronauts in space in the post-test. Because the participating students would have to deal with academic texts throughout their schooling and possibly later in college or university, the Lextutor Compleat (*sic*) (Lextutor.ca) was selected for analysing the compositions quantitatively. *Lextutor* classifies words into four categories: K1, K2, academic word list (AWL) and Off-list Words. K1 and K2 lists contain the 2,000 most frequently used words in English language; K1 (1–1,000) the most frequently used and K2 (1,001–2,000) less frequent. The AWL contains 570 high-frequency words appearing in typical academic texts. *Lextutor* can be used to generate a vocabulary profile showing the total words ('tokens'), different words ('types'), K1 Words, K2 Words, AWL Words and Off-list Words. *Lextutor* K1 and K2 type-token ratio (types ÷ tokens) shows the variety in the text, and the token-type ratio (tokens ÷ types) the lexical density in the text.

A vocabulary profile was generated for each composition. Obvious spelling errors were corrected, first because the aim was not to test children's spelling skills but their vocabulary range and quality. Second, the initial *Lextutor* vocabulary profiles classified the majority of misspelled words in many compositions as Off-list words while the words were clearly of lower levels (e.g. 'alifant' for 'elephant' or 'longe stiks' for 'long sticks'). These were categorized as either K1, K2, AWL or Off-list. Undecipherable words were left as is and excluded from analysis. Compositions were then input into *Lextutor* to generate a vocabulary profile. In the vocabulary profile, non-lexical proper names are included in the K1 list, as per *Lextutor* classification of words. Duplicates/multiples were all counted in tokens but only once in the Off-list means. For example, an Off-list word 'mammoth' appeared eight times in one composition and is counted in tokens eight times but only once in Off-list words.

Quantity and Range of Vocabulary

As expected, there was a clear difference between the two groups in the output quantity as measured in the total number of words, the number of discrete items, K2-list words, and Off-list words. Students in the experimental group outscored their control group peers at statistically significant levels in *Lextutor* Tokens, Types, and K2 list and in AWL words.

When pre- and post-tests were paired, the comparisons revealed that the grade four and five experimental classes made greater gains in Tokens, K2 list words and

AWL words, but the difference in Types was not statistically significant. Similarly, the experimental group in grade six scored higher means than their control peers, but the difference failed to reach statistical significance. The control group scored overall higher in Off-list words, and their words included numerous words related to planets and space, including names of all the planets in the solar system. An inquiry revealed that the grade five control group had spent considerable time in their science class on planets, whereas the experimental group grade five had only began the space unit a week before the post-test. Thus, the control group children may have been exposed to more space-related vocabulary than their experimental group peers and thus may have had an advantage in this regard.

When pre- and post-tests were paired, the comparisons revealed that overall, the experimental group children made statistically greater gains than their control peers in all but *Lextutor* Types. The differences were largely due to the grade four and five experimental groups who made greater gains in Tokens, K2 list words and AWL words at level ($p < 0.01$). While the experimental group scored higher in Types, the difference was not statistically significant.

Quality of Vocabulary

There were also notable differences in the quality of vocabulary between the two groups. In the pretest, the control group's compositions included only one AWL word (finally) and in the experimental group none. However, the post-test revealed fifteen AWL words in the experimental group (author, publish, team, project, job, contact, chemical, element/s, primary, finally, grade, source, theories, cultures, goal) as opposed to only seven in the control group (create, challenge, chart, researching, finally, energy). In the post-test, the control group's AWL words were limited to 'finally', 'computer' and 'project' while the experimental group's compositions featured also words such as 'volunteered', 'survive', 'medium', 'finally', 'sphere', 'occurred', emerged, 'intelligent', 'computers' and 'approach'. There was also a rich variety of Off-list words in the experimental group. It should be noted that the storybook collection available to children during the experiment included three stories featuring issues of environment, but none related to space.

Conclusions

The above data, combined with the data from the studies described in Chapter 6 suggest that reading and appropriate follow-up activities have a beneficial influence on children's receptive vocabulary, and that rich reading texts can promote learning of subject matter vocabulary. In the reading books, children are exposed to a much richer vocabulary than in the ESL books. Gloria, Maya and Sarah reported that they can select the target vocabulary in consultation with the English supervisor to meet the class learning objectives. The expectation is not to cover the whole book, which would be an impossible task considering the time limitations and students' language development. In some schools the same reading book is covered over two school years. In contrast, Houda, Rima and Tanya are expected to cover the whole book while Bassima had some leeway as long as her students passed the end-of-the-year school-wide exams. However, parents of her students often complain if children do not cover the book, because in most cases parents have paid for the imported books and feel that they should 'get their money's worth'. The classroom experiment suggests that even a relatively brief story-based intervention can have a positive influence on children's productive vocabulary.

Recommendations for Practice

Teachers

- Consider the target vocabulary and its importance or significance to your particular students. It may be sensible to omit and/or replace some of it. For example, if the target vocabulary includes concepts or topics not familiar or useful to your students, replace them with words to which your students can relate and which they may need more than the offered target words but keep the grammatical structures. For example, if the target structures include asking and answering questions about breakfast but children are not familiar with the book options, replace them but keep the structures 'What do you like to have for breakfast?' and 'I like to have …'. Needless to say, where common school-wide tests are assigned, such alterations need to be done in cooperation with all teachers involved.
- Ensure that the target vocabulary is repeated as often as possible in a meaningful context.
- Even if target vocabulary is recycled across units, look for opportunities for meaningful, contextualized review.

Materials Developers

- When determining the target vocabulary for a given level, take into consideration the need for repetition and recycling of the words throughout the unit and throughout the coursebook in case of words considered critically important or words that are abstract or not very salient in their introductory context.
- Consider also how much additional language is needed to proceed through the lessons, activities and tasks.
- When developing global coursebooks, aim to include different cultural concepts, and provide activities in which children can compare their own experiences with those of children in the target language culture. For example, a unit on leisure time activities could include children of different backgrounds discussing their favourite activities and comparing them with those of their peers.
- Develop materials that incorporate many different cultures. For example, a group of children can travel from one country to another and explore concepts such as family life, school days, leisure time activities, foods and the like.

8

Instructional Texts as Models for Writing

He was obliged to write with one finger for the rest of the day; and this was of very little use, as it left no mark on the slate.

Lewis Carroll – *Alice's Adventures in Wonderland*

Writing in the First Language

Writing is the creating of original text using the individual's intellectual and linguistic resources rather than copying someone else's text, using prepared lists of words to create sentences or stories. (Hudelson 1989: 5, citing Berthoff 1981)

In the first language context, Graves has argued that children need modelling in order to develop as writers so that they would not perceive writing as magic, as if 'we only need to hold the pen and a mysterious force dictates stories, poems, and letters' (1983: 43). Whitley (1995) believes that children's knowledge of traditional stories provides them with a powerful model for their writing, which resonates with Escott's (1995: 12) argument that 'children's narrative reading is reflected in their writing'. However, when Australian linguist Martin (1984, quoted in Bearne 1995: 13–14) examined the kind of L1 writing children were asked to do in primary school, he found that classroom writings were primarily of 'recount of experience' type. Yet, as he notes, this type of writing does not help children to develop as writers, as apparently 'only a minority of children learn to write successful narratives by the end of Year 6'. Bearne's reaction to this is that actually 'this kind of routine, purposeless activity stultifies any writing' (1995: 14). If this is true about native English-speaking children, then what can be expected from young ELLs?

Bearne quotes American writer Booth who suggests that young writers should be 'nourished' in narrative and says: 'Who I am now can best be seen in the stories I can now tell. Who I am to become can best be seen in the stories I learn to tell' (Bearne 1995: 16). While some of these arguments have been heeded by educators espousing literature-based, holistic approaches to literacy in first language contexts, real-story narratives have not been given much attention in TEYL and TEVYL course. Since the early 2000, these materials have included some stories; however, most are presented in simplified form of present tense as opposed to real narratives, which would sound more natural.

Writing in a Second Language

Writing is a skill given very little attention in TEYL coursebooks, with the available tasks consisting mainly of filling in blanks, compiling lists and composing short messages and letters, which serve merely an exercise function. Children are rarely, if ever, required to narrate something other than 'On Saturday we went to …'. Such writing does not fit Hudelson's above definition of writing. In the 1980s, Samway (1987: 3) argued that even 'the most advanced levels of most ESL texts for elementary grade children present writing in an artificial way'. A look at more recent texts confirms this to be still true. For example, in four TEYL courses produced between 2000 and 2010 by some of the largest international publishers (and still in print at the time of this writing), writing tasks are still very limited. For example, in the highest level of a five-level course, there are a total of seventy-two lessons but only twenty writing tasks in all, ten of which are letters or poems. Teachers' guides reveal no explicit writing instruction (Ghosn 2013). The assumption seems to be that children just somehow pick up the skill on their own, or that writing is not very important for young ELLs.

Yet, research since the 1980s shows that young second language learners also can produce stories early in their L2 development, and that neither sophisticated oral language nor the ability to read seems to be a prerequisite (see, e.g. Edelsky 1982; Hudelson 1984; Rigg 1981; Zamel 1992). In fact, Zamel argues that writing contributes to young L2 learners' reading development, because

> writing requires these beginning readers/writers to make decisions about purpose, sequence, and language, because it helps them to understand how and why texts are written, gives these learners insight into the goals, constraints, and concerns of authors, insight which they apply to their reading. (1992: 469)

Heddie, a nine-year-old language learner, brings her experience to bear upon the L2 writing theory in this poignant statement: 'The more you write, the more you learn how to write. It's like speaking, the more you speak the more you learn to speak' (quoted in Maguire and Graves 2001: 561). Moreover, Hudelson (1984) suggests that writing may also facilitate other schoolwork for young ELLs.

Story-Based Programs and Written Expression

The positive influence of stories on first language development is well documented in the literature. Research shows that exposure to stories of high literary quality significantly improves children's quality of writing, regardless of their reading ability (Dressel 1990), with children's L1 writing reflecting the linguistics structures, format, and style of their reading materials (DeFord 1981; Dressel 1990; Escott 1995; Mikkelsen 1984). When investigating the quality of primary school children's talk during story discussions, Strickland and Mandel Morrow (1989) found that children also developed competence in organizing their explanations, learned to modify their speech according to the purpose and audience and developed analytical ability. It is not unreasonable to assume that these skills can transfer also to their writing. Young ELLs' writing similarly resembles their instructional texts, as Hudelson (1989) and Huie and Yahya (2003) have reported. In the case of both first and second language learners, exposure to stories of high literary quality has been found to significantly improve children's quality of writing, regardless of their reading ability (Dressel 1990).

Findings of Tudor and Hafiz (1989) and Hafiz and Tudor (1990) resonate with those of Hudelson and Huie and Yahya. The researchers report on the influence of extensive reading of graded readers on written expression of sixteen Pakistani children aged ten to eleven years in the UK and fifty adolescents (ages fifteen to sixteen) in Pakistan. They report statistically significant gains from the first study in the story groups' syntactic, semantic and spelling accuracy while children's writing became simpler and more basic, reflecting the structure of typical graded readers. Their second study reports statistically significant gains of the experimental group's writing readiness, vocabulary base, and accuracy of expression, but not on syntactic accuracy. While students wrote more, their vocabulary ratio declined. This is not surprising, bearing in mind the findings of DeFord (1981), Mikkelsen (1984) and Dressel (1990) of children's L1 writing.

By far the most compelling evidence in favour of 'real' as opposed to graded or simplified books as medium of second and foreign-language instruction comes from the 'book flood' studies conducted by Warwick Elley and his colleagues in Niue, Fiji, Sri Lanka, Singapore and South Africa. In these studies, children were exposed to large quantities of high-interest storybooks in an effort to provide extensive exposure to the new language, especially in the challenging FLAPPS contexts. These studies, involving literally hundreds of primary school children, document gains in all four language skills, including writing. The intention here is not, by any means, to diminish the value of simplified or graded readers, as long as they are interesting and presented as narratives that will provide young English learners the past tense verbs they need for their own communication. There is no research evidence to suggest that learners cannot acquire a past tense of a verb they have not encountered in its present tense as long as the words occur in a meaningful context. A good example is Eric Carle's classic *The Very Hungry Caterpillar*, where the verb 'ate' is repeated numerous times.

Children's Narrative Writing

The above-cited studies have not reported on qualitative aspects such as cohesion, amount of detail and style, for example, in children's writing. When Huie and Yahya (2003) compared writing samples of 168 native English-speaking children and 228 limited English proficient (the term used by their school district) children in Florida, they found striking differences between the two groups in these three areas. Native English-speaking children's writing had a clearer organizational structure and they used more adjectives and two-syllable words than their non-native English-speaking counterparts, which produced not only more detailed and lively texts but also texts with more personal style. The authors note that the L2 learners' writing indicated the kind of writing instruction they had received: 'children had been given prepared sentences in which they were asked simply to fill in the blanks' (27), in other words, writing tasks typical in the English-language teaching texts. When 300 compositions from grades four, five and six in two schools in Lebanon were examined for vocabulary, spelling and literate language, a striking difference was noted in the quality of children's narratives. The findings reflect those of Hudelson and Huie and Yahya cited above.

Children in a story-based, reading-focused program wrote not only longer narratives but also narratives that had clear beginnings, cohesion with appropriate transition words and a logical conclusion. The same was observed in the narratives of the children in the experimental group of the fifteen-week story-based intervention described in Chapter 6.

Narratives after Six Years of English and EMI

ESL Group's Writing

Let us first compare narratives in the retrospective study. The following two narratives, both by grade-four girls, were evaluated as among the best in the ESL group in terms of narrative quality. All children's texts are left as they were written with no mistakes corrected. Misspelled words are capitalized.

> PUNISHMUNT of wrong doing
>
> Once APON a time there were people living in danger because there were big elephants that is DANGERS: The woman, babies and animals were afraid from these DANGERS animals. The rabbits and birds were making a plan the rabbit said: 'I know what to do, I will go in the volcano and bring some of the larva and the other rabbits will take the LARVE and put them in the pond and when the elephants want to drink they will die.' They did the plan and the elephants died. From this time in peace.

The text has a title, a clear beginning, a plot and an ending. It even includes a quote from a character. What is interesting is the inclusion of rabbits and birds making a plan. Another girl, apparently an aspiring author, wrote a story also with a clear beginning and ending, as well as a rudimentary plot. However, it is long run-on without any punctuation. Square brackets indicate the author's best guess at a word.

> I'm [name] I'm in grade 4 B and I'm the author of this story and I'm so happy that you want to read my story and I love to PUPLISH it.
>
> Once upon a time there were people were wear just an underwear and they Eat just animals and then they felt hungry and then they went to hunt an elephant they found an elephant they start throwing on him rocks and then the elephant ran away and then they followed him but they didn't found and then they found another elephant but he Escaped and then they return home and they slept the other day they walk up and they went serching and then they found three they began throwing on him rocks and a wood but it is sharp at the front and the elephant began running but they CHAPCHERED [captured] the small elephant and his mom began following them and in the night they made fire and when they want to put the elephant on the fire he began to kick the people but thy roped him and then his mom and dad came and RESCUDE him when the elephant TOUCK [took] his BAB they began hugging him and the people and the elephant were friends and they lived HAPPLY ever after.

However, the majority of the texts produced by the students in the ESL program were similar to the three below. Girl, grade four:

> Once APON a time in a forest there was people killing the ALEPHANT because they are living and drinking in there forest, there was a small river. The African people was killing them with trunk of the tree. They fight and fight and fight at last the elephant goes.

Although the text is in the past tense with the exception of the last sentence, it does not really tell a story. A text by a fifth-grade boy, while beginning with the familiar 'Once upon a time' and using past tense and some punctuation, is not a cohesive narrative with a clear direction.

> Once apon time there was an elephant attack PEPOLE. and the PEAPOLE started to throw sticks on the elephants. and were scared of the elephants and the elephants KIL a person and he fell in the water. and the elephants had big horns and the elephants were huge and fat. and there was a girl WICH had a baby and the BAYBY started to cry. and the elephants BROK the TRES. and the PEPOLE started to run away. and the people didn't have CLOTHE. And there were very big Mountains.

A sixth-grade boy's text is more story-like and includes description of the people, but the reader does not really get a sense what ultimately happened:

> Once upon a time their where an old people that live in the Forest and they CLOTH their where From the animal like the lion, sheep and other they sleep on the ground they eat animal like fish, sheep, and other they drink from river. One day they saw a big animal it called mammoth they didn't get scared the started to fought someone holding a knife big wood sharp they hit him and they take his meet and his bones they get happy because the Hit the mammoth than they saw two mammoth they fought him to get there and they go to the Forest.

Literature-Based Group's Writing

The following reflect the quality of narratives in the literature-based group. The first is from a fourth-grade boy. Despite the spelling mistakes, there is a clear beginning, a plot that builds on the given picture stimulus and a traditional 'happy ever after' ending.

> The Wild Elephants
>
> Long TOME ago there was a pretty village that was named the Western. The people were very kind. After a few weeks an earth QUAQE came, all the neighbors

ran and huddled around. A few strong men came outside they thought that it was a SQUAL but it wasn't there came a large groups of elephants ran like a shot of a gun into the PRARIE. The men held guns and long sticks. The elephants STATED to make PESTY sounds but non was hurt. The VILIGERS were scared and they stared at their large tusks. They ran to their homes to hide. The wild elephants went away. After a few hours they got out and set traps. One saw their large foot prints. They set big big traps and small traps. Then they followed the broken REES because they knew that the Elephants did it they walked a hour and a half. Then they saw the large CCUC [?] They got some poison food and they woke Him up They were hungry They found the food and ate. They counted to five and they were dead. And they all lived happily ever after.

A fifth-grade boy's story sets the scene before actually introducing the plot. Characters are given names and the text tells us what the characters felt and knew. There is also considerable detail and very advanced vocabulary.

The Stone age

During the Stone age, (probably two million years ago) people didn't act like they do now. They used to always wear something that looked like a skirt, and only that. They used to get food by killing stray animals like the elephants above. Even THER weapons weren't the same. They used to throw rocks or sharpened long sticks to fight.

One day, a small village ran out of food supplies. Three people with most unusual names: (Tha, Mog, mand Jiel) volunteered to go hunting. On the way, Mog suddenly stopped and looked into a small forest with tall trees. The other two stopped too, feeling vibrations under THIER feet. And almost instantly they knew what it was making all the vibrations. Three hairy elephants came out from behind the trees. Tie threw a sharpened stick directly at the middle one's stomach. Mog got the same one above the leg. The first one fell to the ground. It was dead. The other two ran away leaving thier friend. But not before one of them hit Tha with IT'S horn and crippled him. Jie and Mog returned home, in THIER carriage not only the dead animal, but Tha he was token to wise man, who could only give him some herbs to decrease the pain, but most unfortunatly, after two weeks, somebody had a solution. The next day Tha was standing up, as good as new.

A fifth-grade girl produced the following story:

People in the Jungle

Long ago in the middle of summer. A group of Vikings went hunting in the forest for some animals. They had in their hands long sharp spears. After walking for hours and hours it became night time, each person went to do things like for example: one went to COLECT timbers to make a fire, one would pitch the tents and many other things. At late night they heard the howling of the wolf and other creepy sounds. Lance went out at night to the deep forest to see what the weird sounds and lights he was seeing and hearing. After walking for ten minutes he tripped over some shoes. I turned out to see his friend Kate trying to find her necklace that she dropped in the river. He asked her what the light was that he saw. She told him that it was his flashlight. They went back to the camp together and slept. The next morning they packed every thing and continued walking. After seven hours of NONE stop walking they found two gigantic mammals they hid behind the bushes and waited till the mammals get out of the pond. The Vikings surrounded the mammals and started stabbing it with the spears. It fell on the floor and died. Now they had a problem it was how they are gonna get it back home. They had no way to bring it back. Gabriel had some rope with her in her bag pack. She said they would tie it from its neck and pull it. When they get half way back the rope got ripped. George said they had to push it from back, and some of them had to pull it from the horns. It was the only way to take it home. They got it home successfully they were very proud that they got it home. Kate realized that lance was missing, but he wasn't. He was just hiding behind the rock. She told him to never ever ever do that again, because he scared her to death now they were really proud and happy from each other.

There is reported speech, and characters are assigned a problem as well as emotions, and there is considerable creative detail. The two narratives are quite creative considering the simplicity of the picture stimulus and the fifty-minute time allocated for the writing. Although the literature group's compositions included also similar weak narratives as the ESL group's writing, they were fewer, and the creative narratives clearly outnumbered them.

Narratives after Fifteen Weeks of Story-Based Intervention

Let us now examine the narratives of two children in the experimental group of the fifteen-week classroom-based experiment. The four narratives reflect the typical differences found between children's narratives before and after the experiment. The first piece is by a ten-year-old girl describing the prehistoric scene. The texts are again left as written by the student:

I see in the picture the people hite the elephant on his STOMAC with the large wood and the tree BIHAND the elephant and the people bake they hold the circled KNIF and they stand and thinking WATE [what?] to do to the elephant to die and same one he have in his hand an rock and he throw the rock to the elephant and the elephet die.

The text is not a narrative but a run-on description of the picture, although children were given specific instruction to 'write a story to go with the picture' and were reminded about story elements. This is what the same girl wrote after fifteen weeks of story-reading and written follow-up activities (emphases added):

> *One day* a man and his friend went to the sky they have a 1 year WEN *they come* to the Sky they see a moon and primary [?] and ROKET and they bring telescope to her family see the moon and primary they fix the thing THEIR and they make a ROKET *because when they WAN'T to come down* they have a ROKET and they see all the planet the MARCALY, venus, Earth, Mars, Jupitar, Saturn, URANYOS, PLOTO, NIPTON. The people is the sky love to come another time and some of the people was going to the Earth in U.S.A. and some they was STELL fixing to take picture because WAN'T to make the the FLORE nice like this they make the FLORE nice and some of them the OXEGEN was Finish and some of them was STELl Fixing and the finish and One year to come to U.S.A. *and they WAN'T to come another time.*

Although the text is still a long run-on with only one full stop, it is clearly a narrative, albeit with plenty of spelling and grammar errors. It tells a story, unlike the first attempt. The word /flore/ ('floor') apparently is used to refer to 'ground', as in colloquial Arabic the word *ard* is used for both, floor and ground. The word 'floor' was also used in other compositions to refer to the ground.

The following two texts were produced by a twelve-year-old boy before and after the story-based intervention (emphases added):

> *In long ago THEIR was a people*, living in The forest with The animals and They don't have a GLOSES [clothes], but one day The large ELEPHENT came to house where The people lived THEIR, The people STARED to fight with the large animal, most of The people died from This animal, They still 4 week EVER day They came one. After four week They DEID The children.

This is what he produced after fifteen weeks of story-based work:

> *Long time ago there were a man named Abbas*, he always dream to be an astronaut, and This dream become True in 1992. After 8 months with his friend in spaceship, They arrived to mars, and The story begins, They start to explore every Thing. *First* They put Lebanons flag, *second* They start to dig, *when they are DIGING*, Abbas found a TREATURE [treasure] under The ground. He showed

to his friend and he said: Hey, hey I found a TREATURE. All his friend come to see. They saw a book, he were happy because he is The first person found a book on mars. *After 12 months* in the earth, They read a magazine That Abbas is the first person on a mars found a book.

Despite the grammar errors, inconsistent capitalization, punctuation and mixed verb tenses, the text clearly tells a story. There is a clear beginning that is grammatically correct and also some transitions words. The text also includes a quote from a character, albeit without quotation marks but indicated with a colon.

In all groups, there were long rambling papers that lacked coherence as well as shorter papers that read better. However, the experimental groups' papers reflected overall clearer organization, more detail to support the main ideas, and, in many cases also more creative expressions, as compared to the control groups in all three classes. The following two texts were written by a ten-year-old girl before and after the intervention.

Pretest:

I see in this PICTECHRE MANS giant ALIFANT and I see some PEPOLE are HOLDEING coodes [?] to KEL the ALFENT and same PEPOLE are KARIEG the BEBS and I see man HOLDE a ROUK [rock?] to KELA these ALIFANT and I see PEPOLE are KAMEING from done and holding WODS to came and KLE the ALEFANTS

Post-test from the same girl after the intervention:

The SPCE ship on the star

ONE OPEN a time there was a PEAPOLE that they want to TRAVIL to the SPCE. One man his name is Maryo. Maryo wants a few people to go with him to the SPCE. One day Maryo TALL [told?] ten people to go with him. One man TALLED him. But we cant go to the SPCE. Then Maryo TALL him Why? Then the man tell because if we want to go to the SPCE we want to bring a ROCK [rocket].

THAN Maryo TOLLED him yes we can bring a ROCK. One day morning Maryo brought a ROCK from his dad Then Maryo went his friend and TOLLED them. Now we want to go to the SPCE Than the people TALLED him. Yes

THAN they riad the ROCK and TRAVIL WEN they ARIAVED all the people BIGAN to work. Maryo he was DIGING and he found a large prayer write on it that a large man he was in 300 old years TRAIVLD to the star, and Maryo shouted to the pepole come and see there was age man hi was in 300 old years travild to the star and all the PEPOLE SURPRIAD and TULLED Maryo LIT us want to the star and Maryo

Although spelling and punctuation clearly still leave plenty of room for improvement, the text is significantly longer and more coherent. The narrative has a title, an opening sentence and an attempt at dialogue and paragraphing. Clearly an improvement from the pretest sample.

Here is another example of imp6

Pretest:

Once apon a time in a forest there was people killing the alephant because they are living and drinking in there forest, there was a small river. The African people was killing them with trunk of the tree. They fight and fight and fight at last the elephant goes.

Post-test:

Long ago there was a man, His name is Jack. He was walking outside he saw rockets MANS and trucks in the water taking of the poison that a plane throw them in the river. He often help them to find that something that pull the poison from the river, He was Happy to help them. He went to the shop and bring the cloth that rockets MANS wears, He was surprise that there was the last one of the clothes. He took it and went to jump of the mountain, He dig and dig and at last he found it, He shout to peter and tony to told them that he found it. They said that they dig and dig and they didn't find them, They tell him you are the best of us all, come on and take of the poison from the water, Theytake them OFE the water, and Jack was Happy after all.

One might argue that the striking differences between the pretest and post-test compositions are a result of children being more familiar with space-related concepts than prehistoric. Yet the pretest compositions featured the word 'mammoth' so many times that is clear children did have some idea about prehistoric concepts.

In one fifth-grade class, students were asked to compare *The Day of Ahmad's Secret* with *Alexander and the Terrible, Horrible, No Good, Very Bad Day*. Children everywhere can relate to Ahmed's joy of learning to write his name and Alexander's miserable day full of disappointments. Students were first guided to use a Venn diagram to plan their responses. Their instructions were to compare country, families and daily activities of the two boys. This is the final draft of one boy after grammar and spelling errors were corrected based on teacher's feedback:

> Two different days
>
> By Hani M.
>
> Miss Manal's Grade 5
>
> Alexander and Ahmad both had a special day, but they were special in a different way. Alexander woke up and went to school, and he had a very terrible day. His brothers were not very nice with him and his teacher did not like his picture. Ahmed lives in Cairo, Egypt. Today he did not go to school. He went to work. But he was very happy because he had a secret. He told his secret at home to his parents. It was that he knows how to write his name. So one boy had an unhappy day and one had a happy day. That's life! (Ghosn 2003b: 19)

Clearly, the student has given some thought about the differences in the two boys' experiences. The student is not listing all of Alexander's disappointments, focusing on two that he might have found most meaningful based on his personal experiences. Note the insightful concluding comment.

Conclusion

The retrospective data illustrate the potential of story-based instruction to provide children with much richer models for their writing than the traditional TEYL materials. Despite the relatively short intervention period, some significant gains were noted also in the experimental group's writing, resonating findings from the retrospective study and further corroborate the findings from the large-scale book flood studies. Findings suggest that story-reading and appropriate follow-up tasks not only contribute to the development of children's second language reading and vocabulary but also develops their writing. This is evidenced by the story-based groups' use of more and clearer opening and closing sentences, transition signals and supporting detail than their counterparts. These are important skills in academic writing in the upper grades. The qualitative differences between the experimental and control groups' writing also reflect Huie and Yahya's (2003) conclusion that students' instructional texts work as models for their writing; simplified texts provide simple models, while stories feature much richer language and thus offer more sophisticated models.

The findings are particularly significant in MENA region, because Arabic rhetorical mode differs significantly from that associated with Anglo-Saxon rhetorical modes. Yet, students in EMI programs in upper-grade levels and in tertiary education are expected to produce writing more in line with the linear Anglo-Saxon model. Further research in different cultural contexts would perhaps shed more light on the issue.

Recommendations for Practice

Teachers

Young second language learners need good and varied models for their writing, something that is lacking in typical TEYL coursebooks.

- Dialogue journals that David Wray has recommended to be exchanged between students and teachers can work well between students as well. Students can have a special notebook for this activity. Once or twice a week students write something that they have experienced or that interests them, and exchange journals with a partner who responds with their comment or describe something that happened to them. (Wray's website has more writing ideas: http://warwick.ac.uk/staff/D.J.Wray/Ideas/audience.html)
- Writing directions is a good exercise in organized thinking. For example, students can write directions from the school to a location not too far from the school. Teachers should guide the students first in how to organize their directions; what should the person do first, second and so on. A simple hand-drawn map with key landmarks labelled will be helpful for the activity.[1]
- A chain story is a fun activity that also develops creativity. It works either as a whole-class activity in a small class or as a row activity in a larger class. The very first time, teacher writes the first sentence on a sheet of paper and passes it to a student in the front row, who writes the sentence that logically continues the narrative. The story is passed from one student to another until the last student either ends the story or passes the paper/s to the first student, until the story comes to a logical (or even absurd) conclusion. Before students can write their sentences, they must read all the previous sentences first. For a more challenging activity, work by phrases.

- If and when the coursebook features a poem or a story, invite students to use that piece of writing as a template to write their own version of it. For example, the classic *Goldilocks and Three Bears* has been used at least by one Lebanese teacher to get her students to write their own similar stories but simply changing the animals and the food (see Chapter 12).

Materials Developers

- Include specific instruction on writing in different genres, including reports, story scripts and the like with models and templates.
- In the upper primary levels, include introductions to outlining and how to use outlines in prewriting phase.
- Present writing as a procedure with more than one 'write about' step.

9

Literate Language from Storybooks

'Contrarywise,' continued Tweedledee, 'if it was so, it might be; and if it were so, it would be; but as it isn't, it ain't. That's logic.'
Lewis Carroll – *Through the Looking Glass*

Without sunlight, most plants could not make their own food. If plants couldn't make food, humans and animals would have nothing to eat. … If you put one plant in a sunny place and another in the dark, what do you think will happen? (Collins 2016: 9)

The above is a quote from a typical primary school science textbook. In primary school science, growing and caring for plants are typically introduced in grade levels three and four. However, conditionals, such as those in the above quote, usually do not appear in TEYL courses before level five.

There is a strong connection between learners' use of literate language features and their reading and academic success. In their seminal studies, both Heath (1983) and Wells (1986) have shown that facility with features of literate language is critical for success in school. Paul (2007) points out that literate language plays an important role in conveying meaning when sharing information about concepts and events removed from the immediate context of learners. This is the case, for example, in subject matter classes, where much of the discourse is often decontextualized. Thus deficits in literate language pose a potentially serious problem for children, limiting their ability to communicate specific meanings, as Paul notes. In contexts where subject matter is taught in English, young English language learners need not only to develop a sizeable vocabulary but also acquire literate language characterizing academic discourse.

Much of previous research on children's literate language has examined young children's first language oral narratives. This chapter examines literate language features in young Arabic-speaking English learners' written narratives.

The chapter first compares literate language in compositions of eighty children (ages nine to eleven) collected in two different English programs; forty from children taught using an internationally marketed American ESL course and the other forty using a literature-based program. All children had been learning English since Kindergarten and were also learning math and science in English. Two significant differences between the groups prompted re-examination of 120 compositions generated in pre- and post-tests during the fifteen-week random-grouping, story-based experiment described in Chapter 6. The aim was to determine whether reading storybooks can enhance literate language features in young English-language learners' narrative texts. The findings show that certain features associated with literate language were more evident in the writing of children in the literature-based program. In the classroom experiment, literature language features increased in the narratives of the experimental group but not in those of the control group.

Literate Language

> Human beings do not live in the objective world alone, nor alone in the world of social activity as ordinarily understood, but are very much at the mercy of the particular language which has become the medium of expression for their society. (Sapir and Mandelbaum 1958: 69)

Whether one buys into the Sapir-Whorf theory that an individual's thoughts and actions are determined by the language or languages that individual speaks, it is clear that language is the basis for thinking, structuring the way we develop, organize and present ideas. It is equally clear that language underpins the whole academic curriculum. Failure or low competence in the language of the curriculum implies either failure or low success in the whole curriculum. According to *Merriam-Webster's Collegiate Dictionary*, to be 'literate' in something, means, for example, 'having knowledge or competence' in something (1994: 680) while 'competence' refers to 'knowledge that enables a person to speak and understand language' (ibid: 234). Therefore, to be 'academically literate' means to have knowledge of and be able to speak and understand the language associated with academic discourse.

Academic literacy implies also facility with literate language. Central to literate language is literate lexicon, which is commonly featured in teacher lectures, textbooks, encyclopedias and other scholarly contexts, and which, according to

Nippold (1993), is a critical component in adolescents' semantic development. Literate lexicon includes abstract nouns, metacognitive and metalinguistic verbs, coordinating and subordinating conjunctions, and adverbs (Greenhalg and Strong 2001). Use of elaborated noun phrases are also evidence of literate language development, as are derivatives, which begin to appear with increasing frequency in textbooks beginning at third grade (Nippold 2007). See Table 9.1 for features frequently associated with literate language.

Research indicates that exposure to narratives facilitates the development of literate language features, and Wallach and Butler argue that 'the most natural and common way of acquiring literate language is through print' (1994: 6).

Greenhalg and Strong (2001) explain why the literate language is important. When constructing a narrative, the use of mental and linguistics verbs make the narrative more explicit and literate; conjunctions, elaborated noun phrases (ENPs), linguistic and mental verbs makes it clearer, help organize and clarify ideas and events, thus enabling the listener/reader develop a 'mental model' of the characters and events. They note that when a child includes adverbs in their narratives, it shows they have developed an 'understanding of subtle differences in meaning'. Temporal conjunctions, such as 'when', 'while', 'before' and 'after' in subordinate clauses provide background for events (Pellegrini 1985), while

Table 9.1 Literate Language Features

Linguistic Form	Examples
Elaborated Noun Phrases – noun phrase with two or more modifiers preceding the noun, or with qualifiers such as prepositional phrases, appositives and relative clauses following the noun	*The big, brown dog* chased the cat. *My friend, Mary,* lives next door. We saw *the girl in the blue dress.* I don't like *people who are mean.*
Conjunctions – coordinating (excl. *and/ then*) and subordinating	Coordinating: *but, so, yet, for* Subordinating: *because, before, after, while, until, if, although (when)*
Adverbs – all adverbs, including those that are structurally in error	*here, now, quickly (quick)loudly (loud), soon*
Mental/Linguistic verbs – verb expressing cognitive and linguistic processes of humans, animals or fictional characters	Mental verbs: *decided, thought, knew, forgot, wished* Linguistic verbs: *said, yelled, called, asked*
Abstract nouns – nouns referring to intangible things, such as feelings, ideals, concepts and qualities	*beauty, courage, patience, belief, happiness, hate, love, dreams*

Source: Adapted from Benson (2009: 174–8).

causal conjunctions such as 'because', 'so that' and others provide psychological motivation or physical reasons for the events (Scarlett and Wolf 1979).

As shown in Chapter 7, children's writing is influenced by the type of instructional texts they encounter in their lesson, with both first and second language learners using their instructional texts as models for their own writing (Hudelson 1983; Huie and Yahya 2003; Samway and Taylor 1993). A vast body of research into children's narrative development and writing has been conducted with first language learners, while research involving second language learners' writing development has concentrated primarily on children in English-dominant contexts. Limited research has explored children's English-language writing in countries where English is a foreign language or spoken as the main language by only a limited segment of the population. To elicit literate language samples from children, storytelling and retelling are frequently used strategies (Muñoz et al. 2003), with the focus being primarily on young children, as mentioned. Limited attention has been given on written narratives generated by young second language learners. This chapter aims to bridge that gap by examining young Arabic-speaking English learners' use of literate language features in their writing.

Literate Language in Young ELLs' Writing

Table 9.2 shows the literate language features in the compositions of eighty children in two different programs. Coordinating conjunctions 'and' and 'but' were equally numerous in both groups and were not included in the counts. Compositions elicited by the picture stimuli from the *TOWL-3 Test of Written Language* (Hammill and Larsen 1996) in the study described in Chapter 7 about

Table 9.2 Literate Language Features in the Two Groups

	Literature Group	ESL Group
Linguistic verbs	33	14
Mental verbs	42	40
Adverbs	16	8
C. Conjunctions	16	12
Sub. Conjunctions	60	31
ENPs	18	18
Abstract nouns	1	0
	186	123

vocabulary were examined for literate language features. The reading-based groups' compositions featured statistically significantly more linguistic verbs and subordinating conjunctions than the compositions of their communicatively oriented ESL course peers, while no significant difference was found in the number of adverbs, mental verbs and elaborated noun phrases. However, while the ESL groups' mental verbs comprised only 'know', 'want', 'love' and one instance of 'believe', the literature groups' mental verbs in addition to these included also instances of 'realized', 'remembered', 'considered', 'feared', 'decided', 'forgot' and 'hoped'. Similarly, the ESL group's linguistic verbs consisted of only 'tell/told', 'say/said' and one 'shout', while the literature group also used 'claimed', 'yelled' and 'screamed/screaming'. In both groups, coordinate conjunctions consisted only of 'and', 'but', 'or' and 'so', and the most common subordinating conjunction in both groups was 'because', with 'until' featuring in two of the ESL compositions and 'when', 'after', 'before' and 'until' in compositions of the literature group. One ten-year-old student in the ESL group used also 'even though' in one sentence. The only abstract noun found in the sample was 'danger' in grade four of the literature group. The only adverbs used by the ESL group were 'quickly', 'happily' and 'suddenly', while the literature group, in addition to these, used also 'hard', 'instantly', 'directly', 'probably', 'successfully' and 'usually'.

Table 9.3 shows the number of instances of literate language items in 120 post-test narratives of the two ESL groups after the fifteen-week exposure to storybooks and follow-up activities. While no significant difference between the groups were found in the pretest, the experimental group's post-test compositions featured overall more literate language items than those of the control group. Statistical analysis revealed a significant difference in the total number of literate language feature items between the two groups in favour

Table 9.3 Literate Language in Children's Narratives Before and After Intervention

	Post-test	
	E	C
Linguistic verbs	105	98
Mental verbs	129	80
Adverbs	104	72
Conjunctions	164	104
ENPs	43	16
Abstract nouns	27	10
	572	380

of the experimental group. Examination of the discrete items revealed also statistically significant difference in the use of mental verbs, conjunctions, elaborated noun phrases and abstract nouns. However, the use of adverbs failed to reach statistical difference.

Examination of the compositions revealed also some interesting qualitative differences. While the control group's conjunctions consisted mainly of coordinating conjunctions 'and', 'but' and 'or', the experimental group employed also coordinating conjunctions, such as 'because', 'if', 'when' and 'after'. Regarding mental and linguistic verbs, the experimental group's compositions featured a richer variety of them, including 'love', 'remember', 'thought', 'decide', 'plan', 'imagine', 'shout', 'ask', 'answer' and 'call'. In contrast, the control group's mental and linguistic verbs consisted primarily of 'think', 'thought', 'tell', 'told' and 'said'. Elaborated noun phrases in the experimental group included 'something hard to find', 'first person to go to the moon', 'people who are on the moon', and other similar phrases. The control group's elaborated noun phrases consisted primarily of 'a man/boy/planet named X'. While twenty-seven abstract nouns appeared in the experimental group's narratives and ten in the control group's narratives, the difference was in the discrete items. While the experimental group's abstract nouns included 'idea/s', 'chance', 'theories', 'opinion', 'challenge' and 'dream', the only abstract noun the control group used was 'dream' (a dream came true; I had a dream).

In addition, the experimental group children's narratives reflected some perspective-taking ability, as shown by them assigning thoughts, emotions and plans to the characters. The following examples from ten- and eleven-year-olds illustrate this (again, the text is left without corrections; emphases added):

> In 3095, the Columbian astronauts decided to make a station on the moon. They prepared themselves to make <u>what they dream for</u> … Carl <u>said in his self</u> [to himself] that <u>if his dad was still alive he was to be happy from</u> [with] him.

Another student wrote: 'The leader has a small son <u>who loves the computer</u> very much. He was walking he saw a machine <u>he thought</u> it is a computer…', showing ability to infer characters' thoughts and moods. The third student wrote about an astronaut named Jack, who found the source of petrol, and about his friends, who found an ancient object she calls 'a ruin':

> They found an expensive ruin they wanted to give it to Jack, but he didn't take it because they found it. He said: 'When I found source of petrol, I didn't say to anyone let it be his chance. <u>Now it's time to be your chance</u>.'

In contrast, the control group's narratives were primarily recounts, with little evidence of thought given to what the characters in the stimulus picture might think and what they might plan or feel. (For more examples of children's writing, see Ghosn 2007, 2013.)

Conclusions

The findings indicate that story reading, accompanied with some follow-up activities, can enhance the literate language features in children's second language narratives even during a relatively short intervention period. This is evidenced by the experimental group's use of significantly more vocabulary and phrases associated with literate language. The quantitative differences, further supported by the qualitative differences, resonate again with Huie and Yaha's (2003) study, which showed that young English-speaking children's writing was modelled after their instructional materials. Typical primary school English-language teaching texts comprise prepared dialogues, which children take turns to practice, brief informational texts, and brief simplified story narratives. Sentences are usually choppy, with conjunctions largely limited to 'and', 'but' and 'or' in the lower grades. The story narratives, if included, are mostly written in the present tense in the lower grades, as already mentioned before. In contrast, quality children's literature features a rich variety of contextualized vocabulary and expressions and enables children to develop also perspective-taking ability, an important real-life skill. Perspective-taking will also be required in academic English, both oral and written. Without this ability, students would have difficulty understanding the viewpoints of others and thus would not be able to present effective counterarguments, for example. Literate language features were very evident in the narratives of children having been taught English for six years using a reading-based program. This is not surprising since during the six years, they would have had plenty of exposure to rich variety of language.

Despite the relatively short intervention period of fifteen weeks, some significant differences were noted between the experimental and control groups. The findings are in line with Lazar's (1994) claim that stories enable learners to develop a more overall awareness of language than typical language teaching activities. The results also add one more reason to Ghosn's (2002: 172) 'four good reasons' to use literature in primary school language teaching, namely that of literate language development. The results are particularly relevant in contexts where children must study all or some of the school subjects in English while learning it as a second or foreign language. Replication of the findings, as well as longer studies, are needed, particularly because not only is English-language instruction spreading to ever younger groups of learners, but also EMI demand is growing in many parts of the world, including in the Arab World. Thus attention must be paid to young language learners' development of literate language.

Recommendations for Practice

Teachers

- If the coursebook includes any features of literate language, teachers can draw student attention to them and activate them in a discussion about the topic at hand and encourage students to use some of them in their own writing.
- If the coursebook is devoid of literate language, teachers can spend a session perhaps once a week (preferable more) to read children stories that include expressions associated with literate language. Then engage children in a discussion about the story and activate the literature language expressions.

Materials Developers

- It would be useful for materials writers to include features of literate language in the coursebook texts and include exercises where the language would be activated.

10

Transfer from Arabic to Children's English Writing

Speak in French when you ca'n't think of the English for a thing
                    Lewis Carroll – *Through the Looking Glass*

Arabic speakers face some challenges when learning to write in English, and research has identified many of the errors stemming from L1 interference. That is not very surprising since Arabic differs from English in several ways, including the alphabet, text directionality, phonology and grammar. Even mechanics differ, with Arabic having no capital letters, for example. Errors in Arabic speakers' English writing have been studied extensively, but much of that research has focused on high school-level and university-level learners of English. This chapter reports on grammar, spelling and mechanics in English writing of Arabic-speaking primary school children learning English in grades four to six (ages nine to twelve) in two different instructional programs. Analyses show that many of the errors students made were, indeed, a result of negative L1 transfer. However, evidence suggests that literature- and reading-focused instructional materials might mitigate the influence of negative L1 transfer as well as facilitate children's spelling development.

Grammar Differences between Arabic and English

When it comes to grammar, there are considerable differences between English and Arabic. First, there are differences in verbs, as Arabic has no verb 'to be' in the present tense, no auxiliary verb 'do', and the verb tense system is also different from that of English (Al-Shujairi and Tan 2017). For example, there is no present continuous verb tense in modern standard Arabic. The in-progress action will be evident from the context, as in *laysa-l-aan, li-annani ashtaghil*: 'Not now, because I work', *laysa-l-aan* (not now) implying an in-progress action. However, in different dialects, present continuous can be expressed by adding a prefix to the verb, such as *ba* or *be* in Egyptian and Gulf dialect, or *amba* or *ambe* in the Levantine dialect as in *mish halla'*, *'ambishtghil*: 'Not now, I am working'. Furthermore, there is no distinction between past activity whether a connection to the present exists or not. For example, 'I have visited Jeddah twice' is the same as 'I visited Jeddah twice': *zurtu jeddah marratayn*. Similarly, 'I have studied Arabic for two years' is the same as 'I studied Arabic for two years': *darastu-l-'arabiyyah sanatayn*. This has been found to be problematic for Arabic speakers (e.g. Ali 2007). Alkhudary and Al-Ajdal (2020) and Ali (2007) found subject-verb agreement and wrong verb forms to be common in Saudi EFL learners' writing and resulting from mother tongue interference.

Moreover, Arabic does not have exact equivalents for modals such as 'can', 'may', 'might', 'must', 'should' and 'would'. Instead, Arabic has words and phrases that function the same way, such as in the following examples: '*May* I borrow your book?': *hal yumkinuni istaaratu hatha-l-kitaab?* in which the phrase *hal yumkinuni* functions as 'may'. 'He *could* speak English at age five': *kaan bi-imkaanihi at-takallumu bil ingliziyya fi sinn al-khaamisah*, in which *kaan bi-imkaanihi* translates roughly into 'was able to' but means also 'could'. 'You *should* see a doctor': *yajibu an tara tabeeban* translates into 'You *must* see a doctor'. Thus, English modal errors are common among Arabic speakers (e.g. Alja'arat and Hasan 2017).

English relative clauses are also problematic for Arabic speakers (e.g. Ala'arat and Hassan 2017; Hamadalla and Tushyeh 1998) and also result from negative L1 transfer. Common errors of older learners featured also in many children's compositions in this study. One was insertion of the unnecessary pronoun because in Arabic words inflect by gender. For example, in *haatha huwa-l-kitabu-llathi qara'tuhu*, *–hu* indicates masculine gender of 'book'; consequently, students write (or say) 'That is the book which I read /IT/'. In *ummi khabazat al-halwa*, the *–at* in the verb indicates feminine gender of 'mother', resulting in 'My mother /SHE/ baked sweets' in English. Another was omission of the relative pronoun as in 'There are many people like football', which in Arabic is *naason katheeroun yuhibbouna kurata-l-qadam* and literally translated as 'People many like football'.

Prepositions are yet another considerable source of problems because not all English prepositions have an Arabic equivalent. While English has about 150 prepositions, Arabic has only seven: *min* (from), *ila* (to), *'an* (about), *'alla* (on/over), *ba/bi* (by, with), *la/li* (of, for), *fi* (in, into). However, in Arabic, some adverbs can be used as prepositions: *khalfa* (behind), *aman* (in from), *bayna* (between) and others (Alkhudiry and Al-Aidal 2020, Essberger 2000). Al-Ahdal and Asmawi (2021), Al-Bayati (2013) and Abushihab et al. (2011) found preposition errors to be the most common errors in university students writing in Saudi Arabia, Iraq, Malaysia and Jordan. Serham, Abdulhafud and Jasim (2019) found that students either omitted or replaced prepositions based on their knowledge of Arabic prepositions. Tahaineh (2010) found also that Jordanian college students use a correct preposition if an equivalent exists in Arabic, but either use an incorrect one or omit the preposition altogether if an equivalent in Arabic does not exist.

Another problem is nouns; English nouns are either singular or plural, whereas Arabic nouns have singular, dual and plural forms. English has three gender pronouns: masculine (he), feminine (she) and neuter (it), and one plural pronoun (they, them). All Arabic verbs and nouns are gendered, and thus nouns are inflected depending on the word gender as well as the number. For example, 'book' is a masculine noun, so *lad<u>da</u>ya <u>kitāb</u> wāhid* means 'I have book one', while *laddaya thalathat <u>kutub</u>* means 'I have three books'. 'Car' is a feminine noun, so *lad<u>ay</u>ha sayyaratun <u>wahida</u>* means 'She has a car', while *ladayha <u>sayyartan</u>* means 'She has two cars' and *lad<u>ay</u>na <u>thalatu sayyarat</u>* means 'We have three cars'.

Grammar Errors in Children's Writing

Data on grammar errors were collected from one hundred compositions randomly selected from a pool of 220 compositions elicited in an earlier study in grades four, five and six in two English-medium schools, fifty from each school. In both schools, children had received the same number of lessons a week since Kindergarten. School A students had been taught English using a widely marketed American content-integrated ESL course, while school B students had been taught with an American reading anthology series (one grade level below the one designated by the publisher). With few exceptions, children were native speakers of the Lebanese colloquial form of Eastern Arabic and had been taught English by teachers whose first language was also Arabic. See Table 10.1 for grammar errors.

Clearly, the biggest number of grammatical errors occurred in singular/plural verb-noun agreement (109), the majority of them in school A. Singular verbs were used with plural nouns, as in 'there /WAS/ many people' and 'they /WAS/ very happy', while no instances of singular nouns linked to plural

Table 10.1 Grammar Errors

	School A			School B			Total
Error grade	4	5	6	4	5	6	
Omission of relative pronoun	3	6	1	0	1	0	11
Replacement of relative pronoun	1	3	0	1	2	0	7
Insertion of unnecc. pronoun	2	2	1	2	1	2	10
Omission of 'to be'	0	4	1	0	0	0	5
Preposition error	5	5	13	7	6	6	42
Plural/singular verb agreement	25	41	12	6	18	7	109

verbs (as in 'My English book /ARE/ lost') were found. An examination of the grade-five papers, where fifty-nine singular/plural errors were found, revealed that eight papers in school A accounted for the forty-one errors, and one paper in school B accounted for half of the eighteen errors in this class. In both classes, there were many papers that had no singular/plural errors. However, it should be noted that in both schools, these errors were fewer in grade six, suggesting that this error might decrease further as children progress to upper grades.

Not surprisingly, preposition errors were the second biggest error group (forty-two). The most common error was the incorrect use of 'from', as in the following examples: 'His mother was so happy /FROM/ him'; 'They were happy /FROM/ me'; 'Be careful /FROM/ the stranger'; 'People died /FROM/ this animals'; 'Something lost /FROM/ many years'; 'They finished /FROM/ oxygen. This again is clearly interference from children's L1. For example, 'His mother is happy *with* him' in Lebanese colloquial Arabic is *ummu mabsouta* <u>minho</u>, *minho* meaning 'from him', so students will say in English 'His mother is happy /FROM/ him'. Similarly, Arabic uses the preposition *min* to refer to something that happened 'long time ago' (<u>min</u> *zamān*), or 'some years ago' (<u>min</u> *kam sini*), thus children say '/FROM/ long time ago'.

Other errors common in older Arabic speakers' English writing were few in these children's compositions. The insertion of a pronoun when not needed in English appeared ten times, as in 'The woman /SHE/ go and told to …'; 'The womens /THEY/ begin shouting and hiting the memouth', and in relative clauses, as in 'The sticks that the men throw / THEM/', and 'saw a big animal

/IT/ called mammoth'. However, many children in school B managed this construction quite well: Few people *that were attacking* elephants; Elephants *that were* behind; from the *mountains that were* very high (grade 4); All the *people who came* to fight them; to find the *necklace that she dropped* in the river (grade 5); Troops of *people who lived* on the island; ... broke the *tree trunk that people put there to use* as a bridge (grade 6). Omission of a relative pronoun occurred only in three instances, all in school A: There were people [who] want to go to the trip; There were many people [who] want to go to space.

Interestingly, most children describing the futuristic scene in which an astronaut appears to be picking up a book or a tablet from the ground used the same expression only in slight variations: 'He found a book something written on it' and 'There was a rock something written on it in chinese'. It appears that the construction 'a book on which something was written' (*wajada kitāban mkatoubon 'alayhi shay'un* or *wajada kitāban 'alayhi kitābāton*) was beyond the children at this age, but they managed to convey the meaning even when relying on their Arabic.

There were also some grammar errors that, while common in older Arabic speakers' English writing, were committed rarely or not at all by children in this study. For example, as Arabic lacks the present tense 'to be', according to previous studies its omission is apparently fairly common in older Arabic speakers' English writing. However, only five compositions out of the one hundred (5 per cent) had this error. There were no errors of genitive construction, such as /BOOK THE BOY/ instead of 'boy's book', and no compositions were found missing the auxiliary 'do', an error featured in older Arabic speakers' writing. Also, modal verbs, although rarely used, were used correctly: 'He could tell the astronaut that ...' and 'People would be proud of you'. Present and past continuous verb tense, when used, were also used correctly: 'He was digging and digging and then he saw ...' and 'He was thinking his father will be happy'. None of the compositions featured attempts at present perfect tense, most likely because the nature of the tasks required mainly use of simple present, past or future tense verbs. So, it is not possible to determine if children would be able to use it correctly. In school B, there were only three relative pronoun replacements and one missing relative pronoun in grade five. All the other errors in relative clauses were in school A. School A grammar errors were more than double of those in school B. It seems that just as children's instructional texts provide models for their writing, the rich, natural language associated with good children's literature may facilitate the acquisition of syntactic features.

Spelling

A wide array of textbooks is available for young learners, but a brief survey of several widely marketed books reveals that little, if any, overt attention is given to spelling or word study. Yet, the knowledge about orthography in both reading and writing is quite important. As Cook aptly notes,

> It is assumed that everyone knows how to spell, how to form letters, when to use capitals – why should it require research? Yet writing forms a complex linguistic system, which is important to all literate language users, and which has to be acquired by all literate people whether in the first or second language. (Cook 2001: 1)

Research from American classrooms shows children's English spelling to be a developmental process happening in clear stages. The awareness of where children are in their spelling development will enable teachers to tailor instruction to meet their needs (Invernizzi, Abouzeid and Gill 1994). However, little research is available on whether young ELLs' spelling is similarly developmental, whether they use any invented spellings and whether instructional texts play a role in it. This chapter explores data collected from 220 compositions in the above-described schools A and B. Children's spelling was analysed based on the Gentry (1982) and Bear and Templeton (1998) models developed in native English-speaker context.

Stages in English Spelling Development

The development of spelling initially involves invented spellings, which are the result of children applying the grapheme-phoneme knowledge they have acquired to words whose conventional spelling they have not yet mastered (Bear and Templeton 1998; Henderson 1985).

Gentry (1982) and Bear and Templeton (1998) models draw on the seminal work of Henderson (1981, 1985) and Bissex's (1980) recount of her son's spelling development in *GNYS at WRK*. Table 10.2 shows the stages in the two models. Figures 10.1, 10.2 and 10.3 illustrate spelling development of young K. G. at age five, six and seven, respectively. In her school, invented spelling was encouraged, and research shows that children encouraged to use invented spelling write longer and more fluent pieces of writing than their counterparts who are not encouraged to do so (He and Wang 2009, citing Paul 1976). Children who

Table 10.2 Gentry's and Bear and Templeton's Stages

Gentry's Stages (1982)	Bear and Templeton's Stages (1998)
Stage 1 Precommunicative	Stage 1 Prephonemic
Stage 2 Semiphonetic	Stage 2 Semiphonetic
Stage 3 Phonetic	Stage 3 Letter name
Stage 4 Transitional	Stage 4 Within-word pattern
Stage 5 Correct (Conventional)	Stage 5 Syllable juncture
	Stage 6 Derivational constancy

use invented spellings can explore phoneme-grapheme relationships and segmentation in their efforts to compose text.

English-Language Learners' Spelling

As He and Wang (2009) note, little research has examined young ELLs' spelling in free writing activities, as much of the research has focused on learners' spelling of pseudo-words. They conducted a study of two six-year-old kindergarten children and two first-grade children who were native speakers of Taiwan Mandarin. Van Berkel (2004) examined English spelling of 1,400 Dutch students in their last year of primary school. No formal instruction was provided in spelling in either case. Findings from both studies showed that spelling development was predictable, and the latter study also showed that students made fewer errors with regular spellings than with irregular ones.

English spelling can be especially problematic for young Arabic-speaking children. In Arabic, there are twenty-eight letters in the alphabet with some having up to four different shapes, depending on whether they appear at the beginning, middle or the end of the word (see Figure 10.4). In English there are about forty-three sounds for the twenty-six letters of the alphabet. In Arabic there are three vowels in speech, but in writing only the long stressed vowels are represented. In lower primary school textbooks, the vowels are identified by diacritical marks, but older readers must infer the vowels from the semantic and syntactic context. While up to three consonants may be between vowels in English, Arabic allows only two.

Al-Busaidi and Al-Saqqaf (2015: 188), who focused on errors in monosyllabic words, found vowels to be more problematic than consonants, 'probably because of the perceptible mismatch between phonemes and graphemes' in university

Figure 10.1 K's spelling at age five

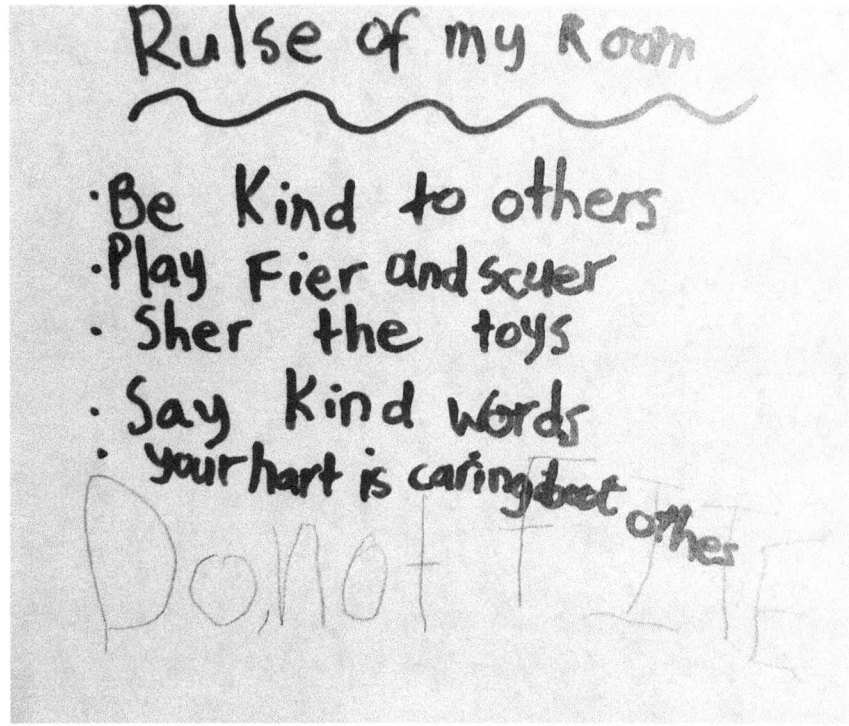

Figure 10.2 K's spelling at age six

students' writing. Alsaawi (2015), Haggan (1991) and Behout (1985) and others have identified the following eight categories of spelling errors:

1. Consonant doubling errors: /DIGING/ for /digging/.
2. Consonant substitutions: /s/ instead of /c/ as in /SENTENSE/ for /sentence/, and /BOT/ for /pot/. The b/p confusion clearly results from Arabic not having /p/ sound.
3. Schwa errors: /COLLAGE/ for /college/ and /UNFAMILIER/ for /unfamiliar/.
4. Silent –e errors, adding an –e to the end of the word when not necessary as in /PLAYE/ for /play/.
5. Misspelled vowels: /WIll/ for /well/ or /INCLOUDE/ for /include/.
6. Letter-order confusion: /THEIF/ for /thief/.
7. Homophone errors, confusion between /their/ and /there/.
8. Idiosyncratic spelling errors not analysable.

Alsaawi (2015) found these to be the most common errors among his university-level students, and Al-Jarf (2010) identified faulty graphemes and phonemes in

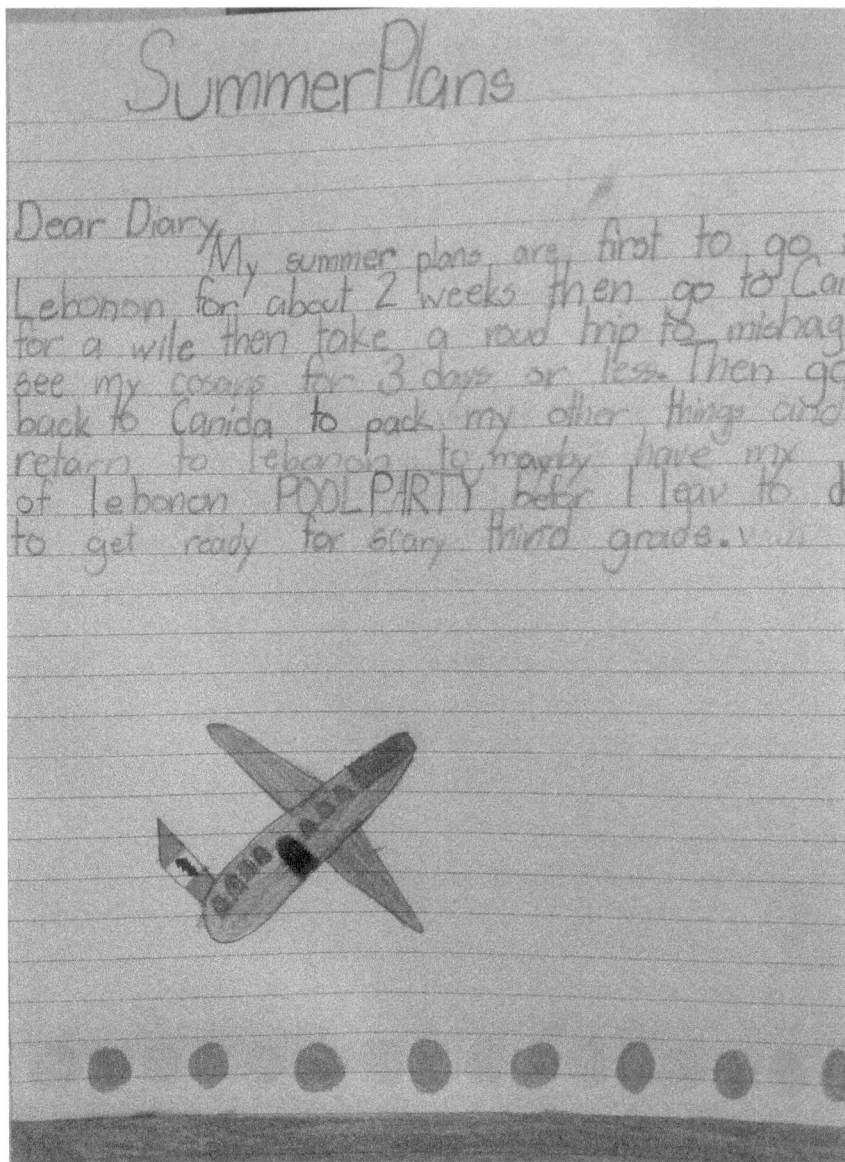

Figure 10.3 K's spelling at age seven

writings of Arabic-speaking secondary school students and undergraduates in Saudi Arabia. When Saigh and Schmitt (2012) examined adult Arabic-speaking ELLs' ability to recognize spelling errors in words where a wrong vowel was used or where a vowel was missing, they found that participants had more problems noticing errors in short vowels than long vowels. Hayes-Harb (2006)

Figure 10.4 Letter positions in Arabic words

came to a similar conclusion about Arabic speakers' lack of awareness of vowels in English texts.

In one reported study, Alenazi (2018) gave twenty English learners (ages between five and ten) in a Saudi school in the UK five English words (sun, school, cat, pig and horse). All twenty children had lived in the country for at least one year. Alenazi's report shows that most of the children's spellings represented Gentry's phonetic stage, which closely corresponds with Bear and Templeton's letter name stage; many children spelled /school/ as /SKOL/, /horse/ as /HOS/, /sun/ as /SON/, and /cat/ as /KAT/. This chapter provides new insight into spelling development of young Arabic-speaking children.

Lebanese Children's Spelling

From 220 compositions written on two different occasions, sixty were randomly selected for analysis yielding 286 different misspelled words. Repetitions of the same errors were omitted. For example, one fourth-grader used the word 'astronaut' in their story eight times, each time spelling it as /ASTRONALD/, and it was counted once. Interestingly, 'once upon a time' used by many children appeared in twelve different spelling versions, including /ONCE UPONE TIME/, /ONE SAPONIE TIME/, /ONCE APONED TIME/ and /ONE SOPONY TIMe/, among others.

Spelling errors occurred in the majority of compositions, and many matched the categories identified in older learners' writing, such as vowel errors: /SHIP/ (sheep), /BAD/ (bed), /DEGGING/ (digging) and /TELL/ (till). The *schwa*-sound errors were also common, as in /AMIRICA/, /AMARICAN/, /METEL/ (metal), /DERTY/ (dirty) and /HUMON/ (human). Errors in 'there/their' and

Table 10.3 Children's Spelling Error Categories

Grade	Errors	Phonetic	Transitional
4	134	68	66
5	57	12	45
6	95	10	85

Table 10.4 Errors According to Bear and Templeton

Grade	Errors	LN	WWP	SJ	DC
4	134	68	37	23	6
5	57	12	28	12	5
6	95	10	48	26	11

'were/where', occurred often, as did omissions of weak or silent letters, as in /DISC(o)VER(e)D/, /TRAV(e)LED/, /C(a)BIN/, /DRE(a)M(e)D/. Switches of letter order occurred fairly frequently as well, as in /SHAVLES/ (shovels), as did omissions of double consonants: DIGING (digging), /MUDY/ (muddy), /PLANING/ (planning), /HITING/ (hitting), but unnecessary doubling was rare. Unlike older learners' errors, such as /tʃ/ 'in action or nation' occurred rarely, and no 'v/f' errors were found. Only two children spelled /b/ as /p/, spelling the word 'tribe' as /TRIPE/.

The words were first categorized according to the Gentry (1982) model and then according to the Bear and Templeton (1998) model. Tables 10.3 and 10.4 show the number of different errors categorized according to the two models. Multiples of same errors were omitted. According to the Gentry model, the majority of the errors were classified as transitional stage (196), with some reflecting the phonetic stage (ninety).

The Bear and Templeton model breaks the errors down into more categories as shown in Table 10.4.

The Bear and Templeton model is more informative than the Gentry model. Following are error examples categorized according to Bear and Templeton model. Letter-name stage: /COLD/ for 'called', /SQUEES/ for squeeze; within-word pattern: /CRIE/ (cry), /CRALL/ (crawl), /GROWND/ (ground), /DECIDED/ (decided); syllable juncture: /ATEND/, /HOPING/ (hopping), /CAPCHUR/ (capture); and derivational constancy: /CHARICTERS/,

/MAIER/ (mayor) and IMMEDIETLY. Findings mirror those from native English-speaker studies.

Of the spelling errors, nearly half were substitution errors, 41 per cent omission errors, 9 per cent insertion errors and 0.5 per cent transposition errors. These are among the most common errors of English-language learners according to Cook (1997: 478–9), which resonates with studies of older Arabic-speaking English learners' spelling errors.

As mentioned, there were a number of problems with *schwa* sound, and these were very prominent as in /DINASOURS/, /PEAPOLE/, /PEPEL/, /PEPOLE/, /PEPOL/,/VILLAGE/RS/, /VILAGE/, /VILIDGE/, /VILLEGE/, /VILIGERS/, /VILIDGERS/. This is not surprising, since Arabic-speaking English learners commonly have difficulty with the sound, as Bebout (1985) found. Yet, the words were clearly readable. The *schwa*-problem in spoken Arabic is not very surprising since it poses a problem for speakers of other languages as well. For example, speakers of Finnish and Turkish have problems with the sound in spoken English.

A little surprisingly, four fourth-graders correctly spelled 'suddenly', 'amused', 'rescued', 'protect', 'thousands', 'discovered', 'suggested' and 'excited', and a fifth grader spelled astronaut as /ASTRONALD/ but correctly spelled 'rocket', 'crushed', 'suddenly', 'amused', 'themselves', 'caught', 'scared', 'rescued' and 'glowing'. One might be tempted to think that children had some help from their teachers, but that is not the case as the researcher administered and monitored children during their writing in all the studies described in this volume.

Unlike high school and university students in previous studies, the children in this study were between the ages of nine and twelve and thus still demonstrating developmental spelling stages in their free writing; in other words, many wrote the words the way they sounded them out. For example, while the omissions of weak or silent letters were common in grade-four students' writing, they appeared less frequently in grades five and six, suggesting clear upward development.

Influence of Arabic

Interestingly, the influence of local colloquial Arabic was evident in many of the children's texts. For example, the word 'clothes' was spelled in many texts as /CLOSES/. Although it may sound surprising, an explanation is found in

Lebanese colloquial Arabic where the /th/ sound is frequently pronounced as a hybrid between /s/ and /z/. For example, a boy's name 'Haytham' is typically pronounced as 'Hay/S/am in many parts of the country, although the correct pronunciation is 'Hay/θ/am'. This is the case also likely with the spellings of /OLEVSEM/ for 'all of them' and /ATHRUNATE/ for 'astronaut' that appeared in some children's compositions. The way children 'hear' words in their texts depends on how their teachers pronounce them, especially if children have little exposure to spoken English outside the classroom.

The addition of a vowel to break a three-consonant cluster appeared in twenty compositions, all but one in school A. The following are examples of this error: She /TOOK-E/ the book, far away /FROM-E/ here, took/-e-/them/ OF-E the water, /SAMART/, /ENED/ (end), give /HIM-E-FLOWERS/, /WORK-E-HARD/, /MONTH-E-S/ and /WAR-E-KS/ (works). Bowen (2011) aptly suggests that such additions of vowels are attempts to make pronunciation easier, since unlike English, Arabic allows only two adjacent consonants. The young writers are mentally or softly voicing the word as they would speak it and thus inserts the extra vowel they hear in their own speech. However, this error decreased from ten in grade four to only three in grade five. Many Lebanese teachers themselves commit this error in their speech. The following classroom transcripts illustrate this.

T1:   Is this/-e-/story a sad/-e-/story or a happy one?
Ss: Sad!!
T1:   Right, this is a sad/-e-/story.
T: No, we don't/-e-say/ 'he come'. What do we say?'

This pronunciation problem is common with many adults. For example, a high-school chemistry teacher was observed demonstrating an experiment and referred to a 'test/-e-/tube' several times. Yet the teacher had obtained a master's degree from a university in the United States.

Mechanics

Arabic and English differ also in mechanics. Arabic writing has no discernable difference between print and cursive, as mentioned, and uses no capital letters even for proper nouns or at the beginning of sentences. While English discourages long list-like sentences, in Arabic it is common to see long phrases and sentences connected only by *wa* (and) without any punctuation.

Capitalization and Punctuation

Incorrect capital letter use was extremely common, and capitalization was inconsistent even within compositions in school A. In many papers, some proper nouns were spelled with capitals in one sentence and not in others, and even in the same sentence, some students capitalized some proper nouns but not others. For example, one boy listed eleven planets in his composition with some names capitalized and others not. Particularly in school A, students randomly capitalized regular words in the middle of sentences, even when some punctuation marks were correct. Many students in school A omitted capitals even in their own names, and some capitalized their surname but not their first name and vice versa as in /Rami youSef bOutroS/. No such instances were found in school B, where there were compositions completely free of punctuation and capitalization errors, and capitalization was applied more consistently. In neither school, there seemed to be little improvement over grade levels in punctuation while the use of capital letters somewhat improved from grade four to six.

Numerous compositions were one single long run-on or two long run-ons broken by one period or a comma. As mentioned earlier, Arabic allows lengthy sentences with the conjunction /wa/ repeated between clauses while English does not. That may explain why there were many run-ons with only /and/ between clauses in both schools. In many compositions, some sentences were correctly punctuated while the rest were run ons. It may be that the reading books incorporating plenty of quality fiction and non-fiction facilitate writing development, especially since the experiment described in Chapters 6 and 7 suggests that even a relatively short exposure to quality storybooks improves children's writing.

Handwriting

Although one might argue that due to the modern communication technology one does not have much need for handwriting. However, there are still many situations where students must use handwriting. School tests and examinations are still largely handwritten, as are some international tests, such as the International Baccalaureate (IB) Program exams. The clearer the handwriting, the easier it is to read by the examiners. Personally, over the twenty-six years of university teaching, I have numerous times sent students home with a copy of their paper to be typed because of handwriting that was too difficult and time-consuming to decipher. In 2020, Olivia Coghlan of tutorsplus.com cites

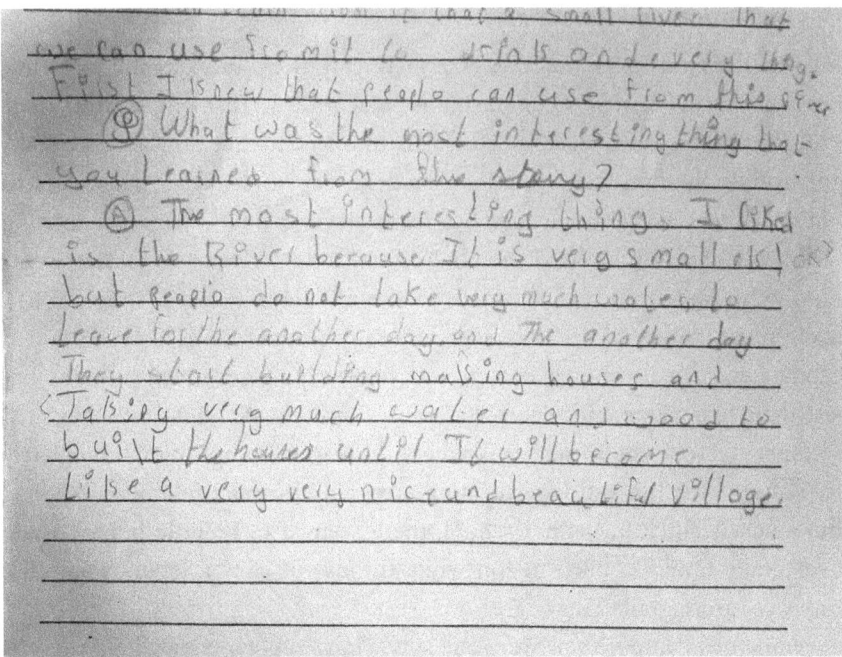

Figure 10.5 Children's handwriting

an IB physics teacher who points out that while the classroom teacher may get used to their students handwriting, that is not so with external readers. Poor handwriting can thus lower the score.

As already mentioned, there is no distinction between print and cursive handwriting in Arabic as all letters in a word are always joined. Thus, children learn the Arabic alphabet letters and then learn to join them into words. However, in English, as in many other languages, children first learn print letters and later transition to cursive writing. In the writing samples collected for this chapter, handwriting often left much to be desired, even in grades five and six. Many words were difficult to discern. For example, in a fifth-grade sample in Figure 10.5, the fourth word of line five and the first letters of lines six and eight take some guessing to figure out the letter /k/. When shown the sample, the class teachers said she had gotten used to their students 'messy handwriting', thus confirming the comments of the physics teacher above regarding classroom teachers getting used to their students handwriting. The teacher further pointed out that she had no time to focus on handwriting because she had to 'finish the book'. Her view was that handwriting should have been taught in kindergarten and first grade.

Concerns

The wide range of grammar and spelling skills within one classroom implies differentiated instruction, which in many contexts will not be easy to achieve. While from an instructional standpoint, classifying misspelled words according to the Bear and Templeton model provides more insight to guide spelling instruction than the Gentry model. However, it will be unreasonable to expect that teachers who teach full weekly load of twenty-five to twenty-eight hours will spend time classifying children's spelling.

Although many publishers produce grammar and spelling books, they are usually not the most desirable option; unless grammar and spelling books are coordinated with the coursebook, their meaningful use may entail teaching considerable new vocabulary before the exercises will be meaningful to students. For example, it does not make sense to teach children to spell words they do not yet understand. The same is true about phonics books used with young beginners in which children are expected to match sounds with pictures when they do not yet have the words for the pictures.

In some cases, even if words are known, the pronunciation may differ so that learners cannot hear the sound similarity. For example, in some US English dialects, the word 'pitcher' (as a jug) often sounds the same as 'picture', and 'prince' may sound like 'prints', and this is reflected in YL phonics books. If young ELLs would have learned the words as distinctly different, the matching exercise will not make sense. In many first language classrooms, spelling books were dropped in the 1990s because of their 'decontextualized nature' (Invernizzi, Abouzeid and Gill 1994: 156). Children also clearly need systematic practice with both punctuation and capitalization to reduce the negative L1 transfer.

Conclusion

Negative transfer from Arabic was evident in children's grammar errors and spelling, with some spelling reflecting negative transfer from spoken colloquial dialect. Similarly, the long run-on sentences and capitalization errors reflect transfer from Arabic where there are no capital letters and lengthy independent clauses linked together with *wa* is common.

The only discernable difference between the two schools was the textbook used for teaching English. While due to other possible confounding variables, one cannot draw any conclusions, the findings do resonate with earlier studies that suggest storybook reading has a positive influence on children's language learning. It would be interesting to examine more closely the link between course materials, associated writing tasks and errors in syntax, spelling and mechanics.

Although children's grammar and spelling errors mirrored some of those of older Arabic-speaking learners of English, many errors identified as common with older learners were rare and some completely absent from these children's writing. Except for preposition and punctuation, errors generally decreased from grade four to grade six. Yet many college-age Arabic speakers continue to make these errors despite having learnt English for a number of years. Finally, students need help in developing their handwriting.

Considering the spread of English-language teaching in primary schools of the MENA region and the growing demand for bilingual Arabic-English instruction in the region, it will be important to identify strategies that will help children develop strong writing skills. This will be especially important for students who need to pass national exit examinations of English and not only gain admission to but also succeed in tertiary education, much of which is now delivered in English in the region.

Recommendations for Practice

Teachers

- First, children's compositions should not be *corrected* by teachers, but marked with indicators for errors, for example, *P* (punctuation), *Cap* (capitalization), *s/v* (subject/verb disagreement), *prep* (preposition) and the like. Children should then rewrite their compositions based on the comments. Correcting children's compositions is a waste of teachers' time, as very few children would look at the corrections, focusing only on the grade received. I have found this to be the case even with university students, except for the most diligent ones.
- Prepositions. Plenty of preposition practice, especially for the correct use of 'with' is necessary. Teachers need to also monitor their own use of prepositions, as observations and interviews reveal that many teachers incorrectly use the preposition 'from' as in 'My students are always afraid /FROM/ the exam' and 'I am afraid/FROM/ snakes'.

- Relative clauses. By grade five, children are typically ten years old and ready for explicit grammar instruction and contextualized practice on relative clauses and correct use of relative pronouns. They will also need exposure to rich language that features relative clauses. High-quality children's stories are a useful source of models for language use.
- Unnecessary pronoun addition. This may, in fact, best be taught directly and providing plenty of practice, possible in a game format.
- Spelling and mechanics. Children will learn to pay attention to word features when they have frequent opportunities for word study from early on.
- Sorting pictures into groups by the sound features in their names is a typical activity in the phonics approach, but problematic if words are unfamiliar to children. If words for sorting are drawn from the instructional texts and children have already learned to pronounce them, the activity will make sense. Sorting can then be done by initial consonant sounds, blends or digraphs. Later on, pictures can be dropped, and word cards are sorted into groups.
- Students need also help in transitioning from print to cursive. In the absence of handwriting in most TEYL books, teachers are the best models for their students when it comes to handwriting. There are also useful handwriting models, such as the *D'Nealian* alphabet, which provides a smooth transition from print to cursive.

Materials Developers

- It would be useful for TEYL coursebooks to include spelling and word study activities that utilize the vocabulary presented in the texts in the above-described ways. Early texts should be rich in rhymes, alliteration and activities that highlight word features.
- It would be also helpful to incorporate handwriting practice in the early levels for children to learn to form letters correctly.

Part 3

Teachers and Students in Action

11

Whole Language Experiences in Kindergarten

'Come back!' the Caterpillar called after her. 'I've something important to say!'
Lewis Carroll – *Alice's Adventures in Wonderland*

Learning 'a Whole' Language

Whole language has been around since the early 1980s, eventually finding its way also to ESL classrooms as evident from numerous conference presentations and publications in educational journals in the 1980s and 1990s. Some textbooks in the late 1990s even claimed to be whole-language-based. However, there have been fierce and extensive debates about whole language and whether it works or not or whether it is just another 'fad'. The approach has been discredited by many researchers (see, e.g. Castles, Rastle and Nation 2018; Ludden 2015). One possible reason for this may be that the critics of the approach have only considered quantitative research, dismissing qualitative research.

'Whole language' is not a method or a set of specific instructional materials but a philosophy about language learning and teaching. This philosophy views language learning as a complex process where learners are actively engaged in using the language in meaningful situations. One of the key proponents of whole language, Kenneth Goodman (1987) has argued that fragmenting language into parts, such as grammatical patterns, vocabulary lists or phonics, results in 'abstractions and nonsense' while Rigg (1991) adds that it destroys the language. The following are the essential points in the whole language philosophy. Listening, speaking, reading and writing are integrated, and language is used for authentic communication and idea sharing, and the learner is in the centre of the curriculum and has choices while the teacher acts as a facilitator (Rigg 1991).

Language learning is viewed as a product of an interactive process and thus learners must have opportunities to share and discuss ideas (Newman 1985).

One of the key issues in the whole language debate has been phonics instruction in the context of native English-speaking children's reading programs. While whole language proponents promote 'embedded phonics', the critics call that a 'guessing game', seeing synthetic phonics as the right way. This may well be true about children learning English as their L1, but it may be less appropriate in the case of young children learning English as a second or foreign language. As mentioned in the previous chapter, for phonics teaching to make sense the words used must be familiar to the children. However, beginning learners have still a very limited knowledge of words. So, for them to be able to match, for example, the sound /o/ in a picture of a 'top' with a same sound in the word 'pot', they would need to know both words. Yet many very young learner courses use a synthetic approach to phonics instruction. Take an example from a grade-one (age six) book. The very first phonics lesson includes pictures of a cat, a mat, a hat and a fat man. Underneath each picture there is a word completion task: /__at/, and children are expected to write the missing letters. There is also a picture of a cat on a mat with a hat next to it and a sentence, 'The fat cat has a hat. The fat cat is on the mat.' At this stage, children have encountered only the word 'cat' in their lessons but none of the other words. Eight pages later, children should circle sixteen words that name the picture next to the words: 'map, nap, lap' next to a picture of a woman sitting with a baby on her lap; 'tin, pin, fin' with a picture of an open sardine tin next to it and so on. With the exception of the word 'pen' none of the words appear in the first lessons of the book. In a whole language approach, phonics would be studied by sorting words familiar for children from their earlier lessons, ideally in a game format.

'Going whole language' is not simple, however, and we should not be fooled into believing that we can switch instantly from a more traditional approach to a whole language approach just as easily as we might change the daily schedule or decide to adopt a new textbook. The switch is slow, and, at times, painful, even in L1 settings, as has been reported by several teachers. In the EFL/ESL setting, it is likely to be more difficult, because the whole language philosophy essentially calls for a student-centred approach to teaching and learning, where the teacher is prepared to provide authentic experiences for language learning and is tuned to students' interests and needs. In a truly whole language classroom, the teacher is ready to take advantage of the real learning situations that occur throughout the year – holiday preparations, field trips, school plays – and allow for student interests, which may range from dinosaurs to sports and Barbie dolls. Learning experiences can be orchestrated by the teacher in such a way as to ensure learning objectives are addressed.

Young English-language learners need to learn to listen, to speak, to read and to write in the new language, often without exposure to English outside school. Vygotsky (1978) and Halliday (1975), among others, view language learning as an intensely social, interactive process. Constructivist theorists argue also that children are able to construct new knowledge best within meaningful interaction with their environment (e.g. Kamii 1991). Given this is true, young language learners need to have plenty of 'opportunities to interact in a meaningful, interesting context and play with the language while developing vocabulary and structures' (Ghosn 1997: 16). We saw in Gloria's, Maya's classes and will see in Rawan's class in the next chapter how meaningful contexts and learner interests create interactive discourse and negotiation of meaning, topic and form, all important in second language learning. Yet many primary school TEYL courses are set up around decontextualized drills and skills exercises and few brief recounts or stories that would invite genuine interaction.

Thematic Instruction

Thematically organized instruction and whole language work well together, because thematic instruction can provide opportunities for frequent repetition and recycling of vocabulary and structures in a meaningful context. This will help learners to internalize the new language and begin to try to use it in their own communication. As Gianelli suggests, thematic instruction works 'because theme-related language and vocabulary are used and reused in new contexts, all of which are meaningfully related' (1991: 13). While children's own, immediate environment is a good source of thematic units, many children's stories are also a rich source for a thematically organized syllabus. Stories that contain predictable, repetitive patterns will reinforce vocabulary and structures, and they are often highly generative and can present plenty of discussion topics that may allow children to link the story to their own lives, which will make the discourse more meaningful to them.

Open-ended activities allow for children's interest and invite their input. Newman (1985) aptly describes such open-ended activities as 'invitations' to learning rather than 'assignments'. Needless to say, 'the instruction must have objectives and goals, but the means through which the objectives are reached can be flexible, and to some extent the objectives themselves' (Ghosn 1997: 16).

Two anecdotal accounts from kindergarten classes illustrate how thematic units can be built around a good picture book. They are not to be understood as lesson plans to be followed by other teachers in other classes but shows how children's interests can mould a lesson while still keeping learning objectives in mind. The first example illustrates children's enthusiasm and how they pick up language from an interesting story. The second example shows how a good story can be linked to subject matter learning within natural, whole language approach. There is no need for each child to have their own copy of the book, because children can be invited to make their own books to take home. This saves a considerable amount of money in situations where the budget is very tight and parent resources are limited.

The Very Hungry Caterpillar

The twenty-six four-year-old children in a KGI class were all native speakers of Arabic spoken in Lebanon and were also learning Arabic alphabet. Eric Carle's *The Very Hungry Caterpillar* served as the starting point, because it included the days of the week, numbers from one to five as well as some prepositions, which were part of the learning objectives for the class. All the vocabulary is presented in salient context that leaves nothing for guessing. (For those unfamiliar with the story, it tells a story about a hungry, little caterpillar which eats through a variety of edibles over a week, gets a stomach ache, and, after spending time in a self-built cocoon, emerges as a colourful butterfly.)

The class was taught by Lebanese-Canadian Betty, who always began her day in the morning with a calendar and weather activity, followed by a story or 'morning conversation'. Betty usually introduced new lessons by saying 'Today we will learn about …'. This time she asked if children would like to hear a new story. As predicted, the children received the idea enthusiastically, and the teacher proceeded to read the story, using a pointer to identify items on the pages and saying things like 'Here, can you see the tiny egg?', and 'See, here are the plums, here are four plums' and so on. At the conclusion of the story, she did not need to ask the usual comprehension questions because children began commenting on the story immediately. Some had already made comments during the reading about the food items. Through the ensuing discussion, Betty followed children's leads whose discourse was primarily in Arabic since children had had only about seven months of English instruction, some instruction in number concepts and basic life science concepts in English. Betty used reflective listening, recasting children's Arabic comments into

English, at the same time validating them, often extending a question to other children:

R:	((Ana ma bhib elkabees)) [I don't like pickles.]
T:	[nodding to Rania]: You don't like pickles?
[To class]:	Does Rania like pickles? [pointing to the pickle in the book.]
Class:	No!
T:	That's right. She doesn't like pickles. Pickles are sour [makes a face to indicate sour taste]. Who likes pickles?
Ss:	((Me! Mee!!))
T:	Ah. You like pickles. Hani, Tanya, and Zeina like pickles. I like strawberries [pointing to strawberries in the book]. They are sweet. Mmmm! Who likes strawberries?
Ss:	Me! ((Me!))
T:	It seems that we all like strawberries. They are sweet. Are strawberries sweet?
S:	Yes! (Ghosn 1997: 18)

Vocabulary was repeated within natural and genuine discourse, and the teacher's approach provided not only modelling but also repetition. There was no out-of-context drill or questions about vocabulary or structures. Children were enjoying themselves and were actively participating. Children's participation was largely due to Betty's knowledge of Arabic, which enabled her to recast children's Arabic contribution into English. With young children with very limited English, similar approach might not work if the teacher does not know the children's L1 or if there are children from several different language backgrounds in the class. Inability to use English or L1 when communicating with the teacher is likely to produce frustration and possible loss of motivation and subsequent disengagement from the lesson. This is especially significant with young children whose communicative skills even in L1 are still developing and who are already facing the stress of being separated from the familiar home environment and their caregiver. However, with children who already have some communicative ability in English, the approach can work even if the teacher is unfamiliar with children's L1. In this case, the teacher can reflect the L1 contributions back to the class and say, for example, 'Who can tell me what Radwan said?' 'Who is this (pointing to an object) called in Arabic?' Time can be given for children to consult each other in small groups to arrive at the answer. I am firmly of the opinion that when teaching languages to young and very young children, regardless of the approach used, it is imperative that the teacher is familiar with the children's L1 in order to be able to validate children's L1 communication attempts. At the same time, I believe that the teacher should only use the target language, as it is often the only model students have aside from the book.

There are many children's books that can encourage children to make predictions, which keep them motivated to listen or read on. When teachers ask questions about what children think will happen next, what the character might do and why they think what they think, children are not only motivated to find out if their predictions were accurate but also engaged in formulating hypotheses and justifying them. In young learner classroom, these hypotheses will, of course, be at children's developmental level. For example, examining the cover of a story such as *The Ugly Duckling*, which shows a young bird looking sad, can generate many different hypotheses from the title and the illustration. Children in Betty's class quickly began to draw items form the book, and some scribbled numbers and 'words' related to the story. During recess periods, several children were observed running around and calling out 'Look! Look! Me butterfly!' Before snack time, Betty reinforced the preposition 'through' as children filed out of the room to wash their hands. She repeated the phrase 'through the doorway' with each student.

It was interesting to observe the children during snack times, as children examined their peers' lunches and eagerly pointed out any of the caterpillar's food they found; apples, cheese and a cupcake. Some of the children who had slices of cheese, ham and flat Arabic bread in their lunch box punched holes through them, saying 'Look! Caterpillar go through [my cheese]!' or 'I go through my "mortadella"!' (Although many teachers and parents may frown at this activity, it does illustrate children's active engagement with the story and their appropriation of some of its language.) Children talked about what foods they liked and what not, and what their favourite lunch box foods were. The discussion was in Arabic, but Betty went around the tables, making comments in English and asking the children questions.

During the time allocated for learning numbers, Betty brought out the book again and invited children to count food items on the pages, and she wrote numbers on a flip chart. She invited children to come and point to the numbers she named. Or she pointed to a number and asked children to name it. At the time, children were all familiar with numbers one and two, and the teacher now focused on the number three. The children were eager to demonstrate their knowledge of numbers and much counting went on. 'Who can come and count three strawberries for me?' 'What about three oranges?' and so on.

During the morning calendar activities, children often remembered what the caterpillar ate on the given day. In order to check which suggestion was correct, the book was brought out. After verifying pears to be correct, children often asked for the story to be read again. This provided an opportunity to reinforce the numbers. During the rest of the week, Betty read the story several times, at times using the pointer to follow the text as she read. Betty introduced a picture bingo activity to the class, and by the end of the week, some children sought out the bingo boards and organized their own game during their free time. Some children sought out the book out during their free time and taking turns to 'read' it to each other. Although children were still at the pre-writing and scribbling phases of their writing development, Betty invited them to make their own caterpillar book. She gave them text from the book enlarged on A4-size sheets of paper stapled together, with the top half of the page left empty. Children were invited to illustrate their own books with Betty occasionally helping with the text: 'Look, it says in the book that the caterpillar ate through *one* leaf on Monday. Here it says the caterpillar ate through *four* strawberries, *four* strawberries. How many strawberries do you see?" By the time the books were ready, most children were able to 'read' their story and take it home. One compiled copy was made for the class library. Figure 11.1 shows children's attempts at writing.

Other activities that were introduced included picture-sorting, number bingo, dramatizations with a sock puppet, painting butterflies and making papier-maché cocoons. A grocery store corner was set up that incorporated concepts related to the story, mainly pictures and plastic fruit available in the toy centre. In this class, children incorporated much vocabulary and many concepts from the story into their daily free time activities from day one, with the number and frequency of words increasing as the days went by. Because children were very interested in the metamorphosis of the caterpillar, Betty introduced the children to silk moths. This was possible because Lebanon has a long history in sericulture, and there are still plenty of mulberry trees in the country. A nursery teacher in the school was growing silk worms and lent Betty three silkworms (larvae) to bring to the class. A box for them was set up in the corner of the classroom, and mulberry leaves were brought in for children to observe

How Big Is a Foot?

How Big Is a Foot? by Myller is an amusing story where a King orders a bed for the Queen. He uses his own foot to measure the size of the bed and gives the measurements in feet to an apprentice. The young apprentice uses his own foot

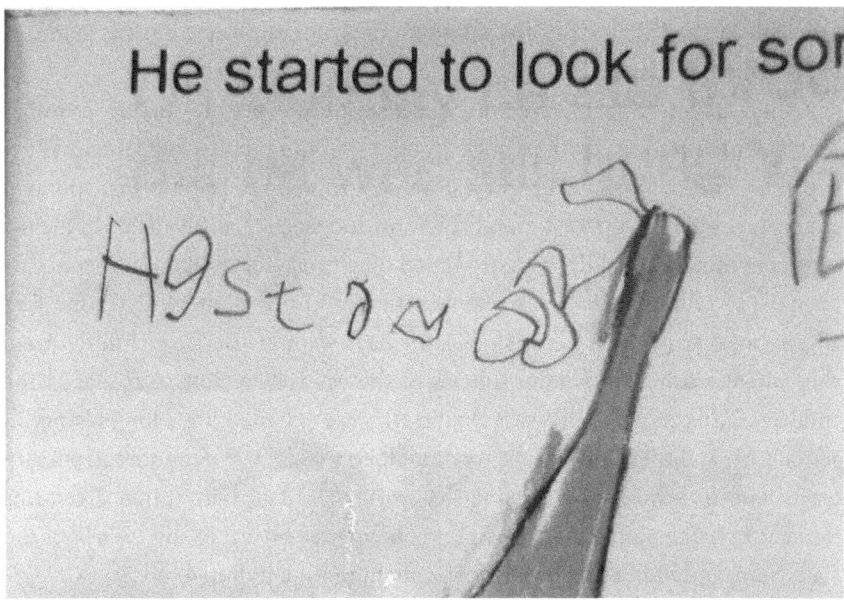

Figure 11.1 (a, b) Children's scribbles

to measure the bed, and, needless to say, ends up in jail because the bed turned out too small. KGII teacher, Nisreen, in an English immersion school used the story with her five-year-olds to introduce them to the concept of standard measurements. She showed children the cover of the book and told the class she was going to read a story:

T: Look, KGII. This story is called *How Big is a Foot?* What do you see in the cover?
Ss: King! Queen! ((Pajamas!))
T: OK, who said queen? [student raises a hand] Oh, Jihad, why do think it's a queen?
S1: Has ((crown)) Miss.
S2: Queen not wear pants!
S1: ((But look at the hair!)) She a queen!
T: OK, everybody. Let's read to find out.

Nisreen reads the first two pages, where it becomes evident that the King wanted to get the Queen a birthday present. She asks the children what a king might get a queen for her birthday. Lively exchange ensues:

T: What do you think the King will give the Queen?
[Several children call out things.]
T: Please, remember quiet hands [demonstrates, and children calm down].
S1: Shoes, Miss Nina! She has no shoes!
S2: No. Shoes are not for birthday! King must give her ((gold bracelet)) or something.
S3: Ring ((diamond))!
S1: But she has no shoes.
S4: She has ((pajamas)). You wear shoes with your ((pajamas))?

Nisreen proceeds with the story, stopping at the point where the poor apprentice is sent to jail for making the bed too small. So Nisreen asks the children why they think the bed was too small.

S1: What mean [tries to pronounce 'apprentice']?
T: Apprentice, well apprentice is a job. This apprentice wants to become a carpenter, so now she is an apprentice, learning to do carpentry.
S1: Like ((carpenter))?
S2: So she new. ((maybe he does not know how to measure well))
T: OK. Let us see if we can help him out.

Nisreen divided the five-year-olds into six groups, and said: 'Let's see if we can figure it out.' She gave each group different objects. One group got large paper clips, one crayons, another pencils of different lengths and another tongue depressors. She then gave each group their measuring tools and a piece of paper with the name and picture of the item they were to measure. Two groups with different measuring tools were given the same object to measure. She modelled the measuring with the paperclips to show how there should be no gaps between the items. As the groups moved around the class to measure their objects, two or three children in the group were measuring with others serving as counters and recorders. When the group was in agreement about their measurement, the recorders wrote down the numbers next to the picture. When the results were compared, some children were surprised about the differences in measurements and insisted that they had measured correctly. The class was interrupted by the recess bell and Nisreen told the class they will talk about this problem more the next day.

The next day, she brought in newspapers and invited children to help each other to draw the outline of one of their feet on folded newspapers, cut it out and glue the pages together. She then invited volunteers to use their foot measure to measure the distance from the door to the board. As the outcomes were still different, she asked the class if anyone remembered what measurement the King and apprentice used. Children called out 'foot/feet' in unison. 'OK. Both used their foot. Yesterday, you used your feet to measure how many feet it takes from the doorway to the boat. But did you all get the same results?' she asked. 'Why not?' Children offer suggestions, many pointing out that not everyone's foot is the same size.

Nisreen brought out the book to point to the illustrations of the King using his foot to measure the width and length of the bed while the apprentice was using his own much smaller foot to measure the required width and length. She points to the illustrations and asks what they see: 'What can you see here ... and here? Is there a difference? Why was the bed too small?' Children note that the apprentice's foot was much smaller than the King's. She then asked the children if they would have any advice to the apprentice, who was in Jail. Children eagerly point out that he should have used the King's foot instead of his own. She suggested they write a letter to the apprentice together and give him some advice. The following letter was generated with Nisreen guiding the children with leading questions and recasting any Arabic utterances into English as she typed the text, which was projected on the whiteboard. The text was then jointly edited with Nisreen's guidance. After the third line of the draft was projected, she asked how the Apprentice could measure with the King's foot when he was in jail.

> Dear Apprentice
>
> You were very nice to make the bed for Queen. But you had a mistake.
>
> The King measured with his foot and told you how big you must make the bed. You must use King's foot to measure the bed.
>
> You must do like this: Ask King to draw his foot on some paper and give it to you. Tell him 'King, then I can make the bed right.' Good luck!
>
> Miss Nina's KG2

This story is perfect for introducing the basic concept of standard measurement. The way Nisreen approached it made it interesting for children because they had experienced the concept in hands-on activities and a story context. Children were now ready to be introduced to the use of a ruler to measure things. I have also observed some teachers reading the whole story and then discussing the need for standard measurements. If this is followed by the hands-on measurement activity, it is only another task to accomplish and the opportunity to generate curiosity and discovery is lost. When asked to do the task, children quickly point out to the teacher that they must use the same measurement tool.

Nisreen used the story to introduce children to the use of a ruler. She provided children with rulers with markings every five centimetres, and over several days, she gave children different measuring tasks. Many of the children needed one-on-one guidance to learn to use the ruler somewhat correctly. Nisreen was fortunate to have a full-time assistant teacher, who was also a graduate student in early childhood education. The assistant was able to provide the individual attention children needed. Nisreen also continued to work with children on letter writing. She read children Lionni's *Cornelius* and guided children to write letters to Cornelius, a crocodile who wanted to learn to walk upright and hang from trees with his tail, or the other crocodiles in the story. She followed this with Lionni's *Fredrick*, a mouse who collected words for winter while other mice collected food.

Caveat

For the above approaches – which can be considered a form of whole language approach – to work as intended, the teacher should be familiar with the children's mother tongue. Without that knowledge, the teacher will not be able to use reflective listening and provide the English words that children need to express their ideas, and thus communication will be limited. This is easy to accomplish where children and teacher share the same language, but in other settings, such as a native English-speaking teacher teaching a multilingual class with several mother tongues, this would be difficult.

Well-prepared local teachers, who not only speak the children's language but are also familiar with the local culture, may find it easier to manage the class than teachers from other cultures, as both the local teacher and students share similar expectations about classroom roles. They can more readily adapt or help children relate to unfamiliar cultural concepts as they can point out similarities and differences. Needless to say, 'well-prepared' implies not only knowledge of pedagogy but also excellent target language skills, including grammar and pronunciation. If this can be accomplished, there should be no need to 'import' native English-speaking teachers. After all, in many countries around the world there are few, if any, foreign teachers, especially in primary schools.

Recommendations for Practice

Teachers

Illustrated picture books and rhymes are ideal for very young learner classes and short thematic units. Many provide also opportunities for movement. The following rhymes and titles lend themselves well for thematic units in very young learner classes, as well as in lower primary school beginners.

- A thematic unit can be built around *The Very Hungry Caterpillar* about healthy food as well as life cycle of insects or frogs, for example.
- Classic Mother Goose rhyme, 'Little Miss Muffet' can initiate a unit on spiders while Carle's (1977) delightful *The Grouchy Ladybug* (*Bad-Tempered Ladybug*) will lead easily to a unit on sharing if coupled with *The Rabbit and the Turnip* (Addison-Wesley). Both offer also plenty of opportunities for movement and dramatizing.
- A retelling of an old classic with a new twist, *Little Hen Gets Help* (Ghosn 2006), can be viewed at http://www.youtube.com/watch?v= RPWH71tUJaE and downloaded as a free PDF from caringkidspublishers.com. It works well as an introduction to a thematic unit on domestic animals, life on a farm, bread, or helping friends and sharing. Taken together, *The Grouchy*

Ladybug, The Rabbit and the Turnip and *Little Hen Gets Help* will form meaningful thematic units either on animals or friendship and sharing, or both. All three feature repetitious refrains that children can pick up for their own use.

Materials Developers

- A very young learner coursebook, if one is necessary, should not consist of fill-in-the-blanks, phonics drills and decontextualized vocabulary practice. A compilation of carefully selected illustrated stories can be used as bases for thematic units. Words for phonics and word study can be drawn from the stories and can be worked on when children have had some time to familiarize themselves with target vocabulary.

12

The Flexibility of Story-Based Instruction in the Classroom

'... and what's the use of a book,' thought Alice, 'without pictures or conversation?'

Lewis Carroll – *Alice's Adventures in Wonderland*

TEYL courses are primarily organized around structured skills-based syllabi although many courses now include some highly simplified stories. It may, however, not be the best option in cultural contexts where classroom interactions are hierarchically oriented and where teachers adhere strictly to the coursebook options, which may limit student engagement as seen in some of the chapters. In contrast, story-based instruction allows teachers to select not only the instructional approaches best suited to their personal preferences but also those that meet the prevailing cultural expectations. As we saw in some of the classroom vignettes in this volume, different teachers may guide discussions around stories in different ways. The common thread, despite the different approaches, is the connected genuine interactions around stories. In this chapter we will first follow two Lebanese teachers to see how one story can be approached in very different ways to encourage student participation. The teachers follow the steps outlined in Ghosn (2013). First, there is some preparation, which can be accomplished in different ways; students can be invited to examine the cover art and the title of the story and do a 'picture walk' through a story (unless there is a surprise ending!) and based on this make predictions about what the story might be about. For example, when Dima, whom we met in Chapter 6, introduced her class to Allard's (2002) *Josh Gets Glasses*, one boy suggested that Josh was getting ready for school, but after a picture walk revised his prediction and noted, 'Oh maybe Josh getting glasses so maybe this is doctor not his mother' (Chaaya 2006: 36). Students can also be invited to tell what they may know about the topic they have identified. After the reading of the story, teachers engage students in reflecting on and discussing the story; what they thought about the story; and what they thought about events or characters' actions, as well as relate the story to their own personal experiences. Then children should be given meaningful reasons to revisit the story and its language. Further follow-up activities will reinforce the language and/or concepts in the story.

Pourquoi Story Experience

Third-grade teachers Zainab and Amal were both given the same version of the classic *pourquoi* story in a local third-grade coursebook about how the rabbit got its short tail and long ears. However, they were not given the teacher's guide or student workbooks. Students were in their third year of formal English and EMI in two small private schools. Although both teachers can be classified as student-centred, Zainab exhibited a more hierarchical approach than Amal.

Preparing for the Story

Zainab is preparing her students to listen to the story. She chose to read the story aloud, first, because her students enjoy listening to her reading them stories, and second, because she felt the language was a bit too challenging for her students to read independently.

Episode 12.1 Zainab Prepares for the Story

T: Grade three, I am going to read you a story, OK?
Ss: Yes, Miss! Yes!
T: OK. Open your books to page thirty-three, please. The story we are going to read is a *pourquoi* story, a *pourquoi* story. Who knows what the word *pourquoi* means?
S1: Miss! Is French it mean 'why'.
T: Very good, Hammoudi. [Reads the introduction about *pourquoi* stories.] OK, now. Does anyone know a *pourquoi* story? A story that tells why something is the way it is? [No response from students.]
T: Who can read the title of the story? Yes, Rana.

S2:	[Reads] *How Rabbit Got its Short Tail and Long Ears.*
T:	Very good. How Rabbit got its short tail and long ears. OK. [reads the first paragraph]
T:	What do we know about rabbit's ears and tail from long ago?
Ss:	Small ears! (small ears) Ears long! Long! [several students calling out answers]
T:	Right, they had small ears and long tails. It says here [reads] *Rabbit liked to show off his tail.* What does it mean 'show off'? Look at the picture.
Ss:	(be proud!)
S3:	Miss! It mean to do like this [stands up and puts her nose up and crosses her arms]
T:	Yes. You are right. It means to be very proud, show off to others. Like he is better than others, OK. Now, what do we know about the fox, the fox? [Several students again call out answers.] Please one at a time. OK.
S4:	Fox he very proud also. He have big nice tail ((like the rabbit)).
T:	Right. Fox was also proud of his beautiful bushy tail, bushy tail. OK. Let's turn to the next page.

She continues like this for the rest of the story, asking also questions about the illustrations. However, she does not solicit any predictions or any student opinions. Yet, students are engaged and eagerly talk about the illustrations, and she listens to them for a brief period and then continues with the story. Students have a two-period block of English, and Zainab spends some time on pronunciation of the word 'bushy', which some children pronounce as rhyming with 'brush'. She then reviews comparatives. For homework, she assigns a worksheet with a cloze exercise.

Episode 12.2 Amal Prepares for the Story

Amal uses a very different approach to the same story with her third-graders:

T:	OK, grade three. What are we going to do today?
Ss:	Story, Miss! Story!
T:	Let's look at the first page, page thirty-three. What do you see in the picture?
S1:	Miss, ((a fox))!
T:	Yes, Zeina. There is a fox. What else can you see? Can you see the rabbit?
S2:	A white animal but ...
S3:	Miss, the story tells us why the rabbit has a short tail and long ears. It says so here.

T: Yes. This is a *pourquoi* story, a *pourquoi* story. *Pourquoi* stories explain why something is the way it is. Does anyone know a *pourquoi* story? [no responses from students] In the picture, does the rabbit look like rabbits you have seen in pictures?

S4: No Miss! My ((grandfather)) he have rabbits. They are different.

T: Oh, your grandfather has rabbits! How nice. How are his rabbits different from this one [points to the picture]?

S4: They have small tail and ears like this [makes a sign of small ears on his own ears]. They not all white.

Ss: Long tail! Small ears!

T: Right. How do you think the rabbit now has a short tail and long ears? Look at the illustrations, the pictures. What do you think happened?

Students eagerly look through the illustrations and offer explanations based on what they observe. Some of the discourse is in Arabic again, and Amal provides relevant English vocabulary.

T: OK, who can read the first paragraph? Yes, Rouba.
     [Student reads the paragraph of four lines.]

T: Thank you Rouba. Look at the fox. How does he look?

Ss: Angry, Miss! Mad!

T: OK. Do you know what rabbits eat?

Students quickly point out in Arabic that rabbits eat carrots and lettuce. Amal offers the English words for both. (In the story rabbits ate fish before the trick played by the fox, and children discovered this on the next page.) Amal continues this way through the story.

Reflections

Although both teachers invite children's reflections, they do it in a different way. Zainab first asks students typical comprehension questions; 'What did the Fox do?' 'Who pulled at rabbit's ears?' In contrast, Amal asks: 'So, what do you think about that?' Most of the students blame the fox for being mean to trick the rabbit this way. Some children suggested that the rabbit should not have been such a show off. When Amal's students responded in Arabic, she validated the response first and then recast it into English:

S: Rabbit she ((deserves it)).

T: Oh, you think the rabbit deserved it? Deserved it because she was a show-off?
S: Yes, Miss.

In contrast, Zainab immediately provided the English words and had children repeat it:

S: Rabbits ((don't eat fish))
Z: Rabbits don't eat fish, right. What do rabbits not eat?
S: Fish
Z: Yes, so Rabbits ... what?

Despite the differences in the two teachers' approaches, all children in both classes appeared engaged and eagerly participating.

Follow-Up

Well-planned follow-up activities that require students to return to the story with a purpose are a key component of successful story-based instruction. During the next lesson, Amal invited children to tell what they remembered about the story. After a brief shred discussion, she invited students to read aloud parts of the story: 'Read the part that shows rabbit was a show-off; Read where we know what fox thinks about the rabbit; Who thinks there was something funny in the story? Read that part.' She asked if others thought that the given part was funny. Students were all engaged. Approaches like this are preferable to the traditional 'round-robin' reading, where students take turns to read a paragraph or few sentences each. During the activity, only one student at a time is engaged while others can easily 'tune out', especially after they have had their turn. Amal then had her students write five questions about the story for their partners to answer. Children wrote their questions and swapped notebooks to answer their peers' questions. To answer the questions, students were able to review the story. When they were finished, Amal had children take turns to read their questions and their partners to read their answers. When a student had read his or her answer, Amal invited the class to assess whether the answer was correct.

Zainab asked her students to tell what they remember about the story by asking specific factual questions. She then had the students take turns to read the story aloud. Although the approach is 'round-robin', she did not select students systematically, row by row but at random, an approach which usually makes students a little more attentive. She asked specific questions about the part that was read, and she also asked students to listen carefully if the reader read his or her part correctly, which may also have engaged students more than the mere 'round-robin'.

Amal's intention had been to have students craft their own *pourquoi* stories in pairs, but that proved too challenging as children did not have any Arabic or other English models of this type of story to draw on. Her second alternative was for children to write one collectively with her guidance. When that did not work either, she explained to students that this was 'probably a fifth-grade activity, so let's do something else!' She invited the class to write a summary of the story with her guidance. This required review of summary and use of quotation marks in direct speech. Later in the week, she had students work in pairs to write a new story by changing something; different characters (rabbit had to stay, of course), different ending, what happened after the story and the like. She reports that both activities worked very well. Class- and student-generated stories are a good source for language activities such as the use of adjectives, adverbs and combined sentences, as well as activities for word study and to introduce proofreading marks. Using students' writing maintains the integrity of the original story and respects the author's art.

Zainab had her students rewrite the story changing direct speech to reported speech. Finally, she simplified the story for children to dramatize. Children were assigned roles, rehearsed them with a partner and took turns to act out the story in front of the class. Children clearly enjoyed the activity although there were a lot of giggles and embarrassed looks when the 'actors' made mistakes or fumbled. For simple props, Zainab could have prepared character cards with the character names and images on the card to hang around students' necks or pinned to their shirts.

Children's Reactions to Stories

The following responses from children of different ages demonstrate the captivating power of stories and shows how stories can generate very diverse reactions from children.

Reader Responses

At the end of the classroom experiment described in Chapter 6, fifth-grade students generated a total of 158 reader responses. They were able to choose from journal entries, letters to and from characters, comparing two stories and in some cases what the author's message in a given story might be. Responses were not graded or edited. When responses were analysed, very different responses to the same story emerged. For example, one story featured resourceful Omar, who with his friends makes a plan to save a mountain from being quarried by a greedy businessman. The majority of the responses were letters addressed to Omar, praising his courage and resourcefulness, journal entries and diary entries from Omar's perspective. Here is an example of a letter to Omar:

> Dear /o/mar
>
> How are you. thank you for you and your /FRENDS/ who were hugging the /MOUNTIN/. How did you think this plan. Was it hard for you to think like this. How many hours or /MINITS/ did you think of this plan, where you /AFRADE/ of /THES/ stupid man who was telling you and your /FRENDS/ to get of the /MOUNTAN/.
>
> I am thanking you for saving this mountain not only this mountain. may be if you and /FRENDS/ /WHERE/ not here they will had broken down this mountain and went on to /BRACK/ other mountains. If you saw /PEPOLE/ /BRACKING/ only mountain do not let them. Just let them /BRACK/ half of it so they can get /SIMENT/ to /BILD/ houses. [name]

Despite the issues of capitalization and spelling errors, the letter clearly indicates that the student had given the story careful consideration before writing his response.

Another story children read featured Heba and her Sri Lankan classmate. Heba snatches her friend's wire art and enters it in an art contest under her own name without her friend's knowledge. Her reason was that the teacher did not allow the friend to take part in the contest because she was from a lower social class. Heba wins the contest and reveals who the true artist was and explains why she did what she did. The moral question here is whether it was right for her to steal the artwork in the first place and then falsely present it as her own, even when her aim was to help her friend. In other words, 'does the end justify the means?' The responses addressing this question were divided. Here are two of the few examples criticizing Heba:

1. *Dear Heba*

> Heba what you did giving the wire of Mallika to Miss Randa was wrong. First you suppose to tell to Mallika that you want to give the wire to Miss Randa. And you were honest when you won, you said for them that wire is to my friend Mallika.

2. From Your Friend [Name]

> Hey Heba, why you did like this? There is problem for you. why you don't tell her? ... The good thing that you make it is when you told the teacher ... so don't /REPAITED/ [repeat?] again.

However, many of the responses expressed different sentiments and focused on the end result and not the means as in the following excerpt:

> Dear Heba
>
> You is very helpful girl and lovely. When you go to Miss Randa and ask her if Mallika can /CHAIR/ [share?] in the contest and she didn't agree because she is the /DOUTER/ for housemaid. And when you put Mallika's dragonfly in the contest and took the first prize and it was 1,000 dollars and gave them to Mallika. it was from the very best works in your life!
>
> /SINSLY/ your [name]

Perhaps the positive reactions to Heba's behaviour stem from the collectivist culture where helping family, friends and the in-group is often taken for granted. Children perhaps related more to this aspect of the story rather than Heba's deceitful behaviour since the ending was happy. See an example of discussion about the same story in Chapter 5 on discourse. The same sentiment was expressed by a university student during the author's moral reasoning class about the question whether it is sometimes necessary to cheat or lie. The student argued that sometimes 'you have to cheat'. She then recounted how during the national matriculation examination, she noticed that a boy next to her did not know some answers, so she helped him. She stated, 'If I didn't do that and he failed the exam, and then I meet him in the street I would be ashamed of not helping him since I knew the answers.'

For Steig's *Amos & Boris*, students had the following options to choose from: 'How did you like the story? If you liked it, what part did you like the most? What do you think the author's message was? If you did not like the story, tell why.' One girl accurately summarized the story but concluded with an honest, 'I am sorry because I didn't answer on the question. But I write what I understand.' It may be that the concept of the story was too unusual for the children, as only very few students had selected this story to read and respond to. Although the responses for stories differed, most of them showed that children had thought about the stories they wrote about. Many of the letters, for example, were quite lengthy and insightful.

Interest in Content

Rowan teaches English in grades three and four in a suburban EMI school and often supplements the ESL coursebook with graded readers and other inexpensive trade books. Rowan described how he used *Slow Little Snail* (Ghosn 1999) with her fourth-graders. The story features a little snail who decides to go for a morning 'walk'. However, despite making several invitations to different critters, none are willing to join the snail until another little snail comes along.

While some children immediately pointed out that snails don't have legs and thus could not walk (consequently a second, revised edition is re-titled *Little Snail's Morning Stroll*, available as free PDF with a lesson plan and student worksheets at caringklidspublishers.com), others said the other critters were mean. When one student said his grandmother cooked and ate snails, one girl pointed out that they were *haram* (forbidden). Rowan avoided discussion about the potentially sensitive issue, immediately moving to a discussion about how it feels to be left out of activities, and many children shared their own experiences. Rowan then invited children to think what the other critters could have said instead of 'You are too slow'. Children's suggestions included 'I am busy now', 'I have something important to do', 'I am sorry, I don't have time now' (some of them in Arabic) and Rowan wrote their suggestions on the board. When one boy suggested 'OK, let's go!' other students immediately responded to him by saying that all the others were fast. However, the boy pointed out,

S: No, look caterpillars not fast. I seen them. Also ((chameleon)) is very slow, I seen one in ((the bushes)) near my house.
T: OK. Rami has seen caterpillars and chameleons. You *have* seen them, right?
S: Yes, I seen them. They are slow.

So, Rowan decided to add Rami's suggestion on the board as well. As homework, he asked children to choose one of one critter's response and change it to a more friendly or polite one. The following day, children shared their work. Here are four examples:

> The ant said 'I am very busy today. Come tomorrow.'
>
> The mantis say to Little Snail 'I am sorry. I like to /GUMP/ [jump]. I come with you if you can /GUMP/.'

Snake /TOLLED/ the snail 'I have important /WRK/'.

Rami, who had seen a chameleon wrote: 'Chameleon say /HAPPLY/ 'OK! Let's go!'"

Since short, illustrated stories lend themselves well to role-play, the teacher had children dramatize the story a number of times. To help children with the dialogue, Rowan printed the two key phrases on the board: 'Would you like to go'; 'You are too slow'. So that if children needed help, they could refer to the board. However, some wanted to use their own responses they had written earlier. Some of the children had great fun taking on the role of the characters that hissed the /s/ sound or lisped the /th/ sound. The phrase 'would you like to' was easily adopted by children, and Rowan reported hearing children use it among themselves, as in 'Would you like to play basket [sic] with me?'

Because many children expressed either fear or even disgust about some of the critters in the story – particularly the praying mantis, the chameleon, the lizard and the snake – Rowan invited the primary school science teacher to do a presentation about various insects and other critters that people tend to fear or avoid in the community. She talked about the role of earthworms, the importance of bees and butterflies in plant pollination and the importance of the animals that eat harmful insects. She also explained that some snakes are actually useful because they eat small rodents like mice and moles. She did, however, point out the importance of not approaching snakes because some have powerful venom that can hurt humans. Some children were still clearly sceptical, but others seemed to show more positive reactions.

Real or Not Real?

In a KGII class, Roula read the classic *Goldilocks and the Three Bears* to her five-year-olds using a big book version of the story from the now out-of-print Addison-Wesley *Amazing English* series (but available online from nany different sources). In preparation for the story, she only asked for predictions based on the cover illustration and the title, and some children were already familiar with the story in Arabic. When reading, she used a dialogic approach, stopping every now and then to point to the pictures and to ask for predictions. She then invited student reactions, and a lively discussion ensued, with much of the children's talk in Arabic.

Episode 12.3

- **S1:** The girl she ((naughty because)) go bear house.
- **T:** Oh, so you think Goldilocks was naughty when she went into the bears' house. Why?
- **S1:** Yes, Miss. She break chair.
- **T:** Yes, she *broke* the chair. So that was naughty.
- **S2:** She eat ((someone else's food!)).
- **T:** Right, she ate the bears' food. True.
- **S3:** Miss, she *must* to go to bear house!
- **T:** So, you think that Goldilocks *had to* go to the bears' house? Why?
- **S3:** Yes, Miss. ((She was tired and hungry and she was in the forest. Maybe a fox will catch her.))
- **T:** I see. So Hassan thinks that it was OK for Goldilocks to go the bears' house. She was tired and hungry, and she was alone in the forest. He thinks that a fox might come and hurt her. So she was safe, safe in the house.
- **S3:** Yes, Miss Roula.
- **S4:** But bear bigger than ((fox))!
- **S3:** ((She didn't know it was)) house for bears!

Clearly, children were very enthusiastically participating, but one little boy was sceptical:

- **S5:** Miss, bears no have house. ((They are lying.))
- **T:** You are quite right, Hani. Bears do not live in houses. But this is a story, it's make-believe. It's not the same as lying. Don't you like stories?
- **S5:** I like ((only stories that are real))
- **T:** I see, OK. You like stories that are real. Did you like *The Very Hungry Caterpillar*? Remember, you read in first grade I think.
- **S5:** Yes. I like ((because it is real)) butterfly come from caterpillar.
- **T:** Oh, I see. You like stories, but only stories that could really happen, yes?
- **S5:** Yes, Miss.

The following day, Roula read the story again, and some children repeated phrases with her. She then invited the children to think: 'What do you think Goldilocks's mother said to her when she came back home? When Goldilocks told her mother about bears?' After a discussion with plenty of Arabic input from children, she handed children cards, some with 'Mother' and some with 'Goldilocks' printed on them. She invited children to pick a card and take turns to act out a dialogue between Goldilocks and her mother. While some 'mothers' were very understanding, others were much less so, even promising harsh punishment for Goldilocks.

Soup from Nails and Stones?

In her fourth-grade class, Bassima is preparing the class to read *Nail Soup*, an old Swedish folktale also known as *Stone Soup*. On her desk, she had set an onion, a banana, a carrot, a potato, a picture of a chicken, an apple, a pinecone and two big nails.

- **T:** OK, kids. What do I have here? Look, what are these?
- **Ss:** [students call out different items]
- **T:** Shh! One at a time please! Yes, Rouba.
- **S1:** Miss, an apple, Miss! And a ((banana)).
- **T:** Right, an apple and a banana. What else?

She goes through all items and then asks the children which ones are edible. Children have no problem with this question, but when she asks which ones could be used to make soup, there is some disagreement because one boy suggests that apples can be used in a soup. Girls all argue against that. Bassima then picks up the two nails and asks if they could be used in a soup. Needless to say, children vehemently object to the idea.

Episode 12.4

- **T:** OK, class. Today we're gonna read a story called *Nail Soup*, *Nail Soup*.
- **Ss:** [giggling and calling out] No, Miss! No! ((nobody can eat nails))! Miss Bassima, you die ((if you eat nails))!
- **T:** Well, let us see. Open your books to page sixty-four, sixty-four. OK. What do you see in the pictures? Mouna.
- **S1:** Two men ((with sacks))
- **S2:** A house, Miss!
- **T:** Right there are two men and they are carrying bags or sacks, and there is a house also. Where do you think the men are going? Nabil?
- **S3:** I think to the house.
- **T:** OK, let's see. Nabil, please read the first page.
- **S3:** [reads] *Long time ago* (xxx) *They saw little house and knocked* [pronounces the /k/ sound]
- **T:** Right, so they are hungry and tired and they see a little house. They *knocked* on the door, *knocked*. The /k/ here is silent. Remember we don't

pronounce it. Does anyone remember another word that begins with /kn/ and the /s/ is silent?

Students call out 'know' and 'knife' and Bassima repeats them. She then asks students to look at the pictures of the two men and an old man at his door and asks them to look at the old man's facial expressions: 'How does his face look in the first picture?' Students are all engaged, scrutinizing the illustrations. They note that in the first picture the man looks angry, but in the second picture he looks different. On each page, Bassima invites children to examine the illustrations and make predictions about what will happen. When they reach the end of the story, some children are laughing and offering comments about how clever the men were.

T: Now, the old man had all this food. Why do you think he first did not want to share it with the hungry men? Please! One at a time, raise your hands quietly. Yes, Rana.
S4: Miss, the man he ((stingy)).
T: So Rana says the man was stingy, stingy. He did not want to share. We call someone like that stingy ((stingy)). Don't want to share with others. But why did he change his mind and gave them potatoes and onions, and even chicken? What do you think?

Several students offer opinions, but their comments are mainly in Arabic. However, they either did not have a clear understanding about why the man changed his mind and even let the men sleep in his bed while he slept on the floor or were unable to express it. Bassima explains that this is a trickster tale, that the men tricked the old man to something he did not normally do.

T: Does anyone remember any other stories where someone tricks another one to do something?
S3: Miss, the *Gingerbread Man*. We took it in KG! The fox trick the Gingerbread man and eat it.
T: Goood! That is also trickster tale, a trickster tale. The fox tricked the Gingerbread man and ate it. How did the fox do it? What was his trick?
S4: Miss, the fox he told gingerbread man 'Jump on my head ((and I take you across the river.'))

Throughout the session, all children are intensely engaged. Bassima then assigns children a cloze exercise from the story as homework. During the next lesson, she planned to review the story and asks questions about it. Her plan could also have included student-generated stories; children could easily work in pairs using *Nail Soup* as a template. They could change the characters and the food items. They could refer to the book for any language they might need for their story. They could then take turns to act out their own stories. Another Lebanese teacher used a storytelling approach to the *Stone Soup* version of the story with students having English as the second foreign language. She used a big soup pot, a ladle and laminated pictures of vegetables as props (Ghosn 2013). In both cases, students could have been taught how to use a simple graph to prepare their own nail or stone soup recipes. This would have been important support for foreign-language math classes.

Depending on the proficiency level of the students, other follow-up activities could include changing the verb tense, changing direct quotes to reported speech, changing the ending, or adding something that happened before the story began or adding what happened to the two men or the old man after the end of the story.

Conclusions

First, the above classroom episodes illustrate the flexibility of the story-based language instruction. It can accommodate to different proficiency levels as well as to different teaching styles. Hierarchically oriented teachers would approach the story differently from more egalitarian teachers in more egalitarian cultures. However, in both cases, a good story will motivate children to engage in the lessons. Discourse around stories flows much more naturally than discourse of language practice activities, as we already saw in earlier chapters. Two other Lebanese teachers were observed when they worked on Hutchins's *The Doorbell Rang* but taking very different approaches (Ghosn 2012: 29–45). Second, it is clear from the observations that children in all observed classes were engaged and participated eagerly. The discourse was natural and student output more elaborate than what could be observed around typical language practice activities as seen around language practice sessions.

In summary, primary school English-language instruction based on authentic children's literature is desirable for a number of reasons. First, stories provide an interesting and motivating medium for instruction, as children are avid consumers of story narrative. Second, research conducted since the 1970s clearly indicates that story-based instruction is more effective than traditional skills-based instruction in developing children's vocabulary, reading comprehension, written expression and grammar awareness. Finally, literature-based approach is flexible in that it enables teachers to select the instructional methods best suited to their personal teaching styles and cultural expectations. It also allows for diverse student reactions and reflection, around which plenty of negotiation of meaning, topics and form could be incorporated as children make language errors or resort to their L1.

Recommendations for Practice

Teachers

- If the coursebook you are using does not feature any stories, bring in some stories. Plenty of high-quality children's books can be bought online with one or two dollars, and some can be viewed and listened to online. Only one copy of the story is needed because it can be shared with the whole class as a read-aloud. In order to preserve the integrity of the original stories, they should not be used for language practice exercises. Instead, students can use the story as a template for their own stories, which can then be used for language activities. Children can also generate a class story if the teacher uses a modified Language Experience Approach. First, the teacher prepares a summary of the story they want to elicit from the students. Then they guide students to produce the summary by asking leading questions. The draft can then be revised and used as a template for new stories.
- If the stories in the coursebook are in simple present tense, they can be retold in the past tense, Students can then use this version as a template for new stories.
- It will be important to identify the key vocabulary and structures the teacher wants to focus on. Children do not need to learn *all* the vocabulary and *all* the structures in a given story, only the ones that are part of the class curriculum.
- It will also be important to allocate sufficient time for all phases of the instructional cycle to be completed in order to enable children to internalize the target vocabulary and structures. Having children generate summaries and stories of their own – whether using class-generated summaries or language ladders as templates – will provide ample opportunities for recycling of vocabulary and structures while respecting the integrity of the original story.

13

Teacher Effectiveness and Learner Engagement

'That's the reason they're called lessons,' the Gryphon remarked, 'because they lessen from day to day.'

    Lewis Carroll – *Alice's Adventures in Wonderland*

I have come to a frightening conclusion. I am the decisive element in the classroom. It is my personal approach that creates the climate. It is my daily mood that makes the weather. As a teacher, I possess a tremendous power to make a child's life miserable or joyous. I can be a tool of torture or an instrument of inspiration. I can humiliate or humor, hurt or heal. In all situations it is my response that decides whether a crisis will be escalated or de-escalated, and the child humanized or de-humanized. (Ginott 1972: 13)

Although written half a century ago, the above quote from Ginott's *Teacher & Child* shows powerfully the crucial role teachers play in their students' educational experience and, subsequently in their learning. In this chapter, we will see how different teachers conduct themselves in the classroom in order to help their students move along and how some teacher behaviours may actually hinder their engagement.

Characteristics of Effective Teachers

Teacher effectiveness is argued to be the most important school-related factor on student achievement (Darling-Hammond 2000; Hanushek 2005; Mourshed, Chijioke and Barber 2010). The perception of what defines an 'effective' teacher, however, has undergone many changes over the centuries. The following are just some of the characteristics associated with effective teachers gleaned from different university centres for teaching and learning. The list is not exhaustive and identifies primarily those characteristics that can be observed in the classroom. First, effective teachers have smoothly paced whole-class instruction and remain task-focused, keeping things moving along without undue interruptions. Second, effective teachers transition smoothly from one activity to another, and their students know what is expected and what to do. Effective teachers also have good classroom management strategies and thus face few or no disruptive behaviours from students. In effective teachers' classrooms, students often initiate interactions with the teacher, and the teacher exhibits a non-evaluative stance.

Effective teachers have not only content knowledge but also pedagogical content knowledge (PCK), that is, the knowledge of how best to convey their subject to learners. Human learning specialist Ormrod (2012: 285) further suggests that good teachers 'modify the directions of discussion to accommodate students' comments and questions and they allow their classes to pursue a topic in depth' even if that would deviate from their original plans. Coursework in general pedagogy will be helpful when planning lessons, classroom management and dealing with children's behaviours. Teachers must have also good verbal ability, and language teachers should have good command of the language they teach. However, this does not mean that only native speakers of the target language should be hired to teach it. All around the world, local teachers with good command of English and relevant teaching credentials successfully teach the language to their students. The same is true also about other languages.

Teachers' knowledge of students' L1 is especially important in the beginning levels when students' English is still very limited. This will enable teachers to validate young learners' contributions and recast them into English without any judgement, as we witnessed in many of the classroom episodes. It would be helpful if teachers were also familiar with the culture within which they work, as that will help them adapt unfamiliar activities and content to be more culturally appropriate. If foreign teachers need to be employed, they would perhaps benefit from some cultural awareness training if they were unfamiliar with the local culture.

Most teachers we observed in the previous chapters demonstrated at least some of the attributes of effective teachers. Gloria and Maya are two exemplars of effective teachers, demonstrating all the above skills. Therefore, it is perhaps not surprising that in the reading test, their students outperformed students in less effective teachers' classes. In contrast, Tanya and Rima exhibited highly judgemental stance, frequently correcting errors overtly and asking students to repeat the correct answers. In their case, the mismatch between the communicative approach and teachers' cultural orientation may offer one explanation for their approach. Sarah did not exhibit characteristics associated with effective teachers. On the contrary, her classes were disorganized, if not chaotic at times, and she was not able to keep the lessons on track. It is therefore not surprising that Gloria's and Maya's students outperformed Sarah's students although Sarah's students had been in a total English immersion program for at least six years. It would have been interesting to know how effective students' previous teachers had been. Perhaps the higher scoring children had benefited from more effective teaching in their earlier classes than their lower scoring peers. We do know that Sarah had taught the same students also in grade four.

Teacher Effectiveness and Student Achievement

Educational Research Newsletter & Webinars (2003: n.p.), which reviewed research conducted in different states in the United States reports that effective teachers' influence is quite significant. For example, groups of first graders in Texas had started with similar percentile ranks, but one group attended classes of teachers identified as effective for three consecutive years, with their peers attending less effective teachers' classes. At the end of the three years, the first group had made significant gains, while their peers in less effective teachers' classes had fallen below their initial percentile ranks. The report also cites a Dallas study, which showed a cumulative influence of effective versus ineffective teachers; students in effective teachers' classes for just one year remained 'ahead of their peers in less effective teachers' classes for at least the next few years'. In contrast, ineffective teacher's influence may similarly last up to three years. Another study in Tennessee found students in effective teachers' classes for three consecutive years scoring in ninety-sixth percentile while their counterparts in less effective teachers' classes scored at forty-fourth percentile (Sanders and Rivers 1996). A study in Virginia schools revealed that students of teachers who ranked in the top percentile quartile in effectiveness scored thirty to forty points higher than expected in the Virginia Standards of Learning Assessment in both math and English. In contrast, their peers in classes of teachers who ranked in the bottom quartile scored twenty-four to thirty-two points lower than expected (Stronge, Ward, Tucker and Hindman 2007). For more on the connection between teacher effectiveness and student achievement, see, for example, Strong, Ward and Grant (2011).

Scaffolding Learning

Classroom interactions, as any human interactions, are social events, within which the patterns of initiation, responses and feedback are constructed jointly by all participants, helping establish the classroom atmosphere. In a language classroom, interactions should create opportunities for learning and using the new language. Vygotsky's (1978) sociocultural theory of learning posits that knowledge is mediated and constructed by and through language in social use. He suggested that children's higher-order functions develop from social interactions, which allows children to confront other people's points of view and discover how others respond in various situations. Similarly, Cummins (1984) argues that social interactions are a key to successful language learning. The processes of developing understanding through social interaction also allow the child to gain new information and provide a level of linguistic interaction that adds a verbal level to their understanding (Echevarria and Graves 1998). In many classes, such interactions were very evident while in some classes no such interactions were observed.

Social learning theory recognizes the unique role adults or more capable peers play in learning. It places emphasis on the importance of modelling and the use of language as a means to learning (Berk and Winsler 1995), rejecting the idea that children learn by passively absorbing information from teacher presentation. It postulates that children are actively engaged in processes that move them to construct new understandings and to make sense of their experiences within their own sociocultural contexts.

Central in Vygotsky's sociocultural theory to learning is the 'zone of proximal development' (Vygotsky 1978: 85), or ZPD, which is the theoretical zone, or area, that lies between the child's current unassisted level of functioning and the level of functioning that the child can reach with assistance. Learning happens within the ZPD as 'the child is interacting with people in his environment and in cooperation with his peers' (ibid: 90). More capable others provide assistance, or 'scaffolding', which assures that the child is interacting within his or her ZPD for the particular task and gradually moving from other-regulation to self-regulation. Although Vygotsky's ZPD is an elusive construct, it has been embraced without any question by many of the theorists who criticized Krashen's theory of 'interlanguage+1' (Krashen 1982: 33) as an elusive construct difficult to measure. Yet, Vygotsky might have well accepted Krashen's 'inerlanguage+1' hypothesis much more readily than have the many second language acquisition theorists.

Drawing on Vygotsky's (1978) sociocultural learning theory, Tharp and Gallimore (1991: 3) suggest that, while a variety of classroom strategies can promote learning, dialogue, 'the questioning and sharing of ideas and knowledge that happen in conversation,' is critical for development of thinking skills required for academic second language literacy. The term 'scaffolding' was originally coined in *The Role of Tutoring in Problem Solving* by Wood, Bruner and Ross (1976) and which Bruner (1978: 19) defined as assistance that enables (students) to 'concentrate on the difficult skill [they are] in the process of acquiring'. The social interaction of dialogue provides learners with such scaffolding. Arguably, scaffolding is an ambiguous construct to operationalize, and to know what might count as scaffolding is not straightforward. In order to determine that scaffolding has, in fact, been successful, one must have some evidence of 'the learner successfully accomplishing the task with the teacher's help' or achieving 'some greater level of independent competence as a result of the scaffolding experience' (Maybin et al. 1992: 188).

Within a language classroom, some form of scaffolding can be provided within meaningful interactions and supportive feedback, which can be accomplished through the teacher 'appropriating' (Newman, Griffin and Cole 1989: 62), or incorporating, learners' ideas into their responses or feedback. This will help learners to construct new understandings. Teacher appropriation includes paraphrasing, summarizing and recapping student utterances and strategies similar to negotiation of meaning or topic discussed in Chapter 5. In the 1990s more attention was focused on application of the scaffolding theory, and Hogan and Pressley (1997) identified key elements of scaffolding to consist of teacher modelling of desired behaviours, offering explanations, inviting students to participate and contribute clues, and verifying and clarifying student understandings. According to Krashen and Terrell (1983), the comprehensibility of linguistic input is influenced by the context and any extra linguistic information available, as well as the learner's knowledge of the world, all of which can function as scaffolding from the Vygotskian perspective. Let us examine interactions in the classrooms of Maya and Gloria, whose classes were observed on three different occasions each. It is difficult to tell whether teachers' scaffolding efforts resulted in student learning, as mentioned earlier, but both Maya and Gloria attempted what they considered to constitute scaffolding. In Table 13.1, a student is reading from the coursebook and pronounces 'custom' as 'costume'. Maya is helping students understand the difference between 'costume'

Table 13.1 Scaffolding Vocabulary Learning

S1:	[reads] This costume started
T:	custom
	A custom is a habit. A CUSTOM is a habit. As I told you, mistletoe is used as a Christmas decoration. CUSTOM. COSTUME is different. For example, COSTUME is what you wear. For example, you wear your COSTUME [school uniform] to come to school, or a Halloween COSTUME or whatever. So they are not the same. It's the –e that makes the difference here. OK. So CUSTOM is a habit [sic].
S2:	Miss, on Sunday me and my friend [unintelligible]
T:	What did you DISGUISE yourself as? What were you DRESSED AS?
S2:	Miss, Cleopatra
T:	Wow! It's very [unintelligible] is Egyptian queen. And your friend, did she have a COSTUME?
S2:	Yes, Miss
	[3 exchanges later, the topic continues]
S3:	We went to [name of village] and [name of town].
T:	Uhm, you had your friends with you?
S3:	Yes, Miss. We were ten and Wissam was wearing an Indian, Miss.
T:	A red [sic] Indian?
S3:	No, Miss
T:	From India?
S3:	Yes, red Indian
S4:	Miss, yesterday Ramzy and Wassim we and some friends we were trick-o-treating and we played [unintelligible; giggling]
T:	They were DISGUISED? They were dressed in different COSTUMES?
S4:	Yes, Miss. (Ghosn 2001: 163–4)

and 'custom'. The capitalized texts indicate what can be considered as attempts at scaffolding.

During the episode, which consisted of several exchanges, most of them longer than one IRF sequence, Maya recycled the word 'costume' several times with examples, while maintaining a conversational tone. One cannot really tell from the observation transcripts whether the scaffolding worked, but it seems clear that the teacher made an effort to facilitate students' comprehension of the concepts at hand. Such scaffolding was observed also in Gloria's class, where the episode in Table 13.2 was recorded as the class was working on a summary exercise featuring a story about Paul Revere.

Table 13.2 Scaffolding a Concept

T:	OK. Page 130, 130. OK. If we all look down at the objective. What's the objective?
Ss:	Summarize
T:	Summarize as well. OK. When we say SUMMARIZE, what do we mean here? Elie.
S1:	We change all the paragraph to one idea.
T:	Do we CHANGE it? Changing or putting
S1:	Putting
T:	Putting it in ONE IDEA. What's this idea?
S1:	The main
T:	The MAIN IDEA. It's putting the whole paragraph into a MAIN IDEA, a MAIN IDEA SENTENCE OK. So this is somehow similar to a story. The story we SUMMARIZED here. It's also working on a SUMMARY. [several exchanges later]
T:	Antoine, did you circle B or C?
S2:	C
T:	Oh? OK. [surprised tone] Do you know why? What is the mistake here? [no response from the student]
T:	Let's hear [nods to another student]
S3:	[reads] *Paul Revere learned from an Englishman who happened to be in Boston* [unintelligible]
T:	That's more DETAILS … and what's the MAIN IDEA? Can you give me the main idea? The SUMMARY of the paragraph.
S4:	[reads] *He learned how to replace missing teeth with teeth from ivory, or the teeth from animals.*
T:	It's also the same idea of learning how to replace teeth, but in C you have who taught him this and where, the place. Listen, What I want to do here is this. I'm going to read C, OK. And you have to follow with me. Follow the second paragraph. Follow me while I'm reading. Just look at the second paragraph and notice if it's THE SAME WORDS, word by word, or if THERE'S a CHANGE [reads] *Paul Revere learned from an Englishman who happened to be in Boston how to carve teeth from ivory or use animal's tooth.*
Ss:	The same!
T:	The same. OK. Word by word. And when you SUMMARIZE you have to USE YOUR OWN WORDS. Other than you have some details, a man, an Englishman, Boston. Clear?

(*continued*)

Table 13.2 Continued

S5:	Number 3
T:	What's number 3? Number 3. Ok. When you choose this sentence you write it here, but we are only circling now. So, why is that summary better than the other choices? Lynn.
S6:	Because it is about the main idea.
T:	So, this is why it's NOT USING THE EXACT WORDS. You are not using the exact words here. It gives the MAIN IDEA without using the exact words. (Ghosn 2001: 166–7)

During another observation, Gloria was teaching children the concept of prediction and how to make logical predictions when reading. The brief story was about a school snow closure day, and two children are putting on warm clothes at home. As the children took turns reading parts of the story aloud, their task was to generate predictions about what might happen. Gloria guided her students by asking questions, such as 'What will happen next?' 'Why do you think that?' 'What did you read that shows something about what they were going to do?' 'What would you do if there was no school tomorrow?' Children were led this way to predict that the children in the story would go out and play in the snow. One student suggested they may build a snowman, and, indeed, the last picture shows a glimpse of a snowman in the yard. Students were engaged, and although Gloria took time to clarify unfamiliar vocabulary, she was able to complete her lesson as planned.

Missing a *chef d'orchestre*?

Let us compare the above teacher behaviours and classroom discourse with those observed in Sarah's class in the English immersion school, where students' vocabulary and reading comprehension outcomes were significantly lower than those of their peers in Gloria's and Maya's classes. Comparison of classroom transcripts from the three classes revealed a notable difference in the three teachers' behaviours. Maya and Gloria kept their students on task and spent little time on classroom management or procedural matters, as their students clearly knew what to expect and what was required of them. In contrast, Sarah spent much time on non-lesson-related matters as the following typical episode in her class illustrates:

Episode 13.1

T: Now this is a paragraph [shows slips of paper]. I have taken these headlines and lead sentences from [local English-language daily] Thursday's issue, all right. I've written down the headlines and I've written … what are you doing? Where is your notebook? Ok, I've written the lead sentences but they are jumbled up. Now you have to match them them like we did yesterday in the comprehension exercise. Do you know what to do?

Ss: Yes

T: Do you know what to do? [to a group of students]
[a lot of noise as groups begin to work]

T: [shouting over the noise] make sure you match the lead sentence (xxx)

T: Who's finished? [moves to one of the tables] what's the problem? What's the problem?

S1: Stephen (xxx)

T: Ok, why don't you change your place. It'll be better. You'll be away from him. Change your place.
[after she collects the slips of paper from students, students take out their reading books]

T: Ok, turn to page 355. This story

S: Which page?

T: page 355, 355 [shouting over the noise]. This story, *The Gold Coin*, was, it is written by a Spanish author
[students do not seem to pay attention]

T: [to a boy] Give it to me, please … Who? This is yours? [picks up a pair of scissors]

S: for Ziad

T: Ziad, is this yours? Ok, I leave it where it belongs to
[to another student] Eric, where is the (xxx) that the nurse gave you?

S2: (xxx)

T: But didn't she sign it?

S2: Yes [point to the teacher's desk]

T: In the box? I'll check it. OK, all right. [another student is reading aloud]

Sarah spent much time circling around the room and paying attention to trivial matters. It appeared that the more she digressed into non-lesson-related issues, the more disengaged, and perhaps confused, the students became. Below is another observation excerpt from Sarah's class. Sarah is introducing new vocabulary her students will encounter when reading a new story in their reading anthology, and she has chosen to do it by providing definitions:

Episode 13.2

T: Martin, where's your vocabulary copybooks?
S:1   ((in my bag))
T: Take it out. [writing on the board]
S2:   (xxx)
T: Yes?
S2:   What's the second word?
T: (xxx) let me just write two more words. Then I can answer [writing on the board]
Ss: [copying words from the board]
T: ((come on)) Yasmina, start, please.
S3:   (xxx) [pointing to the board]
T: Yes. Steven, you haven't started yet. Where's your vocabulary copybook?
S5:   I can't find it [rummaging in his book bag]
T: Then use any other copybook you have, please. You (xxx) which I don't know as long as it is (xxx) [a lot of noise in the classroom]
T: Why can't you find the vocabulary copybook? Where is it?
S1:   I find the language (xxx)
      [Teacher circulates in the room, checking copybooks]
T: You didn't underline the date.
S6:   [under her breath to another student] Nice, underline the date.
T: All right. How many words you used?
S3:   three
T: [Continues to walk around the room] The first one is 'stunned'. You haven't started yet, Steven?
S5:   Miss, Steven is doing with his mouth something, a sound, like this, Miss [makes a sound]
T: Turn around. All right, 'stunned'.
S6:   Miss, I didn't finish.
T: 'Stunned' is shock (xxx) then I'll explain them one at a time. 'Ransacked' – searched very thoroughly. 'Urgently' (xx) quick action. 'Shriveled' – shrunk and wrinkled. 'Herbs' – plants used for medicines and seasoning. 'Hoe' – a tool with a wide blade across a stick used to loosen soil. 'Lumbered' – moved in a heavy, clumsy way.
S7:   Is it after 'heavy' comma?

T:	Heavy, yes. Why?
S7:	Miss, because the
T:	Heavy and clumsy, what are they?
S7:	Two nouns
Ss:	Adjectives!
T:	Adjectives. And what do we separate two adjectives with?
Ss:	Comma!
	[Student shows something to the teacher]
T:	A paper for me from your mother. [Walks over to get the paper] Thank you.
S8:	((how))
T:	Shh! All right tell your mother that we haven't done adverbs yet, but on Friday you will know answer of these questions, because we do adjectives starting tomorrow (xxx) adverbs. OK.

The process was very tedious, and one has to question whether in an immersion class, after six years of English, students would have been served better by being guided to use context clues instead. At times, Sarah seemed more concerned about correct dates and underlining of words rather than their meaning. During the remainder of the activity, much time was again spent on students expressing concerns about what to underline, looking for pencils and so on. The bell rang before students ever started reading. The observer was left with the impression that little was accomplished during the lessons. Thus, the teacher approach might have been one of the contributing factors in these students' lower performance in the *TORC-3* described in Chapter 6. Keeping in mind the above-cited research about the influence of ineffective teachers, it is not far-fetched to predict Sarah's students falling further behind as they move to grades six and seven, even if they would be lucky to have more effective teachers.

With few exceptions, the observed teachers met many of the criteria of effective teachers outlined at the beginning of the chapter, but Sarah's approach can best be described as *laissez-faire*. Although she did not directly criticize the students or outright reject their contributions, she clearly was not 'with-it'. Naturally, all teachers can have bad days once in a while, but when an observer is known to visit the class and record it, most teachers would try to showcase the best they can do. Knowing the long-term impact of an ineffective teacher on student achievement, one can only hope that the teacher taking over Sarah's students the following year would be very effective. In contrast, one can assume that even if some of the other teachers' students were passed on to a less effective teacher, their effectiveness would carry over to the following year.

Conclusion

Clearly, one cannot underestimate the influence a teacher has in student learning. Instructional materials, no matter how sophisticated or advanced, cannot replace an effective teacher. An effective teacher knows how best to make use of the materials available in order to motivate and engage their students and promote learning. The two teachers whose students scored the highest in vocabulary and reading comprehension were observed to engage their students and maintained a smooth pace while giving students plenty of opportunities to explore the language. As a matter of fact, these teachers were also the ones who asked more referential and cognitively demanding questions than their peers in the other four schools described in Chapter 3. Most of the teachers who worked with stories demonstrated the ability to keep the lesson moving along while also allowing student questions and initiations. Their feedback to students was also non-judgemental.

Recommendations for Practice

Teachers

- Good classroom management skills are required for successful teaching. There are plenty of books and articles on the subject. One free resource is *Reach a Child – Teach a Child* (Ghosn 2013) downloadable from Researchgate.com
- Try to provide scaffolding through repetitions and questioning as Maya and Gloria demonstrated.
- When using stories in instruction, rather than begin with the often tedious vocabulary definitions, guide students to use titles, illustrations and the like to make predictions about the story. Teach the use of context clues to figure out meanings of new vocabulary. As students read, they will either get confirmation for their predictions or will need to revise their understanding.

Materials Developers

- It might be worth considering to include some classroom management tips in the teachers' guides, as not all TEYL and TEVYL teachers have extensive pedagogical training in classroom management and positive discipline.

Conclusion

And certainly, the glass was *beginning to melt away.*
                                  Lewis Carroll – *Through the Looking Glass*

To understand the dynamics and learning outcomes in a young language learner classroom, it is helpful to examine them from a systems perspective. The language classroom is a complex system with many interacting variables and is embedded within wider systems that influence classroom dynamics and the subsequent learner motivation, engagement and achievement. Within the classroom system, prevailing cultural norms, instructional materials, and teacher questions and effectiveness all interact with the learners to orchestrate the discourse which, in turn, plays a role in determining the learning outcomes. Instructional materials can either hinder or facilitate the factors influencing language learning, and interesting children's stories with their narrative structure promote not only cognitive development but also vocabulary and reading comprehension, provide models for children's writing, activate academic language functions, and foster development of literate language. In addition, exposure to rich, natural language characterizing good children's stories may help mitigate negative L1 transfer. Perhaps most importantly, story-based instruction is also flexible in that it adapts easily to different cultural contexts and teaching styles. The following sections attempt to tie the various factors together.

Teacher – Materials – Culture Triangle?

Teachers' cultural background may determine to some extent the approaches they use to the instructional materials they have available. Hierarchically oriented teachers adhere more closely to the coursebook options and tend to reject students' own contributions, even if those contributions are valid. More egalitarian teachers may be comfortable taking on a more observer role when students are to practice dialogues. In contrast, story narratives, even when simplified, may encourage some hierarchically oriented teachers to engage students in more genuine discourse than when they work with language practice activities and prepared dialogues. For example, Zainab in Chapter 12 demonstrated a fairly hierarchical stance, but when given a story, she was able to engage her students well without relinquishing her authority. After all, we are *Homo narrans*, so stories attract all ages across cultures.

Lesson content can also be problematic from a cultural perspective. The communicatively oriented coursebooks authored in countries where egalitarian culture is predominant (e.g. the United States, UK and Australia) are marketed widely internationally. The content of the dialogue practice activities in these courses often reflect the source country concepts and topics. For example, the US-produced books often feature either typical Anglo-American concepts or concepts familiar to immigrant children from Asia and Latin America. Apparently, the number of Arab immigrant children in American schools is not big enough to merit inclusion of content familiar to these children. When topics and concepts in the language activities are unfamiliar to young learners (sometimes even for their teachers) the result is an artificial, drill-like dialogue practice with teachers' focus firmly on the form.

Examination of teachers' questioning and feedback strategies suggest that the way given materials were used may have influenced the outcomes, negatively in some cases but positively in others. Questions in the ESL course teachers' guides are mostly at lower cognitive level, limiting student output while questions suggested in teachers' guides of literature-based coursebook include questions at a variety of cognitive levels and generate more elaborate student output. However, when teachers work with stories (or other content interesting to learners), they tend to ask more higher-order questions than they do during the communicative language practice lessons. Even when the teacher's guide presented limited questions, some teachers deviated from the teacher's guide when they worked with simplified stories, asking a variety of questions, including open, data processing questions.

Teacher feedback to student output has a significant effect on the subsequent discourse. Hierarchical teachers' explicit error correction or other forms of rejecting feedback does not encourage further student output, with some students completely disengaging from the lesson. Egalitarian teachers engage in negotiation of meaning and topic and encourage student questions, which promotes further output from students. In all observed classes where teachers were using stories, student engagement was obvious, and the discourse was much more natural than during language practice activities. When working with dialogue practice and other communicative activities, egalitarian teachers are comfortable taking an observer or facilitator role and engage their students in the lessons the way intended by the coursebook authors, as we saw, for example, in Lebanese Canadian Joanna's class.

Discourse around stories as well as novel non-fiction topics is more interactive and genuine, and students often initiate discourse by asking clarifying questions, offering opinions and sharing personal narratives. Students may also initiate questions during explicit instruction of language usage that is an integral part of the story-based reading programs, and much negotiation of topic, meaning and form was observed.

One more factor stood out in the observations and test data: teacher effectiveness. In the case of the three literature-based classes, students in full English immersion program performed less well in general and subject-specific vocabulary and reading comprehension than their peers in the other two classes. Yet all three classes used the same reading anthology series for English instruction. Observation data show that the immersion class teacher demonstrated highly ineffective classroom management strategies, focusing often on trivial, non-lesson related issues than the lesson itself. Students were not engaged and appeared confused and distracted by peer behaviours. Their low performance was, therefore, not surprising, especially since this teacher had also taught the same group of students in grade four, and research shows long-term influence of ineffective teaching. In contrast, her two colleagues kept their students firmly on task, even while allowing them to ask questions and relate personal experiences. Both were clearly in charge and were able to complete their lesson plans. Several additional observations in different classes show that children are highly motivated by stories and are curious about unfamiliar content, as long as they are able to remain in their own persona and the teacher allows them to ask questions and initiate interactions.

Instructional Materials and Learner Achievement

The data suggest that story-based, reading-focused instruction results in better language learning outcomes over time than communicatively focused instruction. Students in literature-based programs and story-based interventions scored higher in general and subject-specific vocabulary and reading comprehension. There was also significant difference in the quality of narratives, grammar use and literate language features in the writing of children in the literature-based classes and story-based intervention. Even a relatively short intervention of story-based work can have a positive influence, and stories with natural, narrative language may also provide students with models for their own writing. Story narratives seem to be particularly beneficial for students who must learn other school subjects in English as there is an established link between narrative ability, cognitive development and academic achievement. The data further suggest that story-based instruction may mitigate negative L1 transfer and possibly help students' spelling development. However, more research is needed on this.

Interesting picture books can be used to introduce young learners to some basic math and science concepts, as well as concepts related to other school subjects. Small-group instruction with books on children's instructional level, coupled with explicit instruction on reading strategies, enables children of different reading levels to make progress at their own pace. Such small-group instruction, however, is difficult, if not impossible, in classrooms of thirty to forty children and no assistant teachers.

One example for the different outcomes can be found in the discourse that instructional materials generate. As mentioned, discourse around stories is more interactive and genuine than discourse during language practice activities characteristic of communicatively oriented young learner courses. Legutke, Thomas and Candlin (1991: 7) have wondered whether it is 'possible to turn L2 classrooms into whole-person events, where body and soul, intellect and feeling, head, hand and heart converge in action'. Observations indicate that this is possible using children's literature, apparently even when the story narratives are simplified. When decades-long research on story-based instruction and the importance of negotiated interactions is taken together with the earlier cited classroom episodes, there is reason to believe that one key to the positive influence of stories may well be found in the interactions that stories can generate. Talking about stories provides a meaningful and personally relevant context to interaction in the new language. Carefully selected readings can maintain motivation while providing an appropriate level of challenge, particularly if the teacher gives scaffolding feedback and keeps the focus on meaning. Form errors can be addressed by teachers recasting them into correct English in a non-judgemental way and extending the discourse to provide more contextualized modelling. Story discussions generate negotiation not only of form but also of meaning and topic. In contrast, the prepared dialogues and other language practice activities typical of young learner courses generate artificial discourse, with students repeating words and phrases from the book even when topics and concepts in the dialogues are familiar to them. The more unfamiliar the topics are, the more artificial and drill-like the discourse becomes. During these language practice activities, hierarchically oriented teachers' focus remains firmly on the form, whereas during story lessons, teachers focused more on meaning. This is not to say that accuracy need not be addressed; the question is more about the approach. In the young learner classroom, story-based instruction is flexible, allowing teachers to select the approaches that are aligned with prevailing cultural norms and their own preferred teaching strategies.

Considering Horowitz's (1990) resilient versus vulnerable children theory, one can assume that frequent and overt corrections and other rejecting feedback by the teacher may influence shy children and those with low self-esteem more negatively than their more resilient, outgoing and self-confident peers. However, conclusions about this cannot be drawn here since no data were collected about children's dispositions or their state of mind during the lessons. However, viewing of the transcripts suggests that the teacher response to student questions and personal contributions played a role in shaping the classroom discourse.

Beyond the Information Given

As interesting as the above findings are, they do not, however, take into consideration many other factors entangled in the complex web of classroom system. For example, we have no information about the student language aptitude, motivation to learn English or about the level of support they received at home for schoolwork, or how much English they were exposed to outside school. It is possible that the highest scoring children not only had effective teachers but may have had additional support at home. In contrast, the lowest scoring children may have been in less effective teachers' classes and received less support at home.

Teachers do not operate in a vacuum but are in a reciprocal relationship not only with their students but also with variables outside the classroom, such as colleagues, administrators and their own families. They are also influenced by level of administrative support, resources, level of autonomy and job satisfaction, for example. All these are influenced by wider sociocultural factors. As discussed earlier, cultures differ in terms of how interpersonal relations are perceived, and what is considered appropriate and what is not in different contexts. Although the

Lebanese culture is in a flux, with exposure to many cultures having introduced new values and norms, especially among the younger generations, the culture is still quite hierarchical.

World Bank Group report points out that in MENA region, political, economic and social factors, while emanating from outside the educational system, 'interact with and shape educational system and its outcomes' creating tensions between tradition and modernity; skills and credentials; discipline and inquiry; and central and autonomy (2019: x). Some of these tensions may be at play in what was observed in the classrooms. Some principals, who espouse modern, non-traditional approaches may choose to adopt non-traditional textbooks for language teaching, such as books intended for native English-speaking children. They may also involve teachers in the materials selection and give them more autonomy in terms of how to put the materials to use. Other principals may favour more traditional, top-down approaches to administration and give teachers little or no autonomy in materials selection and use. For example, Rima, Tanya and Houda reported not having any say in the adoption of the coursebooks and were expected to cover the whole book, regardless of how feasible it may have been. Gloria and Maya had participated in the coursebook selection, Dima was able to carry out a months-long action research project in her class, and Betty and Nisreen were able to select stories they believed were interesting to children while also introducing useful concepts. When Ballan (2005) explored two kindergarten teachers' beliefs and practice about early literacy instruction of ESL learners, she discovered that both teachers shared similar philosophies, but only one of them was able to implement her philosophy while the other was constrained by both school policy on literacy and lack of resources. The discipline versus inquiry tension can be seen in the classes of Rima, Tanya and Houda; students should follow the textbook and not offer their own ideas or raise questions.

Teachers were not interviewed or surveyed about their salaries, job satisfaction or their personal lives. So, it is entirely possible that some of the teachers, including Sarah, may have been less satisfied with their job and level of autonomy than others, which may have influenced their classroom effectiveness. Similarly, we have no information about teachers' personal lives and what stressors may have influenced their classroom behaviours.

When all the chapters are taken together, a picture emerges that illustrates the complex, reciprocal interwoven web of culture, expectations set by teaching materials, teacher strategies, classroom discourse, and student engagement and achievement. The available data weave an incomplete web, with many strands missing. However, we can research only a few variables at a time because it will be difficult, possibly unethical, or even impossible, to design studies that would take into account all the above-mentioned factors possibly involved in children's language learning. For example, we cannot knowingly expose children to ineffective teaching but can study the effects only retrospectively. Similarly, we cannot subject some children to frequent rejecting feedback to compare their achievement to children who received less rejecting feedback. Designing comparative studies that would consider learner achievement, instructional materials, teacher effectiveness, level of autonomy and the role of culture in all of this would be tedious at best. However, the findings indicate some possible explanations for learner achievement. Further studies with larger groups and different settings and added variables are needed to shed more light on why some children in the MENA region fail to develop adequate English-language skills despite years of study.

Pedagogical Implications

While young learner courses often begin with explicit language practice and gradually move to literacy, the reverse may, in fact, be a desirable alternative. Although many might argue that a structured syllabus is more appropriate for beginning learners, it is not necessarily so. A young learner syllabus can be built around amusing stories with limited vocabulary and structures and plenty of repetitious refrains. Repeated shared readings and follow-up activities, such as dialogues drawn from the stories and vocabulary games, will provide ample practice for target vocabulary and structures. As children's literacy develops, longer stories can be gradually added with a variety of follow-up activities, both oral and written. If children are given a choice in such activities, the activities can also be meaningful and relevant to them. First language research shows that native English-speaking children who are exposed to extensive story experiences perform better not only in language but also in abstract thinking. This is an important point particularly where young learners must study some school subjects in the new language.

In hierarchical cultures, language instruction based on illustrated children's books and other interesting content may be more appropriate than the communicatively oriented coursebooks. When working with stories, teachers can remain in their culturally expected roles, regardless of the cultural context. Children can remain in their own *persona* when talking about stories and role-playing, unlike when they are expected to dialogue about unfamiliar topics. Stories that feature culturally unfamiliar content will arouse children's natural curiosity, prompting them to ask questions about the new and unfamiliar things, which will not only generate genuine discourse but will also provide opportunities for culture learning. Dialogues, role-play and other language practice activities can be drawn from the stories. The activities will then be meaningful as the topics are now familiar for children.

Notes

Chapter 5

1 For a detailed review, see Ghosn (2001).

Chapter 7

1 For detailed description of these studies, see Ghosn (2013).

Chapter 8

1 More sophisticated exercises in thinking can be found in *Critical Thinking Activities to Improve Writing Skills* series from Critical Thinking Press & Software. www.criticalthinking.com.

References

Abushihab, I., El-Omari, A. H., and Tobat, M. (2011), 'An Analysis of Written Grammatical Errors of Arab Learners of English as a Foreign Language at Alzaytoonah Private University of Jordan', *European Journal of Social Sciences*, 20 (4): 543–52.

Al-Ahdal, A., and Asmawi, A. (2021), 'Spatial and Temporal Prepositions: CLT for Arab English Learners', *Journal of Language and Linguistics Studies*, 17 (4): 2286–96.

Al-Bakri, S. (2013), 'Problematizing English Medium Instruction in Oman', *International Journal of Bilingual & Multilingual Teachers of English*, 1 (2): 55–69.

Al-Bayati, W. A. (2013), 'Errors Made by Iraqi EFL Undergraduates in the Use of Prepositions', *Bulletin of the Transilvania University of Brasov Series IV: Philology and Cultural Studies*.

Al-Busaidi, S., and Al-Saqqaf, A. H. (2015), 'English Spelling Errors Made by Arabic-Speaking Students', *English Language Teaching*, 8 (7): 181–99.

Alenazi, O. S. (2018), 'Spelling Difficulties Faced by Arab Learners of English as a Foreign Language', *Arab World English Journal*, 9 (2): 118–26.

Ali, N. (2007), 'Some Linguistic Problems Facing Arab Learners of English'. Available online: http://www.iasj.net/iasj?func=fulltext&aId=33586 (accessed 25 February 2021).

Alja'arat, S. M. S., and Hasan, S. H. (2017, Aug.), 'The Influence of Mother Tongue on Learning English Language by Arab Learners', *International Journal of Scientific and Research Publications*, 7 (8): 31–7.

Al-Jarf, R. (2010), 'Spelling Error Corpora in EFL', *Sino-English Teaching*, 7 (1): 6–15.

Alkhudiry, R. I., and Al-Ajdal, A. A. (2020), 'Analyzing EFL Discourse of Saudi EFL Learners: Identifying Mother Tongue Interference', *Asian ESP Journal* 16 (2.1): 89–109.

Allwright, D. (1984), 'The Importance of Interaction in Classroom Language Learning', *Applied Linguistics*, 5 (2): 156–71.

Almarzouki, A. (2015), 'Toward Professionalizing the Teaching in the UAE: An Investigation of Emirati Public Secondary School Teachers' Understanding of Their Profession in Dubai', doctoral dissertation, The British University in Dubai.

Alsaawi, A. (2015), 'Spelling Errors Made by Arab Learners of English', *International Journal of Linguistics*, 7 (5): 55–67.

Al-Shujairi, Y. B. J., and Tan, H. (2017), 'Grammar Errors in the Writing of Iraqi English Language Learners', *International Journal of Education & Literacy Studies*, 5 (4): 122–30.

Anstrom, K. (1997), 'Academic Achievement for Secondary Language Minority Students: Standards, Measures and Promising Practices', National Clearinghouse for Bilingual Education. Available online: http://www.files.ericed.gov/fulltext/ED417 596.pdf (accessed 11 May 2022).

Araujo, L. (2002), 'The Literacy Development of Kindergarten English-Language Learners'. *Journal of Research in Childhood Education*, 16 (2): 232–47.

Armstrong, J. O., and Armbruster, B. B. (1991), *Making Frames for Learning from Informational Texts*. Technical report No. 542, University of Illinois at Urbana-Champaign. Available online: http://.files.ericed.gov/fulltext/ED335650.pdf (accessed 20 June 2021).

Arnold, W., and Rixon, S. (2008), 'Materials for Teaching English to Young Learners', in B. Tomlinson (ed.), *English Language Learning Materials: A Critical Review*, 38–58, London: Continuum.

August, D. (2003), *Supporting the Development of English Literacy in English Language Learners: Key Issues and Promising Practices*, Baltimore, MD: Center for Research on the Education of Students Placed at Risk.

August, D., and Hakuta, K. (1997), *Improving Schooling for Minority Children*, Washington, DC: National Academy Press.

Bacha, N., Ghosn, I.-K., and McBeath, N. (2008), 'The Textbook, the Teacher and the Learner: A Middle East Perspective', in B. Tomlinson (ed.), *English Language Learning Materials. A Critical Review*, 281–99, London: Continuum.

Ballan, R. (2005), 'Early Literacy: Two Kindergarten Teachers' Beliefs and Practices', MA dissertation, School of Arts and Sciences, Lebanese American University, Beirut.

Barnes, D., Britton, J., and Rosen, H. (1969), *Language, the Learner and the School*, Harmondsworth: Penguin.

Bassnett, S., and Grundy, P. (1993), *Language through Literature: Creative Language Teaching through Literature*, Harlow, Essex: Longman.

Beach, L. R., Bissell, B. L., and Wise, J. N. (2016), *A New Theory of Mind: The Theory of Narrative Thought*, Newcastle upon Tyne: Cambridge Scholars.

Bear, D. R., and Templeton, S. (1998), 'Explorations in Developmental Spelling: Foundations for Learning and Teaching Phonics, Spelling and Vocabulary', *Reading Teacher*, 52 (3): 222–42.

Bearne, E. (ed.) (1995), 'Introduction. Greater Expectations: Reflections on Difference. Greater Expectations', in *Greater Expectation. Children Reading and Writing*, 2–10, London: Cassell.

Bebout, L. (1985), 'An Error Analysis of Misspellings Made by Learners of English as a First and as a Second Language', *Journal of Psycholinguistic Research*, 14 (6): 569–93.

Belhiah, H., and Elhami, M. (2015), 'English as a Medium of Instruction in the Gulf: When Students and Teachers Speak', *Language Policy*, 14: 3–23.

Benson, S. (2009), 'Understanding Literate Language: Developmental and Clinical Issues', *Contemporary Issues in Communication Science and Disorders: CICSD*, 36: 174–8.

Bergeron, B. S., and Wolff, M. B. (2002), *Teaching Reading Strategies in the Primary Grades*, New York: Scholastic Professional Books.

Berk, L. E., and Winsler, A. (1995), *Scaffolding Children's Learning: Vygotsky and Early Childhood Education*, Washington, DC: National Association for the Education of Young Children.

Berthoff, A. E. (1981), *The Making of Meaning: Metaphors, Models and maxims for Writing Teachers*, Montclair, NJ: Boynton/Cook.

Bettleheim, B. (1986), *The Uses of Enchantment. The Meaning and Importance of Fairy Tales*, New York: Vintage Books.

Bishop, D., and Edmundson, A. (1987), 'Language Impaired Four-Year-Olds: Distinguishing Transient from Persistent Impairment', *Journal of Speech and Hearing Disorders*, 52: 156–73.

Bissex, G. (1980), *GNYSat WRK: A Child Learns to Write and Read*, Cambridge, MA: Harvard University Press.

Boud, D. (2002), 'Sustainable Assessment: Rethinking Assessment for the Learning Society', *Studies in Continuing Education*, 22 (2): 151–67.

Bowen, H. (2011), 'Spelling It Out! Accounting for Spelling Difficulties for Arabic Learners of English', ACADEMIA. Available online: http://www.d1wqtxts1xle7.doudfront.net/54783898/Spelling-it-out-Accounting-for-Spelling-Difficulties-for-Arabic-Learners-of-English (accessed 4 April 2021).

Brock, C. A. (1986), 'The Effects of Referential Question on ESL Classroom Discourse', *TESOL Quarterly*, 20 (1), 47–59.

Bronfenbrenner, Y. (1979), *The Ecology of Human Development*, Cambridge, MA: Harvard University Press.

Brookfield, S. D. (2005), 'Learning to Think Critically in Adult Life', in S. D. Brookfield and S. B. Merriam (eds), *Critical Thinking in Adult Education*, 41–52, Hoboken, NJ: Wiley.

Brown, G., and Wragg, E. C. (1993), *Questioning*, London: Routledge.

Brown, V. L., Hammill, D. H., and Wiederholt, J. L. (1995), *TORC-3 Test of Reading Comprehension*, 3rd ed., Austin, TX: Pro-ed.

Bruner, J. (1978), 'The Role of Dialogue in Language Acquisition', in A. Sinclair, R. Jarvella and W. J. M. Levelt (eds), *The Child's Conception of Language*, 241–56, New York: Springer-Verlag.

Bruner, J. (1986), *Actual Minds, Possible Worlds*, Cambridge, MA: Harvard University Press.

Butzow, C., and Butzow, J. (2000), *Science through Children's Literature. An Integrated Approach*, 2nd ed., Englewood, CO: Teacher Ideas Press.

Cameron, L. (2001), *Teaching Languages to Young Learners*, Cambridge: Cambridge University Press.

Cameron, L., Moon, J., and Bygate, M. (1996), 'Language Development of Bilingual Pupils in the Mainstream: How Do Pupils and Teachers Use Language?', *Language and Education*, 10 (4): 221–35.

Cant, A., and Charrington, M. (2014), *MacMillan Next Move 2*, London: Macmillan.

Carroll, S., and Swain, M. (1993), 'Explicit and Implicit Negative Feedback: An Empirical Study of the Learning of Linguistic Generalizations', *Studies in Second Language Acquisition*, 15: 357–86.

Carter, R., and McRae, J. (2002), 'Reading Language: A Fifth Skill', *IATEFL Issues*, 165: 10.

Castles, A., Rastle, K., and Nation, K. (2018), 'Ending the Reading Wars: Reading Acquisition from Novice to Expert', *Psychological Science in the Public Interest*, 19 (1): 5–51.

Chaaya, D. (2006), 'How Young English Language Learners Experience Reading Instruction in a Mixed Reading Ability Classroom. Implementing the Guided Reading Approach', MA thesis, Lebanese American University, Beirut.

Chaaya, D., and Ghosn, I.-K. (2010), 'Supporting Young Second Language Learners' Reading through Guided Reading and Strategy Instruction in a Second Grade Classroom in Lebanon', *Educational Research and Reviews*, 5 (6): 329–37.

Chambers, A. (1985), 'The Child's Changing Story', *Signal*, 40: 59.

Chaudron, C. (1988), *Second Language Classrooms*, Cambridge: Cambridge University Press.

Chen, Su-Yen (2007), 'Extracurricular Reading Habits and Reading Interests of College Students in Taiwan: Findings from Two National Surveys', *Journal of Adolescence & Adult Literacy*, 50 (8): 642–55.

Chiappe, P., Siegel, L. S., and Wade-Woolley, L. (2002), 'Linguistic Diversity and the Development of Reading Skills: A Longitudinal Study', *Scientific Studies of Reading*, 6 (4): 369–400. Available online: https://doi.org/10.1207/S1532799XSSR0604_04 (accessed 12 February 2019).

Clay, M. (1991), *Becoming Literate: The Construction of Inner Control*, Portsmouth, NH: Heinemann.

Cline, B. (2021), 'Asking Effective Questions', Chicago Center for Teaching and Learning. Available online: https://teaching.uchicago.edu/resources/teaching-strategies/asking-effective-questions/ (accessed 10 January 2018).

Collier, V. (1995), *Acquiring a Second Language for School*, Washington, DC: National Clearinghouse for Bilingual Education, ERIC ED 394 301.

Collins International Primary Science SB3 (2016). Glasgow: Collins Learning.

Cook, V. (2001), 'Knowledge of Writing', *International Review of Applied Linguistics*, 39: 1–18.

Cook, V. J. (1997), 'L2 Users and English Spelling', *Journal of Multilingual and Multicultural Development*, 18 (6): 474–88.

Cullinan, B. E., Farr, R. G., Hammond, W. D., Roser, N. L., and Strickland, D. S. (1989), *The HBJ Reading Program, Laureate Edition*. Orlando, FL: Harcourt Brace Jovanovich.

Cummins, J. (1984), *Bilingualism and Special Education: Issues in Assessment and Pedagogy*, Bristol: Multilingual Matters.

Damen, L. (1987), *Culture Learning: The Fifth Dimension in the Language Classroom*, Cambridge: Cambridge University Press.

Darling-Hammond, L. (2000), 'Teacher Quality and Student Achievement: A Review of State Policy Evidence', *Education Policy Archives*, 8 (1): 1–44.

Davidson, A. J., Walton, M. D., Kansal, B., and Cohen, R. (2017), Narrative Skills Predict Peer Adjustment across Elementary School Years, *Social Development*, 26 (4): 891–906.

DeFord, D. (1981), 'Literacy: Reading, Writing and Other Essentials', *Language Arts*, 58: 652–8.

Dégh, L. (1994), *American Folklore and the Mass Media*, Bloomington: Indiana University Press.

deVilliers, J. G., and deVillliers, P. (2000), 'Linguistic Determinism and Understanding of False Beliefs', in P. Mitchell and K. J. Riggs (eds), *Children's Reasoning and the Mind*, 191–228, Hove, UK: Psychology Press/Taylor & Francis.

Diallo, I. (2014), 'Emirati Students Encounter Western Teachers; Tensions and Identity Resistance', *Learning and Higher Education: Gulf Perspectives*, 11 (2): 46–59.

Dickinson, D., and McCabe, A. (1991), 'The Acquisition and Development of Language: A Social Interactionist Account of Language and Literacy Development', in J. F. Kavanagh (ed.), *The Language Continuum: From Infancy to Literacy*, Communicating by Language 13, 1–40, Parkton, MD: York Press.

Dickinson, P. (2010), *Evaluating and Adapting Materials for Young Learners*, Center for Educational Studies, University of Birmingham, United Kingdom.

Dietz-Itza, E., Martinez, V., Pérez, V., and Fernández-Urquiza, M. (2018), 'Explicit Oral Narrative Intervention for Students with Williams Syndrome', *Frontiers in Psychology*, 8, Article 2337.

Dressel, J. H. (1990), 'The Effects of Listening and Discussing Different Qualities of Children's Literature on the Narrative Writing of 5th Graders', *Research in Teaching of English*, 24: 397–414.

Echevarria, J., and Graves, M. (1998), *Sheltered Content Instruction: Teaching English Language Learners with Diverse Abilities*, Needham Heights, MA: Allyn & Bacon.

Edelsky, C. (1982), 'Writing in a Bilingual Program: The Relation of L1 and L2 Texts', *TESOL Quarterly*, 16 (2): 211–28.

Educational Research Newsletter & Webinars (2003), 'Effective Teachers Are the Most Important Factor Contributing to Student Achievement', *Educational Research Newsletter & Webinars*, 16 (6): n.p. Available online: https://www.ernweb.com/educational-research-articles/effective-teachers-are-the-most-important-factor-contributing-to-student-achievement/ (accessed 23 August 2021).

Eisele, B., Eisele Yang, C., York Hanlon, R., and Hanlon, S. M. (2019), *Hip, Hip, Hooray!*, London: Pearson.

Elley, W. (1997), *In Praise of Incidental Learning: Lessons from Some Empirical Findings on Language Acquisition*, Report Series 4.9. Available online: http://www.files.ericed.gov/?id=412563 (accessed 5 December 2021).

Ellis, R. (1994), *Understanding Second Language Acquisition*, Oxford: Oxford University Press.

Emerging Trends and Contemporary Issues in Language Learning: The EFL Context (2020), Available online: https://www.mec.edu.om/tesol2020/ (accessed 5 January 2021).

Enever, J. (ed.) (2011), *ELLiE. Early Language Learning in Europe*, London: British Council.

Erickson, F., and Mohatt, G. (1977), *The Social Organization of Participation Structures in Two Classrooms of Indian Students*, Ottawa, ON: Department of Indian Affairs and Northern Development, ERIC No. ED192935.

Escott, C. (1995), 'Bridging the Gap: Making Links between Children's Reading and Writing', in E. Bearne (ed.), *Greater Expectations. Children Reading and Writing*, 18–42, London: Cassell.

Essberger, J. (2000), 'English Prepositions List', *An English Club.com eBook*, Available online: www.englishclub.com (accessed 12 February 2019).

Exton, G., and O'Rourke, P. (1993), 'KAL' and 'Real' Books/Reading Schemes', *Literacy*, 27 (2): 27–9.

Facione, P. A. (2004), *Critical Thinking: What It Is and Why It Counts*, Millbrae, CA: Insight Assessment.

Faltis, C., and Hudelson, S. J. (1998), *Bilingual Education in Elementary and Secondary School Communities: Toward Understanding and Caring*, Boston, MA: Allyn & Bacon.

Farahian, M., and Rezaee, M. (2012), 'A Case Study of an EFL Teacher's Types of Questions: An Investigation into Classroom Interaction', *Procedia-Social and Behavioral Sciences*, 47: 161–87.

Fazio, B. B., Naremore, R. C., and Connell, P. J. (1996), 'Tracking Children from Poverty at Risk for Specific Language Impairment: A 3-Year Longitudinal Study', *Journal of Speech and Hearing Research*, 39 (3): 611–24.

Fountas, I. C., and Pinnell, G. S. (2002), *Leveled Books for Readers. Grades 3–6*, Portsmouth, NH: Heinemann.

Friedman, E. (1997), 'What Is the Math Moral of the Story?', *Childhood Education*, 74 (1): 33–5.

Gallagher, J. (1965), 'Expressive Thought by Gifted Children in the Classroom', *Elementary English*, 42 (5): 559–68.

Gallick, J. (1999), 'Do They Read for Pleasure? Recreational Reading Habits of College Students', *Journal of Adolescent & Adult Literacy*, 42: 480–8.

Garcia, A. (2020), 'A New Era for Bilingual Education in California', *Phi Delta Kappan*, cappanonline.org. Available online: https://kappanonline.org/a-new-era-for-bilingual- education-in-california/ (accessed 5 January 2022).

Garvie, E. (1990), *Story as Vehicle*, Clevedon: Multilingual Matters.

Gentry, J. R. (1982), 'An Analysis of Developmental Spelling in GNYS at WRK', *Reading Teacher*, 36: 192–200.

Ghaleb, M., Ghannage, R., Abu Khalil, Souky Rafeh, N., and Yakzan, J. (1998–2000), *Let's Learn Together 1, 2, 3*, Beirut: CERD.

Ghosn, I.-K. (1997), 'ESL with Children's Literature: The Way Whole Language Worked in One Kindergarten Class', *English Teaching FORUM*, 35 (3): 14–20.

Ghosn, I.-K. (2001), 'Teachers and Students Interacting Around the Textbook: An Exploratory Study of Children Developing Academic Second Language Literacy in Primary School English Language Classes in Lebanon', PhD thesis, University of Leicester School of Education. UMI Dissertation Service No. 3049590.

Ghosn, I.-K. (2002), 'Four Good Reasons to Use Literature in Primary School ELT', *ELT Journal*, 56 (2): 172–9.

Ghosn, I.-K. (2003a), 'What Is the Use of a Book without Stories or Conversation? Making a Case for Story-Based Instruction', *Folio*, 7 (1/2): 9–13.

Ghosn, I.-K. (2003b), 'Socially Responsible Language Teaching Using Literature', *The Language Teacher*, 27 (3): 15–20. The Japan Association for Language Teaching.

Ghosn, I.-K. (2004), 'Story as Culturally Appropriate Content and Social Context', *Language, Culture and Curriculum*, 17 (2): 109–26.

Ghosn, I.-K. (2006), 'Young Learners Developing Foreign Language Literacy'. Paper presented at the 2016 IATEFL Conference, Harrogate, UK, 8–12 April 2006.

Ghosn, I.-K. (2007), 'Output Like Input: Influence of Children's Literature on Young L2 Learners' Written Expression', in B. Tomlinson (ed.), *Language Acquisition and Development. Studies of Learners of First and Other Languages*, 171–86, London: Continuum.

Ghosn, I.-K. (2012), 'Storybrigde to Second Language: A Tale of Two Teachers', in R. Al-Mahrooqi and A. Roscoe (eds), *Teaching Literature in the EFL Context: New Perspectives*, 29–45, Oman: Sultan Qabous University Press.

Ghosn, I.-K. (2013), *Storybridge to Second Language Literacy. The Theory, Research and Practice of Teaching English with Children's Literature*, Charlotte, NC: Information Age.

Ghosn, I.-K. (2017), 'They Do Talk – When There's Something Worth Talking About', The Curious Case of Language Class Discourse', in H. Masuhara, F. Mishan and B. Tomlinson (eds), *Practice and Theory for Materials Development in L2 Learning*, 211–29, Newcastle upon Tyne: Cambridge Scholars.

Gianelli, M. (1991), 'Thematic Units: Creating an Environment for Learning', *TESOL Journal*, 1 (1): 13–15.

Ginott, H. (1972), *Teacher & Child*, London: Macmillan.

Goforth, F. (1998), *Literature & the Learner*, Belmont, CA: Wadsworth.

Goodman, K. (1987), *Language and Thinking in School*, New York: Richard C. Owen.

Graves, D. (1983), *Writing: Teachers and Children at Work*, Portsmouth, NH: Heinemann.

Greenhalg, K. S., and Strong, C. J. (2001), 'Literate Language Features in Spoken Narratives of Children with Typical Language and Children with Language Impairments', *Language, Speech and Hearing Services in Schools*, 32 (2): 114–25.

Gregory, E. (1996), *Making Sense of a New World. Learning to Read in a Second Language*, London: Paul Chapman.

Hafiz, F. M., and Tudor, I. (1990), 'Graded Readers as an Input Medium in L2 Learning', *System*, 18 (1): 31–42.

Haggan, M. (1991), 'Speaking Errors in Native Arabic-Speaking English Majors: A Comparison between Remedial Students and Fourth Year Students', *System*, 19 (1): 45–61.

Hakuta, K., Butler, Y. G., and Witt, D. (2000), *How Long Does It Take English Language Learners to Attain Proficiency?* The University of California Linguistic Minority Research Institute Policy Report 2.

Hall, J. K. (2000), 'The Role of Classroom Discourse in Learning Additional Languages', TESOL Applied Linguistics Academic Session, TESOL Conference, Vancouver, Canada, March 2000.

Halliday, M. (1975), *Learning How to Mean*, London: Edward Arnold.

Hamadalla, R., and Tushyeh, H. (1998), 'A Contrastive Analysis of English and Arabic Relativization', *Papers and Studies in Contrastive Analysis*, 34: 141–52.

Hammill, D. D., and Larsen, S. C. (1996), *TOWL-3 Test of Written Language*, 3rd ed., Austin, TX: Pro-ed.

Hanushek, E. A. (2005), 'Why Quality Matters in Education', *Finance and Development*, 42 (2): 15–28.

Harcourt Science Student Edition, Level 3 (2002), Orlando, FL: Harcourt School.

Hardy, B. (1978), 'Narrative as a Primary Mode of the Mind', in M. Meek, A. Warlow and G. Barton (eds), *The Cool Web: The Patterns of Children's Reading*, 12–33, New York: Atheneum.

Hatch, E. (1978), *Second Language Acquisition: A Book of Readings*, Rowley, MA: Newbury House.

Hayes-Harb, R. (2006), 'Native Speakers of Arabic and ESL Texts: Evidence for the Transfer of Written Words Identification Processes', *TESOL Quarterly*, 40 (2): 321–38.

He, T., and Wang, W. (2009), 'Invented Spelling of EFL Young Beginning Writers and Its Relation with Phonological Awareness and Grapheme-Phoneme Principles', *Journal of Second Language Writing*, 18 (1): 44–56.

Heath, S. B. (1983), *Ways with Words*, Cambridge: Cambridge University Press.

Hemphill, L., Picardi, N., and Tager-Flusberg, H. (1991), 'Narrative as an Index of Communicative Competence in Mildly Mentally Retarded Children', *Applied Psycholinguistics*, 12: 263–79.

Henderson, E. (1981), *Learning to Read and Spell. The Child's Knowledge of Words*. DeKalb: Northern Illinois University Press.

Henderson, E. (1985), *Teaching Spelling*, Boston, MA: Houghton Mifflin.

Hiebert, E., and Fisher, C. (2005), 'A Review of the National Reading Panel's Study on Fluency', *Elementary School Journal*, 105 (5): 443–60.

Hoey, M. (1991), 'Some Properties of Spoken Discourse', in R. Brown and C. Brumfit (eds), *Applied Linguistics and English Language Teaching*, 64–84, London: Modern English Publications in association with British Council.

Hofstede, G. (1980), *Culture's Consequences: International Differences in Work-Related Values*, Beverly Hills, CA: Sage.

Hofstede, G. (2002), 'Dimensions Do Not Exist: A Reply to Brendan McSweeney', *Human Relations*, 55 (11): 1–8.

Hogan, K., and Pressley, M. (eds) (1997), *Scaffolding Student Learning: Instructional Approaches and Issues*, Cambridge, MA: Brookline.

Holliday, A. (1994), *Appropriate Methodology and Social Context*, Cambridge: Cambridge University Press.

Holliday, A. (2002), 'The Struggle against 'Us'-'Them' Conceptualization in TESOL as the Ownership of English Changes', Paper presented at the 8th International Conference of TESOL Arabia, Abu Dhabi, March 2002.

Holt, R. (2005), *Blue Skies 4*, Harlow, Essex: Pearson Education.

Horowitz, F. D. (1990), 'Developmental Models of Individual Differences', in J. Colombo and J. Fagen (eds), *Individual Differences in Infancy: Reliability, Stability, Prediction*, 3–18, Hillsdale, NJ: Erlbaum.

Hudelson, S. (1983), 'Janice: Becoming a Writer of English', Paper presented at the 17th Annual Meeting of the Teachers of English to Speakers of Other Languages, Toronto, Canada, March 1983.

Hudelson, S. (1984), 'Kan yu ret an rayt ingles: Children Become Literate in English as a Second Language', *TESOL Quarterly*, 18 (2): 221–38.

Hudelson, S. (1989), *Write on. Children Writing in ESL*, Englewood Cliffs, NJ: Prentice Hall Regents.

Huie, K., and Yahya, N. (2003), 'Learning to Write in the Primary Grade: Experience of English Language Learners and Mainstream Student', *TESOL Journal*, 12 (1): 25–31.

Invernizzi, M., Abouzeid, M., and Gill. J. T. (1994), 'Using Students' Invented Spellings as a Guide for Spelling Instruction That Emphasizes Word Study', *Elementary School Journal*, 95 (2): 155–67.

Jarrah, A. M. (2020), 'Elementary School Mathematics and Sciences Teachers' Perspectives on Using English as a Medium of Instruction', *Humanities & Social Sciences Review*, 8 (4): 473–82.

Kaderavek, J., and Sulzby, E. (2000), 'Narrative Production by Children with Language Impairment: Oral Narratives and Emergent Readings', *Journal of Speech and Language and Hearing Research*, 43 (1): 34–49.

Kamii, C. (1991), 'What Is Constructivism?' in C. Kamii, M. Manning and G. Manning (eds). *Early Literacy: A Constructivist Foundation for Whole Lang*uage, 17–30, Washington, DC: National Education Association.

Kolman, L., Noorderhaven, N., Hofstede, G., and Diencs, E. (2003), Cross-Cultural Differences in Central Europe, *Journal of Managerial Psychology*, 18 (1): 76–88.

Krashen, S. (1982), *Principles and Practice in Second Language Acquisition*, Oxford: Pergamon Press.

Krashen, S., and Terrell, T. D. (1983), *The Natural Approach*, Hayward, CA: Alemany Press.

Kubota, M. (1989), 'Question-Answering Behavior in ESL and EFL Classrooms', MA research paper, Georgetown University, ERIC Document Reproduction Service No. ED313913.

Kumaravadivelu, B. (2002), 'Method, Antimethod, Postmethod', in *IATEFL Conference York Conference Selections*, 11–19, Canterbury, UK: IATEFL.

Lazar, G. (1994), 'Using Literature in Lower Levels', *ELT Journal*, 48 (2): 115–24.

Lederer, R. (1989), *Crazy English*, New York: Pocket Books.

Legutke, M., Thomas, H., and Candlin, C. (1991), *Process and Experience in the Language Classroom*, New York: Routledge.

Lehman, A. (2014), 'Cultural Anthropology and Narratology', in K. Schiever and S. Cayela Sánchez (eds), *Perspectiva Antropológicas:Herramientas para el Análisis de las Sociedades Europeas* [*Anthropological Perspectives: Tools for the Analysis of European Societies*], 69–92, Murcia, Spain: Ediciones de la Universidad de Murcia / Münster: Waxmann Verlag.

Lemke, J. L. (1990), *Talking Science: Language, Learning, and Values*, New York: Ablex.

Lesaux, N. K., and Siegel, L. S. (2003), 'The Development of Reading in Children Who Speak English as a Second Language', *Developmental Psychology*, 39 (6): 1005–19.

Lewis, S. C. (1963), 'On Three Ways of Writing for Children', *Horn Book Magazine*, 39 (5): 460.

Lextutor. Compleat [*sic*] lexical tutor, www.lextutor.ca.

Livo, N. J., and Riertz, S. A. (1986), *Storytelling: Process and Practices*, New York: Libraries Unlimited.

Long, M., and Sato, C. J. (1983), 'Classroom Foreigner Talk Discourse: Forms and Functions of Teacher Questions', in H. W. Seliger and M. Long (eds), *Classroom Oriented Research in Second Language Acquisition*, 268–85, Rowley, MA: Newbury House.

Ludden, D. (2015), 'Whole Language or No Language? Something Is Rotten in the State of Literacy Education', *Psychology Today*. Available online: https://www.psychologytoday.com/us/blog/talking-apes/201507/whole-language-or-no-language (accessed 5 June 2020).

Lustig, M., and Koester, J. (1993), *Intercultural Competence*, New York: HarperCollins.

Lynch, T. (1991), 'Questioning Roles in the Classroom', *ELT Journal*, 45 (3): 201–10.

Lyster, R. (1998), 'Negotiation of Form, Recasts, and Explicit Correction in Relation to Error Types and Learner Repair in Immersion Classrooms', *Language Learning*, 48 (2): 183–218.

Lysterm R., and Ranta, L. (1997), 'Corrective Feedback and Learner Uptake: Negotiation of Form in Communicative Classrooms', *Studies in Second Language Acquisition*, 19: 37–66.

Maguire, M., and Graves, B. (2001), 'Speaking Personalities in Primary School Children's L2 Writing', *TESOL Quarterly*, 35: 561–93.

Mar, R. A. (2004), 'The Neuropsychology of Narrative: Story Comprehension, Story Production, and Their Interrelation', *Neuropsychologia*, 42 (10): 114–34.

Mar, R. A., Oatley, K., Hirsch, J., dela Paz, J., and Pederson, J. (2006), Bookworms versus Nerds: Exposure to Fiction versus Non-fiction, Divergent Associations with Social Ability and the Simulation of Fictional Social Worlds', *Journal of Research in Personality*, 40: 694–712.

Martin, P. (1999), 'Bilingual Unpacking of Monolingual Texts in Two Primary Classrooms in Brunei Darrussalam', *Language and Education*, 13 (1): 38–58.

Maybin, J., Mercer, N., and Stierer, B. (1992), 'Scaffolding Learning in the Classroom', in K. Norman (ed.), *Thinking Voices*, 186–95, London: Hodder & Stoughton.

McConaghy, J. (1990), *Children Learning through Literature*, Portsmouth, NH: Heinemann.

McKay, S. (1986), 'Literature in the ESL Classroom', in C. Brumfit, and R. A. Carter (eds), *Literature and Language Teaching*, 192–8, Oxford: Oxford University Press.

Meek, M. (1988), *How Texts Teach What Readers Learn*, Stroud: Thimble Press.

Mehan, H. (1979), ' "What Time Is It, Denise?" Asking Known Information Questions in Classroom Discourse', *Theory into Practice*, 28 (4): 285–94.

Merriam-Webster's Collegiate Dictionary (1994), 10th ed., Springfield, MA: Merriam-Webster Inc.

Mikkelsen, N. (1984), 'Literature and the Storymaking Powers of Children', *Children's Literature Association Quarterly*, 9: 9–14.

Miller, L. (2003), 'Empathy and Self-Expression: Confessions of a Sometimes Angry Self Psychologist, *Progress in Self Psychology*, 19: 57–84.

Mourshed, M., Chinezi C., and Barber, M. (2010), *How the World's Most Improved School Systems Keep Getting Better*, London: McKinsey.

Mullis, I. V. S., Martin, M. O., Foy, P., and Hooper, M. (2016), *TIMSS 2015 International Results in Mathematics*, Boston College: TIMSS & PIRLS International Study Center. Available online: http://timssandpirls.bc.edu/timss2015/international-results/ (accessed 15 August 2020).

Muñoz, M. L., Gillarn, R. B., Peña, E. D., and Gulley-Faehnle, A. (2003), 'Measures of Language Development in Fictional Narratives of Latino Children', *Language, Speech and Hearing Services in Schools*, 34 (4): 332–42.

Nagy, W. E., and Scott, J. A. (2000), 'Vocabulary Processes', in M. Kamil, P. Mosenthal, P. D. Pearson and R. Barr (eds), *Handbook of Reading Research, Vol. III*, 269–84, Mahwah, NJ: Lawrence Erlbaum.

Nation, I. S. P., and Wang, K. (1999), 'Graded Readers and Vocabulary', *Reading in a Foreign Language*, 12 (2): 355–80.

Nation, P. (1990), *Teaching and Learning Vocabulary*, New York: Newbury House.

National Council of Teachers of Mathematics (1991), *Professional Standards for Teaching Mathematics*, Reston, VA: Author.

National Science Teachers Association (1991), *Scope, Sequence and Coordination of Secondary School Science*, Washington, DC: Author.

Nelly, E., and Smith, A. (2000), *PM Benchmark Kit 1*, UK: Nelson Thomson Learning.

Newman, D., Griffin, P., and Cole, M. (1989), *The Construction Zone*, Cambridge: Cambridge University Press.

Newman, J. (1985), *Whole Language in Use*, Portsmouth, NH: Heinemann.

Nippold, M. A. (1993), 'Developmental Markers in Adolescent Language: Syntax, Semantics and Pragmatics', *Language, Speech and Hearing Services in Schools*, 24: 21–8.

Nippold, M. A. (2007), *Later Language Development: School-Age Children, Adolescents, and Young Adults*, 3rd ed., Austin, TX: Pro-Ed.

Oatley, K. (2002), 'Emotions and the Story Worlds of Fiction', in T. Brock, J. Strange and M. Green (eds), *Narrative Impact: Social and Cognitive Foundations*, 39–69, Mahwah, NJ: Erlbaum.

Orlich, D. C., Harder, R. J., Callahan, R. C., Kauchak, D. P., and Gibson, H. W. (1994), *Teaching Strategies: A Guide to Better Instruction*, 4th ed., Lexington, MA: D.C. Heath.

Ormrod, J. E. (2012), *Human Learning*, 6th ed., Boston, MA: Pearson Education.

O'Sullivan, K. (2015), 'Bilingual Education – Mismatch between Policy and Practice in the UAE?', *International Journal of Arts & Sciences*, 8 (7): 425–38.

Oxford Dictionaries, Available online: www.oxfordlanguages.oup.com/google-dictionary-en.

Özcan, S. (2010), 'The Effects of Asking Referential Questions on the Participation and Oral Production of Lower-Level Language Learners in Reading Classes', MA thesis, Graduate School of Social Sciences of Middle East Technical University, Ankara, Turkey.

Padres Unidos (2002), 'Colorado Upholds the Right to Bilingual Education'. Available online: www.rethinkingschools.org (accessed 11 January 2022).

Paul, R. (1976), 'Invented Spelling in Kindergarten', *Young Children*, 31: 195–200.

Paul, R. (2007), *Language Disorders from Infancy through Adolescence: Assessment & Intervention*, 3rd ed., St Louis, MO: Mosby.

Pauls, L., and Archibald, L. (2022), 'Cognitive and Linguistic Effects of Working Memory Training in Children with Corresponding Deficit', *Frontiers in Education*, 6: 821760.

Pearson, B. Z., and deVilliers, P. A. (2018), 'Language Acquisition: Discourse, Narrative and Pragmatics'. Available online: documents.pub/document/language-acquisition-discourse- narrative-and-pragmatics-a-language-acquisition.html (accessed 20 November 2020).

Pellegrini, A. D. (1985), 'Relations between Preschool Children's Symbolic Play and Literate Behavior', in L. Galda and A. D. Pellegrini (eds), *Play, Language, and Stories*, 79–97, Norwood, NJ: Ablex.

Pinto, G., Tarchi, C., and Bigozzi, L. (2016), 'Development in Narrative Competences from Oral to Written Stories in Five- to Seven-Year-Old Children', *Early Childhood Research Quarterly*, 36: 1–10.

Plato (1992), *Republic*. (G. M. A. Grube, Trans., C. D. C. Reeve, Rev.). Indianapolis, IN: Hackett. (Original work published *c*.377.)

Read, C. (1975), *Children's Categorization of Speech Sounds in English*, Urbana, IL: National Council of Teachers of English.

Richards, J., and Lockhart, C. (1994), *Reflective Teaching in Second Language Classrooms*. Cambridge: Cambridge University Press.

Rigg, P. (1981), 'Beginning to Read in English the LEA Way', in C. W. Twyford, D. Diel and K. Feathers (eds), *Reading English as a Second Language. Moving from Theory. Monographs in Teaching and Learning*, 4: 81–90, Bloomington: Indiana University School of Education.

Rigg, P. (1991), 'Whole Language in TESOL', *TESOL Quarterly*, 25 (3): 5–23.

Rixon, S. (2013), *British Council Survey of Policy and Practice in Primary English Language Teaching Worldwide*, London: British Council.

Roth, F. P., and Spekman, N. J. (1986), 'Narrative Discourse. Spontaneously Generated Stories of Learning-Disabled and Normally Achieving Students', *Journal of Speech and Hearing Disorders*, 51 (1): 8–23.

Saigh, K., and Schmitt, N. (2012), 'Difficulties with Vocabulary Word Form: The Case of Arabic ESL Learners', *System*, 40 (1): 224–36.

Samway, K. Davies (1987), 'Formal Evaluation of Children's Writing: An Incomplete Story', *Language Arts*, 64 (3): 289–98.

Samway, K. Davies, and Taylor, D. (1993), 'Inviting Children to Make Connections between Reading and Writing', *TESOL Journal*, 2 (3): 7–11.

Sanders, W. L., and Rivers, J. (1996), *Cumulative and Residual Effects of Teachers on Future Academic Achievement*, Research progress report, Heartland.org. Available online: http://heaeartland.org/sites/all/modules/custom/heartland_migration/files/pdfs/3048 (accessed 10 September 2021).

Sapir, E., and Mandelbaum, D. G. (1958), *Culture, Language and Personality*, Berkeley: University of California Press.

Scarlett, W., and Wolf, D. (1979), 'When It's Only Make-Believe: The Construction of a Boundary between Fantasy and Reality in Storytelling', in E. Winner and H. Gardner (eds), *Fact, Fiction, and Fantasy in Childhood*, 29–30, San Francisco, CA: Jossey-Bass.

Schleppegrell, J., and Simich-Dudgeon, C. (1996), 'What's a Good Answer? Awareness of Behavioral and Content Features of Successful Classroom Iinteraction', *Journal Language and Education*, 10 (4): 273–86.

Serhan, M. D., Abdulhafud, B. A., and Jasim, S. T. (2019), 'Errors in Prepositions in EFL Arab Students' Spoken Discourse', *Journal of Anbar University for Language and Literature*, 29: 325–45. Available online: http://www.researchgate.net/publication/337669758_Errors_in_Prepositions_in_EFL_Arab Students'_Spoken_Discourse (accessed 16 May 2022).

Sexton, T. L., and Stanton, M. (2016), 'Systems Theories', in J. C. Norcross, G. R. VandenBos, D. K. Freedheim and B. O. Olatunji (eds), *APA Handbook of Clinical Psychology: Theory and Research*, 213–39, Washington, DC: American Psychological Association.

Shomoossi, N. (2004), 'The Effect of Teacher Questioning Behavior in EFL Classroom Interaction: A Classroom Research Study', *Reading Matrix*, 4 (2): 96–104.

Short, D. (1994), 'Expanding Middle School Horizons: Integrating Language, Culture, and Social Studies', *TESOL Quarterly*, 28: 581–608.

Shrable, K., and Minnis, D. L. (1974), 'Cognitive Levels Analysis Interaction Model (CLAIM)', in A. Simon and E. G. Boyer (eds), *Mirrors for Behavior III, An Anthology of Observation Instruments*, 539–41, Wyncote, PA: Communication Materials Center.

Sirotnik, K. A. (1983, Feb.), 'What You See Is What You Get – Consistency, Persistency, and Mediocrity in Classroom', *Harvard Education Review*, 53 (1): 16–31.

Solomon, J., and Rhodes, N. C. (1995), *Conceptualizing Academic Language*, Santa Cruz, CA: National Center for Research on Cultural Diversity and Second Language.

Spanos, G., Rhodes, N., Dale, T., and Crandall, J. (2013), 'Linguistic Features of Mathematical Problem Solving. Insights and Applications', in R. R. Cocking and J. P. Mestre (eds), *Linguistic and Cultural Influences on Mathematics Learning*, 221–40, New York: Routledge.

Strickland, S., and Mandel Morrow, L. (eds) (1989), *Emerging Literacy: Young Children Learn to Read and Write*, Newark, DE: International Reading Association, ERIC ED305602.

Stronge, J. H., Ward, T. J., Tucker, P. D., and Hindman, J. (2007), 'What Is the Relationship between Teacher Quality and Student Achievement? An Exploratory Study', *Journal of Personnel Evaluation*, 20: 165–84.

Stronge, J. H., Ward, T. J., and Grant, L. (2011), 'What Makes Good Teachers Good? A Cross-Case Analysis of Connection between Teacher Effectiveness and student achievement', *Journal of Teacher Education*, 62: 339.

Tahaineh, Y. S. (2010), 'Arab EFL University Students' Errors in the Use of prepositions', *Modern Journal of Applied Linguistics*, 1 (6): 76–112.

Tennant, M., and Pogson, P. (1995), *Learning and Change in the Adult Years: A Developmental Perspective*, San Francisco, CA: Jossey-Bass.

Tharp, R., and Gallimore, R. (1991), *The Instructional Conversation: Teaching and Learning in Social Activity*, Research Report 2, National Center for Research on Cultural Diversity and Second Language Learning. Available online: http://www.ncbe.gwu.edu/ miscpubs/ncrcdsll/rr2htm (accessed 10 January 2022).

The Bullock Report. A Language for Life (1975), London: Her Majesty's Stationery Office.

The Swann Report (1985), *Education for All*, London: Her Majesty's Stationery Office.

Thomas, W. P., and Collier, V. (1997), *School Effectiveness for Language Minority Students*, Washington, DC: National Clearinghouse for Bilingual Education.

Tsui, A. B. M. (1995), Introducing Classroom Interaction, London: Penguin.

Tudor, I., and Hafiz, F. (1989), 'Extensive Reading as a Means of Input to L2 Learning', *Journal of Research in Reading*, 12 (2): 164–78.

Uhl Chamot, A., and O'Malley, M. (1994), *The CALLA Handbook. Implementing the Cognitive Academic Learning Approach*, New York: Addison-Wesley.

Van Berkel, A. (2004), 'Learning to Spell in English as a Second Language', *IRAL*, 42: 239–57.

Vandergrift, K. (1990), *Children's Literature: Theory, Research, and Teaching*, Englewood, CO: Libraries Unlimited.

Verplaetse, S. L. (1998), 'How Content Teachers Interact with English Language Learners', *TESOL Journal*, 7 (5): 24–8.

Vine, H. A., and Faust, M. A. (1992), 'Situating Readers: Introduction and Invitation, *English Journal*, 81 (7): 62–7.

Vygotsky, L. S. (1978), *Mind in Society. The Development of Higher Psychological Processes*, M. Cole, V. John-Steiner, S. Scribner and E. Souberman (eds), Cambridge: Harvard University Press.

Wallach, G. P., and Butler, K. G. (1994), *Creating Communication, Literacy and Academic Success*, New York: Macmillan.

Wells, G. (1986), *Meaning Makers. Children Learning Language and Using Language to Learn*, Portsmouth, NH: Heinemann.

Whalen, L. M. (2010), 'Reading Narratives Supports Cognitive Development among College Students', *LiBRI. Linguistic and Literary Broad Research and Innovation*, 1 (1): 11–18.

Whitley, D. (1995), 'Bringing Out the Beast in Them: Reflections on Gender and Children's Use of Traditional Stories', in E. Bearne (ed.), *Greater Expectations. Children Reading Writing*, 57–69, London: Cassell.

Wolf, M. (2007), *Dyslexia, Fluency, and the Brain*, Timonium, MD: York Press.

Wood, D., Bruner, J. S., and Ross, G. (1976), 'The Role of Tutoring in Problem Solving', *Journal of Psychology and Psychiatry*, 17 (2): 89–100.

World Bank Group (2019), *Expectations and Aspirations. A New Framework for Education in the Middle East North Africa. Overview*, Washington, DC: Author.

Wurzel, J., and Fischman, N. (1995), *A Different Place. The Intercultural Classroom*, Newtonville, MA: Intercultural Resource Corporation.

Yang, C. C. (2010), 'Teacher Questions in Second Language Classrooms: An Investigation of Three Case Studies, *Asian EFL Journal*, 12 (1): 181–201.

Zamel, V. (1992), 'Writing One's Way into Reading', *TESOL Quarte*rly, 26: 463–85.

Zimmerman, C. B. (2009), *Word Knowledge. A Vocabulary Teacher's Handbook*, Oxford: Oxford University Press.

Children's Books Mentioned

Allard, S. (2002), *Josh Gets Classes*, Tucson, AZ: Learning Page.

Anno, M. (1995), *Anno's Magic Seeds*, New York: Penguin Putnam Books.

Bell Mathis, S. (1975), *The Hundred Penny Box*, Toronto: Penguin Random House.

Burns, M. (1997), *Spaghetti and Meatballs for All*, New York: Scholastic.

Butterworth, N. (1989), *One Snowy Night*, London: HarperCollins.

Carle, E. ([1969] 1987), *The Very Hungry Caterpillar*, New York: Philomel Books.

Carle, E. (1977), *The Grouchy Ladybug*, New York: HarperCollins.

Cowley, J. (1999), *Mrs. Wishy Washy*, New York: Wright Group.

Dean, J., and Dean, K. (2014), *Too Cool for School*, New York: Scholastic.

Estes, E. ([1940] 1973), *Hundred Dresses*, New York: Scholastic.

Ghosn, I.-K. (1999a), *Children Who Hugged the Mountain*, Beirut: Dar El-Ilm Lilmalayin.

Ghosn, I.-K. (1999b), *Dragonfly Surprise*, Beirut: Dar El-Ilm Lilmalayin.

Ghosn, I.-K. (2009), *Little Hen Gets Help*. Available online: http://www.youtube.com/watch?v= RPWH71tUJaE.

Holmlund Minarik, E. ([1957] 1977), *Little Bear*, Tadworth, Surrey: World's Work Ltd Windmill Press.

Hutchins, P. (1986), *The Doorbell Rang*, New York: Scholastic.

Jewell, N. (1978), *Bus Ride*, New York: Harper & Row.

Levine, E. (1993a), *If You Traveled on the Underground Railroad*, New York: Scholastic.

Levine, E. (1993b), *If You Traveled West in the Covered Wagon*, New York: Scholastic.

Martin, B., and Carle, E. (1967), *Brown Bear, Brown Bear, What Do You See?* New York: Doubleday.

McGovern, A. (1969), *If You Sailed on the Mayflower in 1620*, New York: Scholastic.

Myller, R. (1990), *How Big Is a Foot?* New York: Dell Yearling.

Park, B. (1994), *Junie P. Jones and Some Sneaky Peaky Spying*, New York: Random House.

Parrish, P. (2012), *Amelia Badelia, I Can Read Book*, New York: Harper and Row.

Robinson, B. (1996), *The Best [Worst] School Year Ever*, New York: Scholastic.

Roop, P., and Roop, C. (1998), *If You Lived with the Cherokee*, New York: Scholastic.

Sans Souci, R. D. (1990), *Talking Eggs*, New York: Scholastic.

Slobodkina, E. ([1940] 1987), *Caps for Sale*, New York: Scholastic.

Steptoe, J. (1987), *Mufaro's Beautiful Daughters*, New York: Scholastic.
Viorst, J. (1972), *Alexander and the Terrible, Horrible No Good, Very Bad Day*, New York: Aladdin Books.
Walker, M. (1987a), *Gingerbread Man*, New York: Addison Wesley.
Walker, M. (1987b), *The Rabbit and the Turnip*, New York: Addison Wesley.
Zion, G. ([1956] 2002), *Harry the Dirty Dog*, New York: Scholastic.

Index

abbreviations xiv
academic language
  competence 45–6
  functions 41–2
  of school subjects 42–7
academic language functions and
    literature 41–2, 57–60
academic L2 proficiency 47–9
academic literacy
  general 41
  mathematics 43–5
  sciences 45–6
  social studies 46–7
Arabic 129–31, 159–61

background knowledge in reading 85–6
Bear and Templeton spelling stages
    134–5, 140
bilingual education 50–1
BISC-CALP Model 48–9
Bronfenbrenner 3–4

children's literature
  contextualized vocabulary 30–2,
    127, 157
  and culture learning 11, 13, 26, 200
  defined 26–7
  insights from 26, 34, 77–8, 118
  and knowledge centres 34–5
  language 27–9
  motivational appeal 30–1, 178
  significance 25–6
children's literature and classroom
    discourse 11, 19, 67, 72–8, 155,
    159, 166–9
classroom
  ecosystem xi, 3–4
  interactions 12, 65, 165, 184
classroom experiment outcomes
  general vocabulary 102–4
  literate language 125–7
  reading comprehension 89–91

  subject-specific vocabulary 90
  written expression 114–18
classroom and culture 9–11
classroom discourse and instructional
    materials 70–2, 196
classroom discourse
  IRF sequence 55, 65
  question-answer-feedback pattern.
    See IRF
  student initiations 11, 67–9, 75–7, 155,
    159, 175
  and teacher feedback 78–80
  and teacher questions 59–61
classroom exchanges observed 66–9
classroom as ecosystem xi, 3–4
cognitive academic language proficiency
    (CALP) 48–9
communicatively oriented materials xi, 16,
    21, 79, 94, 125, 194–6, 199
cultural expectations 12–15
cultural patterns
  communication 12–13, 20–1
  egalitarian vs. hierarchical 14–15
  interpersonal relationships 14–15
  power distance 14
  taxonomies 13–15
  uncertainty avoidance 15
culture in the classroom 9–11,
    15–17, 232

dialogue practice and cultural content
    48, 68
dialogue practice in egalitarian
    classroom 17–19
dialogue practice in hierarchical
    classroom 9–10, 16, 69–71
dialogue practice modified 22

effective teacher
  characteristics 181–3
  long-term influence 183
emotional perception 35

English-medium-instruction (EMI)
　challenges 39–40, 42–6, 87
　and children's literature 41–2
　spread 51, 128, 146
error treatment 63, 194

FLAPPS 29, 35, 43, 50, 96, 110

Gentry spelling stages 135–40
grammar
　errors of Arabic ELLs 130–3
　L1 transfer 132

Homo narrans 25, 194
Horowitz model 3, 197

instructional materials and
　classroom discourse 74–5, 193–4
　culture 4, 13, 21–2, 200
　learner achievement 50–1, 193, 195–6
　learner engagement 66–8, 75
　models for writing 109, 127
　motivation xi
interest 173

knowledge centres 40–1

L1 transfer
　grammar 132
　mechanics 142–4
　pronunciation 142
　spelling 139–42
language environment 3, 88
learner engagement and
　instructional materials 9–11, 16
　motivation 29, 31, 62, 74, 155, 193
　teacher feedback 55, 59–61, 234
　teacher questions 55
　topics 67, 69, 73–4, 75–7
learning outcomes in
　communicatively oriented programs 111–12, 124–5
　MENA region 1–2
　reading-focused, story-based programs 88–9, 100–1, 112–14, 124–5
Lebanon xi, 31, 43, 45–6, 49, 59–60, 85, 89, 99–100, 110, 154, 157
levelled books 91–2
Lextutor 103–4

literate language
　features 123–4
　influence of instructional texts on 127–8
　significance 122–4
literate language in communicatively oriented programs 124–5
literate language after fifteen-week story experiment 125–7
literate language in story-based programs 124–5

MENA region 1–2, 46, 50, 87, 99, 119, 146, 198–9
Modern Standard Arabic (MSA)
　alphabet 129
　capitalization 129
　grammar 129–31
　punctuation 129
　reading directionality 129
motivation
　and learner engagement 29, 31, 62, 74, 155, 193
　and stories 28–9, 31, 196

narrative
　human need for 25–6
　significance 25–6, 32
narrative and
　academic achievement 33
　cognitive development 33–4
　language proficiency 33
　writing development 33–4
narratives of young Arabic speakers 111–18
negotiation of
　form 66–8
　meaning 66–9
　topic 66–8

past tense 11, 27, 29–30, 36, 44, 46, 95, 110, 179
perspective taking 32–3, 126–7
phonics 145, 147, 151–2, 163
power distance index (PDI) 14–16
Prism Model 49–50

reader responses to stories 170–6
reading
　background knowledge 36, 85–6
　challenges of for L2 learners 104

dialogic 95, 174
  'round-robin' 169–70
  strategies 91–2
reading comprehension after six years of English 88–91
reading comprehension in second language 85–6
recommendations for practice 22–3, 36–7, 51–2, 63–4, 95–6, 105–6, 119–20, 128, 146–7, 162–3, 179, 192

scaffolding 184–7
social environment 65–6
social interaction 14, 90, 184–5
spelling
  Bear and Templeton model 135, 140
  developmental process 134–5
  Gentry model 135, 140
  invented 134–5
  L1 transfer 141–2
  stages 135
spelling books 145
spelling of young Arabic speaking ELLs 139–41
spelling problems of Arabic speaking ELLs 135–9
story-based instruction
  academic language functions 41–2
  'culture-friendly' medium 21, 79
  and discourse 72–5, 78–9, 196–7
  flexibility of 165–6
  in hierarchical classrooms 19–20
  and language learning 40–2, 88–91, 93, 101–4
  literate language 124–7, 193
  and motivation 32, 35–6
  negotiations 66–7
  young Arabic speakers' narratives 110–17
story-based instruction and student initiations 22, 66–8, 72, 75, 77, 182, 195
story-based instruction and written expression 124–6, 109–10
strategy instruction 91–2
student initiations 11, 67–9, 75–7, 155, 159
systems theory 3–4

teacher
  classroom management 182, 188, 192, 196

cultural background 18–19, 232–3
effectiveness 181–3
questioning strategies 72
turn allocation strategies 61–2
teacher feedback 20, 62–3, 50, 55–9, 62–3, 65–6, 78–80, 185, 192, 194, 196–7, 199, 234
teacher questions
  classifying 65–8
  closed 56, 59
  cognitive demand of 56
  convergent 56–8
  data processing 56
  data recall 56, 58–9
  display 55, 57, 58–9
  divergent 56, 58
  factual 56
  and learner engagement 59–61
  open-ended 56
  reasoning 56–7
  referential 55–6, 58–9
teacher-student exchanges observed 66–9
tensions in MENA region influencing education 198–9
thematic instruction 153–4, 162
TIMSS 43, 95
TOWL Test of Written Language 103, 124
TORC 3 Test of Reading Comprehension 88, 90, 101–2, 191
transcription conventions xv

uncertainty avoidance index 14–15

vocabulary 20, 23, 27, 44–6, 52, 69, 86, 88, 94, 97–8, 100–5
vocabulary
  challenge of 97–9
  exposure time 99–100
vocabulary after fifteen-week story-based experiment 102–4
vocabulary after six years of English instruction 100–1
vocabulary in TEYL coursebooks 99–100
vocabulary of young Arabic speakers
  productive 102–3
  quality of 104
  range of 103
  receptive 100–1

whole language 151–2
word knowledge 97–8
writing
  in first language 107–8
  handwriting 143–4
  mechanics 129, 142–4
  in second language 108–9
  and story-based instruction 109, 116
  in TEYL coursebooks 108

young learner coursebooks
  aural/oral focus 87
  authors' assumptions 18
  culturally unfamiliar topics 4, 13, 21, 22, 46, 48–9, 80, 162, 194
  dialogue practice 48
  language of 46, 84
  questions in 60–1, 194
  structure 4, 99–100, 108–9, 121, 147, 153, 165
  topics 2, 4, 13, 29–30, 37, 48, 83, 194
  vocabulary 94, 99, 105, 127
  writing instruction in 108

Children's Book Index

Alexander and the Horrible, Terrible, No Good Very Bad Day 11, 35, 41
Amelia Badelia 27
The Best [Worst] School Year Ever 92
Brown Bear, Brown Bear, What Do You See? 92
Bus Ride 34
Caps for Sale 28
Children Who Hugged the Mountain 72
The Doorbell Rang 45, 178
The Gingerbread Man 29, 100, 177
Harry the Dirty Dog 92
How Big is a Foot? 45, 157–60
If You Sailed on the Mayflower 47
If You Traveled on the Underground Railroad 47
If You Travelled West in the Covered Wagon 47
Junie P. Jones and Some Sneaky Peaky Spying 92
Mrs. Wishy Washy 92
Mufaro's Beautiful Daughters 34
One Snowy Night 28
Rabbit and the Turnip 29, 162
Spaghetti and Meatballs for All 45
Too Cool for School 83–4
The Very Hungry Caterpillar 31, 46, 110, 154

www.ingramcontent.com/pod-product-compliance
Lightning Source LLC
Chambersburg PA
CBHW062214300426
44115CB00012BA/2062